Scotland
Glory, Tears
& Souvenirs

This book is dedicated to our families as well as fellow Scotland supporters.

Scotland
Glory, Tears & Souvenirs

**Robert Marshall
& David Stuart**

Pitch Publishing Ltd
A2 Yeoman Gate
Yeoman Way
Durrington
BN13 3QZ

Email: info@pitchpublishing.co.uk
Web: www.pitchpublishing.co.uk

First published by Pitch Publishing 2017
Text © 2017 Robert Marshall and David Stuart

Robert Marshall and David Stuart have asserted their rights in accordance with the Copyright, Designs and Patents Act 1988 to be identified as the authors of this work.

All rights reserved. No part of this publication may be reproduced, stored in a retrieval system, or transmitted in any form or by any means, electronic, mechanical, photocopying, recording or otherwise, without the prior permission in writing of the publisher and the copyright owners, or as expressly permitted by law, or under terms agreed with the appropriate reprographics rights organization. Enquiries concerning reproduction outside the terms stated here should be sent to the publishers at the UK address printed on this page.

The publisher makes no representation, express or implied, with regard to the accuracy of the information contained in this book and cannot accept any legal responsibility for any errors or omissions that may be made.

A CIP catalogue record for this book is available from the British Library.

13-digit ISBN: 9781785313318
Design and typesetting by Olner Pro Sport Media.
Printed in Malta by Gutenberg Press Ltd.
Print managed by Jellyfish Print solutions

Scotland Glory, Tears & Souvenirs

INTRODUCTION

There are no restrictions on supporting Scotland's national football team – your race, creed, colour, religion, gender, sexual orientation or political views matter not. If you wish to come along and support international football's greatest underachievers then you are most welcome. That said, it's not for everyone though – it's not for faint-hearted, easily-offended, glory-hunters. Scotland's glory tends to be sporadic and sometimes it is not even obvious but it is to be savoured. You need a mental toughness to be able to stick with Scotland or then again maybe you just need to be daft...

The authors – Robert Marshall and David Stuart – are a couple of dafties who derive much pleasure from supporting Scotland. We also derive pleasure from the pain that often occurs when supporting Scotland. Are you still with us?

Robert attended his first Scotland match, at Hampden Park, Glasgow in 1971 when he was twelve years old. His Uncle David took him to what was Tommy Docherty's first game in charge of the national team, a Euro Championship qualifier against Portugal which Scotland won 2-1. Since then he has attended over 200 Scotland games home and away.

David saw his first Scotland game aged ten in June, 1973 against world champions Brazil at Hampden Park. Taken by his Dad, if truth be told David was going to see Brazil, but since supporting Brazil wasn't a realistic option he stuck with Scotland. He has seen Scotland on many occasions but cannot describe himself as a Tartan Army Foot Soldier, although he does walk to every home game he goes to, as Hampden Park is at the bottom of his street.

Of course there's more to supporting Scotland than turning up at Hampden Park [or wherever] to see 90 minutes of football and to sing, shout, swear, cheer, hug, cry and eat pies – sometimes humble ones. There's also the pre- and post-match rituals and festivities. There's the collecting of associated souvenirs & memorabilia and the talking of enjoyable nonsense about it all and if you are so inclined you can even write about it as well. So here's the writings of a couple of Partick Thistle supporting, ex-schemies from North Glasgow who have evolved into two dark blue anoraks and who still willingly pay good money to see eleven of their countrymen kick a ball about..

We hope that you enjoy reading our take on Scotland the football team. We make no pretentious claims about it being a uniquely insightful, definitive or seminal piece of work – we don't have coaching badges, journalist degrees or PhDs in English. It is however an honest, off-beat account of many of the various aspects relating to the ongoing Mount Florida saga which has been cobbled together by two supporters who will continue to suffer for the cause as long as it is physically possible. We have done our utmost to ensure that the contents are factually [though possibly not politically] correct. If you do spot any errors however, we [a] apologise, and [b] ask that you keep quiet about it!

In this online, electronic nightmare of a world of ours, it's good to see that there is still room for paper and print. There are still discerning individuals out there who will appreciate and hold on to this tangible piece of football memorabilia. So thank you for buying this hardback book, you free-thinking anarchist you!

Shaun Maloney celebrates scoring Scotland's first goal of the game against the Republic of Ireland during a 2016 UEFA European Championships qualifier at Hampden Park.

Scotland Glory, Tears & Souvenirs

KEY FEATURES

- A selective history/alternative encyclopedia of Scotland's national football team through two separate themes written by a couple of supporters who have suffered for the cause [at home and abroad] since the early 1970s

- A humorous reminder of how Scotland, despite producing some great footballers over the decades, have surprisingly yet to win a major title with reviews of all their World Cup and Euro Championship campaigns to date as well as a peek into the future

- An offbeat look at associated aspects of Scottish international football from individual players, managers and rival teams to football collectables and personal experiences

- Extensive use of mostly colour images from the authors' own varied collections of football memorabilia

10	ISOLATIONISM
11	BRAZIL 1950
12	SWITZERLAND 1954
14	SWEDEN 1958
16	CHILE 1962
17	ENGLAND 1966
19	ITALY 1968
21	MEXICO 1970
22	BELGIUM 1972
24	WEST GERMANY 1974
26	YUGOSLAVIA 1976
27	ARGENTINA 1978
30	ITALY 1980
31	SPAIN 1982
35	FRANCE 1984
36	MEXICO 1986
39	WEST GERMANY 1988
40	ITALY 1990
44	SWEDEN 1992
46	USA 1994
48	ENGLAND 1996
51	FRANCE 1998
56	BELGIUM/NETHERLANDS 2000
58	JAPAN/SOUTH KOREA 2002
59	PORTUGAL 2004
61	GERMANY 2006
62	AUSTRIA/SWITZERLAND 2008
64	SOUTH AFRICA 2010
66	POLAND/UKRAINE 2012
67	BRAZIL 2014
68	FRANCE 2016
70	RUSSIA 2018
72	EURO 2020

CONTENTS

A TO Z

78	A&BC FOOTBALL CARDS- THE SCOTTISH CONNECTION
79	ABANDONED AND POSTPONED MATCHES
81	ADVERTISING & PUBLICITY
82	AGING PROCESS – PLAYERS AND SUPPORTERS
83	ANFIELD 77
84	ANGLO CONFECTIONERY
85	ANNUALS
88	BEATTIE, ANDY
88	BEVY OF BEERMATS
90	BLAZERS
91	BROWN, BOBBY
92	BRITISH HOME INTERNATIONAL CHAMPIONSHIPS
94	BROWN, CRAIG
96	BURLEY, GEORGE
98	CAPTAINS COURAGEOUS AND OTHERWISE
102	CARLING NATIONS CUP
103	CENTENARY CELEBRATIONS
104	CHIX
105	CIGARETTE CARDS [THE SWEET KIND]
107	COMIC CAPERS AND COLLECTABLES
109	COMMENTATING LEGENDS
109	CZECHOSLOVAKIA
110	DALGLISH, KENNY – THE 30 GOALS
112	DOCHERTY, TOMMY
115	EAST GERMANY
116	ENGLAND
118	FANZINES
119	FATHERS & SONS, WEE BROTHERS AND THE OCCASIONAL NEPHEW TOO
120	FKS STICKERS
122	GOALKEEPERS' GRAVEYARD
124	HAMPDEN PARK
125	HOME VENUES [OTHER THAN HAMPDEN]
126	IRELAND/NORTHERN IRELAND
127	JORDAN, JOE
130	KICK-OFF TIMES AND MATCH DAYS
131	KIRIN CUP
132	LAW, DENIS – THE 30 GOALS
135	LEVEIN, CRAIG
137	LYONS MAID
140	MACLEOD, ALLY
141	MAKE MINE MONTY
143	MASCOTS

145	MCCOLL, IAN
146	MCLEISH, ALEX
148	NATIONAL ANTHEMS
148	NEARLY MEN
150	ONE CAP ONLY
152	ORMOND, WILLIE
154	OVERLAPPING FULL-BACKS
155	PANINI, ME AND THE WILDERNESS YEARS
156	PENALTY HEROES AND VILLAINS
158	PHOTOGRAPHS – SUPPORTERS' SOUVENIRS
159	PRE-MATCH AND HALF-TIME ENTERTAINMENT
161	PROGRAMMES
162	QUEUING FOR TICKETS
163	RANKINGS
164	REPUBLIC OF IRELAND
164	ROUS CUP
166	ROXBURGH, ANDY
168	SCOTCARDS 1972
169	SCOTLAND SUPPORTERS CLUB
170	SEASIDE PREPARATIONS
170	SMITH, WALTER
172	SPONSORSHIP AND PARTNERSHIPS
174	STADIA – AWAY GAME DELIGHTS
175	STEIN, JOCK
177	TARTAN ARMY
178	TEA FOR TWENTY-TWO
179	TEAM PHOTOS
181	TELEVISION AND PUNDITRY
182	TESTIMONIALS
186	THE TOEPOKE
187	TICKET STUBS AND TICKET PRICES
189	TOPPS TRADING CARDS
191	USSR
192	VINYLS: WORLD CUP VINYLS
194	VOGTS, BERTI
195	WALES
196	WAR AND VICTORY
197	WEMBLEY 67
199	WONDERFUL WINGERS
203	X- RATED TACKLES
204	YUGOSLAVIA
205	ZED NOT ZEE

ISOLATIONISM

There is the suspicion that for decades, the British looked down their collective noses at 'foreign' football. It's certainly a fact that no home nation took part in the first three FIFA World Cups [1930, 1934 and 1938] whilst Scotland also skipped the first two UEFA European Championships [1960 and 1964].

FIFA were founded in 1904 and the Scottish Football Association became members in 1910 before resigning in 1920. We re-joined in 1924 then spat the dummy again in 1928 when we resigned [along with the other three 'Home' Associations] following a disagreement over the status of amateur footballers. The SFA eventually re-joined FIFA as a permanent member in 1946 but I suspect that if we took the huff one more time there would be no getting back in – unless we called ourselves the United Kingdom, but that is another story.

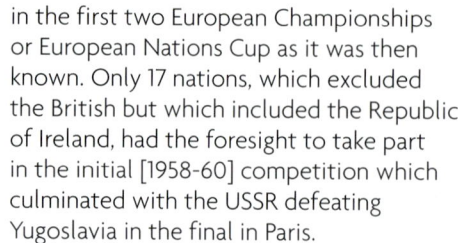

As a result of our less than splendid isolationism we were unable to prevent Uruguay from becoming world champions in 1930 nor Italy from lifting the trophy in 1934 and 1938. We can only wonder at what could have been achieved by the Wembley Wizards of 1928 or the 1930s Scotland teams which demolished both Czechoslovakia and Hungary – runners-up in the 1934 and 1938 World Cup Finals respectively.

Despite being a founder member of UEFA in 1954 Scotland chose not to participate in the first two European Championships or European Nations Cup as it was then known. Only 17 nations, which excluded the British but which included the Republic of Ireland, had the foresight to take part in the initial [1958-60] competition which culminated with the USSR defeating Yugoslavia in the final in Paris.

For the 1962-64 competition 29 of UEFA's 33 member nations took part – the absentees being Cyprus, Finland, Scotland and West Germany! On this occasion Spain defeated the USSR in the final in Madrid's Estadio Santiago Bernabeu. Twelve months earlier at the same venue Scotland had crushed Spain 6-2 in a friendly match with six different Scotland players getting on the scoresheet. Wha's like us?

Of course you could argue that we've kind of went full circle, from self-imposed isolationism to a wilderness where our quality of football is such that every second summer we're now on the outside looking in – women's team excepted. Let's end on a positive note however with the thought that when Scotland's renaissance comes it really will be something to savour...

BRAZIL 1950

Not long after the four home nations re-joined FIFA and then bailed-out football's world governing body with a revenue-raising Great Britain v Rest of Europe match at Hampden Park in 1947, it was agreed that the 1949/50 British Championship would double-up as World Cup qualifying group 5 and that the top two teams would go to the finals. Well you can't say fairer than that, can you? Furthermore, with the qualifiers being played over just the one season it meant that Scotland [and Wales] would enjoy two home

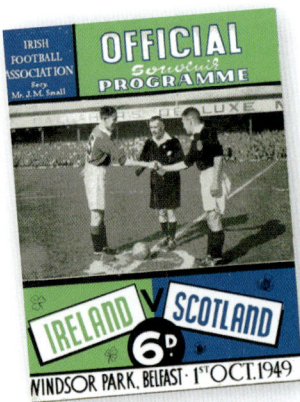

Scotland Glory, Tears & Souvenirs

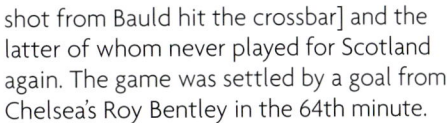

matches whilst England and Northern Ireland would have just one each.

Unfortunately however, the SFA then decreed that Scotland would only travel to Brazil if they were British champions – arrogance, stupidity plus added pressure for the Scotland players. Here we go! Here we go! Here we go!

So just over a year after the creation of the UK's National Health Service and against a backdrop of post-war austerity Scotland played their first-ever World Cup qualifying match, against Northern Ireland at Windsor Park, Belfast on 1st October 1949 and in front of a crowd of 55,000 we duly won 8-2! Rangers' Willie Waddell netted a brace whilst East Fife's Henry Morris managed a hat-trick, on his debut... and never played for Scotland again. You couldn't make this up.

The following month Wales came to Hampden for only the second time where a crowd of 73,781 saw the Scots win 2-0. The goals came from Celtic's John McPhail and Alex Linwood of Clyde both of whom were making their debuts. McPhail would win four more Scotland caps and score another two goals whereas Linwood – you've guessed it – would never play for his country again.

England also defeated Northern Ireland and Wales and with the Irish and Welsh drawing with one another a month prior to the Scotland-England game it meant that both the big two had 'qualified' in advance of the Hampden showdown.

The Hampden showdown on 15th April 1950 turned out to be the Hampden letdown when a crowd of 133,300 witnessed an English victory. The Scottish Selection Committee gave debuts to three players – Ian McColl [Rangers], Willie Bauld [Hearts] and Willie Moir [Bolton Wanderers] none of whom scored [although a shot from Bauld hit the crossbar] and the latter of whom never played for Scotland again. The game was settled by a goal from Chelsea's Roy Bentley in the 64th minute.

In the match programme under the heading 'Terracing Titbits' we were advised that if Scotland qualified we would sail from Southampton on the RMS *Alcantara* [which had seen action during World War Two as an armed merchant cruiser and then as a troopship] – whilst England would fly to Rio. Adeus Brasil.

To their credit, the English FA and some of their players pleaded with the SFA to change their mind and accompany England on the South American adventure but the 'Tartan Blazers' stubbornly refused to see sense.

The finals themselves [the fourth overall] were a somewhat chaotic, lopsided affair with only thirteen nations taking part. Travel

logistics and costs had resulted in several withdrawals/declined invitations.

England were one of the favourites to win the competition but it all went beautifully wrong, er, I mean there was a shock result when our neighbours and friends lost 1-0 to the USA in Belo Horizonte. Three days later a 1-0 defeat by Spain in Rio de Janeiro saw the English Out! Out! Out! Sorry, sometimes I just can't help myself.

Anyway, the competition concluded by way of a round-robin, mini-league involving Brazil, Spain, Sweden and Uruguay. Come the final match at Rio's Maracana Stadium a draw would have given the hosts the trophy whereas Uruguay had to win to top the group – which they did 2-1 after going behind. Of course better World Cups lay ahead for Brazil but just not in their own country. There would be World Cups for Scotland too – appearances at the finals that is for unlike Brazil we're still awaiting our first trophy win. [It could happen…hic!]

SWITZERLAND 1954

For the second successive World Cup our friends at FIFA decreed that a British Championship would double-up as a qualifying group with the top two teams going to the finals. Yippee! With no alteration to the scheduled 1953/54 British Championship fixtures it meant that like four years previous, Scotland [and Wales] would have the advantage of two home games to England and Northern Ireland's one. Hurrah! Furthermore ….cue drum roll…. unlike in 1950, the SFA agreed that Scotland would go to the finals even if they did not finish the season as British champions. Praise the Lord!

On 3rd October 1953 [just four months after the coronation of Queen Elizabeth the Second but only the FIRST of Scotland] a good start was made when Scotland travelled to Belfast's *Windsor* Park [did you see what I just did there?] and defeated Northern Ireland 3-1. 58,248 saw two of Scotland's goals scored by East Fife's Charlie Fleming on his debut and as was the 'custom' in those days, Charlie never played for his country again!

Wales visited Hampden on 4th November and a six-goal thriller ensued in front of 71,387. Scotland were 2-0 up at half-time thanks to goals from Allan Brown [Blackpool], and Bobby Johnstone [Hibernan]. John Charles pulled one back early in the second half for Wales before Hibs' Lawrie Reilly restored the Scots' two-goal cushion. Ivor Allchurch cut the deficit to one in the 73rd minute and then John Charles got the equaliser two minutes from time.

Scotland had two debutants against the Welsh – Johnny MacKenzie of Partick Thistle who would play for Scotland at the World Cup finals and centre-half Willie Telfer of St Mirren who would never play for Scotland again. With Telfer the story goes that he was a 'gentleman-player' who refused to commit a 'professional foul' to prevent one of John Charles' goals and so

Scotland Glory, Tears & Souvenirs

incurred the wrath of the Scottish selectors.

England defeated both Wales and Northern Ireland to head the group at this stage and on 31st March 1954 [three days before the Scotland-England encounter] Wales missed their chance to draw level with Scotland [and ultimately force a play-off] by losing 2-1 to Northern Ireland in Wrexham.

So both England and Scotland had qualified prior to them taking to the field at Hampden on 3rd April and Scotland now had our first manager – Andy Beattie – albeit on a temporary basis and with the actual title of 'Official in Charge'. Allan Brown gave Scotland the lead against the English after only seven minutes but then England took control and raced to a 4-1 lead before a last-minute goal from Willie Ormond of Hibernian made the final score semi-respectable in front of 134,544.

In a similar scenario to the Wales game, Scotland gave debut caps to two players – the aforementioned Willie Ormond who would go on to play at the World Cup finals [and indeed manage Scotland at a World Cup finals 20 years later] and Celtic defender Mike Haughney who would be filed under S for scapegoat and never play for Scotland again.

At the finals although each team was allowed to bring a squad of 22 players – the SFA decided however that 13 [which included only one goalkeeper] would be sufficient for our purposes. The squad was weakened further by the absence of any players from Glasgow Rangers who went instead on a close-season tour of Canada which clashed with the World Cup in Switzerland.

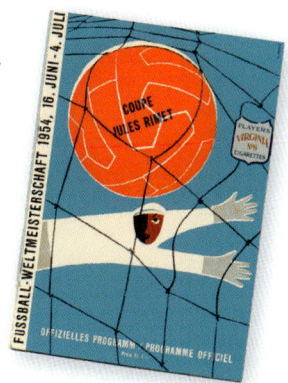

Just to add to the pantomime of it all, the Scotland players were forced to train in their club jerseys which earned them the nickname of 'The liquorice allsorts'. Also, Scotland in conjunction with England threatened to walk out of the World Cup if FIFA adopted a last-minute proposal to allow substitutes.

Anyway, Scotland were drawn in group 3 along with Austria, Czechoslovakia and Uruguay. However, FIFA had decided that the two seeded teams in each group should not play one another and consequently only two rather than three matches would be played so Scotland avoided fellow non-seeds Czechoslovakia. No, I don't understand the logic of it either.

On 16th June 1954 at the Sportzplatz Hardturm, Zurich Scotland played their first-ever match at a World Cup finals in front of a crowd of 25,000... and lost 1-0 against Austria. Scotland, [skippered by Preston's Willie Cunningham in the absence of Rangers' George Young] played well and came close to scoring on several occasions. Apparently back home the narrow defeat was greeted as a minor victory. Aaaargh!

Things then got farcical again however when just before the Uruguay game, Andy Beattie resigned his Scotland duties citing internal disagreements with SFA officials with lack of control over team selection a particular problem.

For that historic game against the Austrians the team comprised of seven home Scots with Aberdeen,

13

Celtic, Dundee, Hibernian and Partick Thistle all represented. Scotland's line-up was unchanged for the game against Uruguay in the Saint Jacob Stadium in Basle, so the unlucky/lucky duo who didn't see any World Cup action were George Hamilton of Aberdeen and Celtic's Bobby Evans who was the most experienced player in the squad. Amazingly, Scotland were the only finalist whose squad included players from clubs outwith their own national league – the previously mentioned Cunningham and Tommy Docherty [Preston North End], John Aird [Burnley] and Allan Brown [Blackpool].

The game against Uruguay was shown live on British television – a rare 'treat' in those black and white days of austerity and in the sweltering Swiss heat and with 34,000 in the stadium watching [and no doubt laughing] Scotland had their arses well and truly felt. Apparently the Uruguayans had body-checked, handled frequently, kicked and gouged throughout but they also put the ball in the Scotland net no fewer than SEVEN times without reply. Oh those fiendish foreigners, why they even resorted to using the ball and making it do all the work.

So Scotland's first World Cup was a bit of a disaster, well actually it was a total disaster but surely we would learn from our mistakes? Aye, right.

Uruguay would defeat England in the quarter-finals and ultimately finish fourth with the Austrians besting them in the play-off for third place. The surprise winners of the competition were West Germany who defeated the much-vaunted Hungary 3-2 in the final.

1954 wasn't a total write-off for north of Hadrian's wall however as apparently that was the year the Osprey recolonized Scotland. Better them than the English....again.

SWEDEN 1958

For Scotland's third attempt at winning the World Cup, FIFA abandoned their British Championships-doubling as a qualifying group approach and so we were all pitched into proper European qualifying sections for the first time. Somewhat ironically all four home nations qualified to comprise exactly one quarter of the 16 finalists. Rock n Roll!

Scotland were drawn in qualifying group 9 alongside Spain and Switzerland and we played three of our four qualifying matches in May 1957 with the final game in November of that year.

On 8th May [with petrol rationing still in place because of the Suez crisis] Scotland got off to a flier with a win at Hampden against Spain [who had surprisingly drawn their opening qualifier 2-2 at home to the Swiss]. A crowd of 88,890 saw Scotland twice take the lead and twice get pegged back before two late goals from Jackie Mudie meant a hat-trick for the Blackpool inside-forward and a 4-2 victory for the Scots – Charlton Athletic's John Hewie got the other goal.

On 19th May [just four days after Britain tested its first hydrogen bomb] Scotland travelled to the Saint Jacob Stadium, Basle and defeated Switzerland 2-1. The home side had taken the lead after only 12 minutes but that man Mudie drew Scotland level before half-time. Celtic's Bobby Collins then got the winner in the 71st minute to ensure a much more pleasing visit to Basle than the previous sojourn three years earlier when we took a 7-0 doing from Uruguay at the 1954 World Cup finals. Scotland were skippered by

Scotland Glory, Tears & Souvenirs

Rangers' George Young who was winning his 53rd and final cap.

On 26th May [six days before the first Premium Bond winners were selected by the computer ERNIE], Scotland lost 4-1 to Spain in the Estadio Santiago Bernabeu, Madrid. This time the Scots were run ragged by Alfredo Di Stefano and Ladislao Kubala. Scotland's goal came from Hibernian's Gordon Smith.

Going into the final qualifier against Switzerland, Scotland knew a victory would ensure a trip to Sweden the following summer and on 6 November 1957 [with Sputnik 1, the first artificial Earth satellite visible in the night skies] a crowd of 58,811 at Hampden Park saw the Scots triumph 3-2. Archie Robertson of Clyde gave Scotland the lead after 29 minutes but the sides went in at the break level. Second-half goals from Jackie Mudie and Alex Scott of Rangers gave Scotland a comfortable lead before a strike from Roger Vonlanthen made for a nervous last ten minutes or so.

Scotland were on their way to Sweden [without a manager] but three months before the World Cup finals commenced disaster struck.... when Elvis Presley was conscripted into the US army. Fortunately we would have the likes of the Everly Brothers and Lord Rockingham's XI to fall back on. In Sweden all four British sides avoided one another with Scotland going into group 2 alongside France, Paraguay and Yugoslavia.

On 8th June 1958 Hearts' Jimmy Murray scored Scotland's first-ever goal at a World Cup finals when he netted the equaliser in the 1-1 draw with Yugoslavia at the Arosvallen Stadium, Vasteras in front of a crowd of just 9,591. It was the only goal Jimmy would manage in his five Scotland appearances. With Scotland chasing a winner, Jackie Mudie had a perfectly good goal disallowed – apparently.

Three days later Scotland took to the field at the Idrottsparken, Norrkoping where a crowd of 11,665 witnessed Scotland lose 3-2 to Paraguay, who had topped a qualifying group which included Uruguay and Colombia. The South Americans were supposedly the weakest team in the group but two errors from goalkeeper and captain, Tommy Younger of Liverpool saw the ball end up in the back of the Scotland net.

It was Younger's 24th and final Scotland appearance. A goal from Mudie had made it 1-1 whilst another from Bobby Collins pulled it back to 3-2 with 14 minutes remaining.

On 15th June Scotland met France in the Eyravallen Stadium, Orebro needing a win to stay in the tournament. 13,554 saw a 2-1 victory for France however with their first-half goals coming from the great Raymond Kopa and the even greater Just Fontaine. In between, John Hewie hit the post with a penalty before Rangers' Sammy Baird pulled one back in the second half.

So Scotland finished bottom of their group whilst France and Yugoslavia progressed to the quarter-finals where they defeated Northern Ireland and lost to West Germany respectively. [Wales also made it to the quarter-finals whilst England did not.] France would lose to eventual tournament winners Brazil in the semi-finals but would clinch third place with a win over the Germans.

Scotland still had a lot to learn about the intricacies of tournament football not least maintaining discipline. Indeed it has been suggested that some of Scotland's players over-indulged at the well-stocked restaurant in their Swedish hotel – not alcohol mind you, but food which included large breakfasts, three course lunches and dinners plus generous portions of creamy Swedish cakes and sandwiches at the 10.00pm suppertime. Trust Scotland to pig their way out of a World Cup....

CHILE 1962
There were only 56 entrants overall for the seventh FIFA World Cup which would be hosted by Chile in 1962. A weird and wonderful qualifying draw involved some European qualifying groups having African or Asian sub-groups which would result in 'group finals' of Spain v Morocco and Yugoslavia v South Korea. For Ian McColl's Scotland however things were more straightforward as we were placed in a three-team group along with Czechoslovakia and the Republic of Ireland and all four of our scheduled matches were played one right after the other between 3rd May and 26th September 1961.

Scotland kicked off their qualifying campaign against the Irish at Hampden with Cliff Richard and The Shadows riding high in the UK music charts and less than three weeks after a 9-3 humping from the old enemy at Wembley. Scotland put their Wembley woes behind them though and ran out comfortable 4-1 winners with two goals apiece from Rangers' Ralph Brand and David Herd of Arsenal. Celtic's Pat Crerand made his Scotland debut and 46,696 were there to see it.

Four days later and again the Scots enjoyed another comfortable victory over the Irish, winning 3-0 at Dublin's Dalymount Park. Ralph Brand was on the scoresheet again whilst Everton's Alex Young weighed in with a double.

Seven days after the Dublin success however Scotland travelled to Bratislava and got thumped 4-0. Rangers supplied six players that day and two of them were amongst a group of five who never played for Scotland again.

By the time the Hampden game against Czechoslovakia came around in September, the Berlin wall had gone up and Denis Law had returned to the fold - as a Torino player. Scotland twice went behind with Liverpool's Ian St. John then 'The Lawman' himself drawing us level before Denis the Menace struck the winner with seven minutes remaining. Again Hampden was less than half-full with 51,590 in attendance. This would be the last World Cup qualifier

Scotland Glory, Tears & Souvenirs

at Mount Florida that anyone would travel to by tram as Glasgow's tramways closed the following year. [One for the public transport enthusiasts amongst us.]

Anyway, in October Czechoslovakia then defeated the Republic of Ireland home and away to draw level on points with Scotland and as their superior goal difference was not part of the qualification process a one-game play-off was required and the Heysel Stadium, Brussels was the chosen neutral venue.

On 29 November 1961 in front of a disappointing crowd of 7,000 [where were cheap flights or the Channel Tunnel when you needed them?] Dunfermline Athletic goalkeeper Eddie Connachan made his Scotland debut as did Dundee winger Hugh Robertson, indeed Dundee supplied three players that day. Twice Ian St. John gave Scotland the lead and on the second occasion we held it until eight minutes from the end when Adolf Scherer equalised. Into extra time we went, Spurs' John White hit the bar before Czechoslovakia scored twice more and Scotland checked into Heartbreak Hotel…again.

At the actual finals in Chile, Czechoslovakia went all the way to the final itself where they took the lead against Brazil before eventually going down 3-1. Could have been us, matey…

ENGLAND 1966

By the time our qualifiers for the eighth FIFA World Cup kicked-off in October 1964, the Beatles had conquered the world. However, Liverpool's contribution to Scotland's attempt at world domination would be restricted to Everton's Alex Scott being capped against Finland in the opening qualifier and an appearance by Anfield's Ron Yeats in the final qualifier against Italy. Poland were Scotland's other qualification rivals and just to make things more difficult for ourselves, Scotland's managers worked in a part-time capacity – Ian McColl for the opening qualifier then Jock Stein for the remaining five.

And so the attempt to win an invite to our next door neighbour's big party began with a routine 3-1 victory over Finland at Hampden. 55,332 saw Scotland go 3-0 up by half-time thanks to goals from skipper Denis Law [Manchester United], Celtic's Stevie Chalmers and David Gibson of Leicester City.

A debut cap was awarded to central defender Jackie McGrory of Kilmarnock whilst his club-mate Robert Forsyth played in goal winning his third cap. At the end of season 1964/65 the Ayrshire club would be crowned champions of Scotland – yes really!

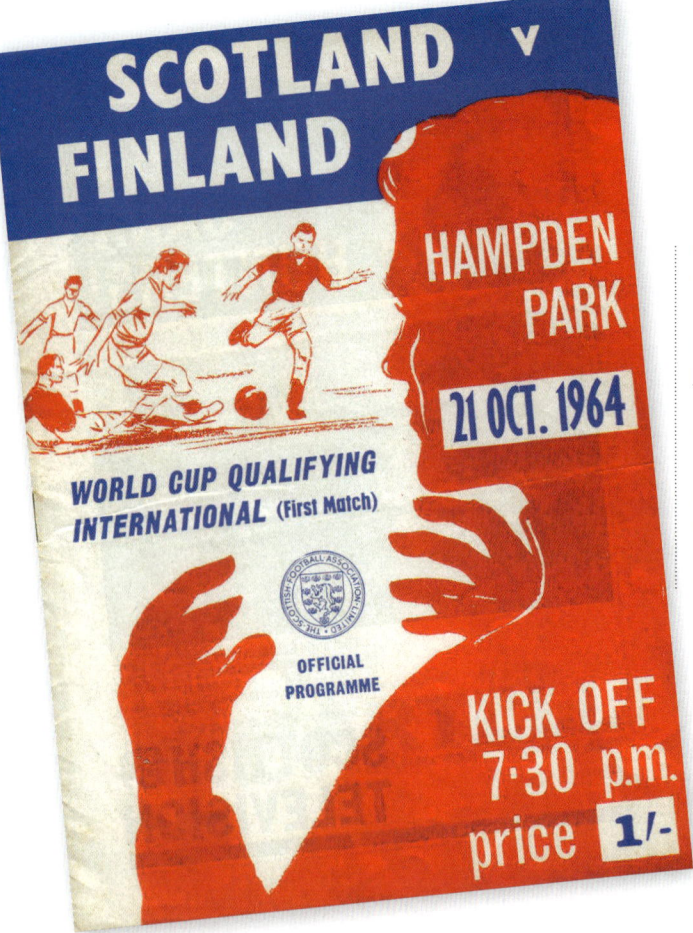

On 23rd May 1965 Scotland travelled to the Slaski Stadium, Chorzow, Poland where they earned a creditable 1-1 draw thanks to a Denis Law equaliser. Four days later the Scotland roadshow moved on to the Olympic Stadium, Helsinki where we came from behind to win 2-1 with goals from Rangers' duo Davie Wilson and John Greig. Wilson's goal was his ninth in 22 Scotland appearances however the winger never played for his country again.

So far so good then, however on 13th October Scotland made a complete arse of things at home to Poland. In front of a crowd of 107,580 Celtic and Scotland skipper Billy McNeill gave his team the lead in the 14th minute which we held for 70 minutes until Jan Liberda equalised. Worse was to follow however a mere two minutes later when Jerzy Sadek hit the winner for Poland. Disaster for Scotland – to coin a phrase. Rangers' 18 year old Willie Johnston made his debut on that woeful Wednesday evening.

Two games against Italy in November and December remained and Scotland would have to win both of them to top the group and qualify for England 66 – a win and a draw would earn us a play-off. Scotland managed to achieve the first victory, in dramatic fashion at Hampden Park when two minutes from time John Greig unleashed a powerful shot past William Negri in Italy's goal.

A crowd of 100,393 had seen Scotland successfully complete part one of the Italian job. Unfortunately however part two would be beyond us, when a weakened Scotland team [no Billy McNeill, Jim Baxter, Willie Henderson or Denis Law] travelled to Naples and saw their World Cup dreams die – 3-0 at the Stadio San Paolo.

It was of little or no consolation that come July 1966 Italy would have a disastrous World Cup finals at Roker Park, Sunderland where they lost to the USSR and Ayresome Park, Middlesbrough where a North Korean victory ensured that the two communist cousins progressed from the group stage at the expense of Italy [and Chile]. As for the remainder of the tournament, well a two-goal hat-trick by Geoff Hurst in

Scotland Glory, Tears & Souvenirs

the final against West Germany gave our nearest and dearest the cup – but mercifully for us, they seldom mention it...

Incidentally, the month before the Queen presented the Jules Rimet trophy to Bobby Moore she did a decent thing by officially opening Glasgow airport and thereby offering up another escape route.

ITALY 1968
Scotland deemed the third European Championship worth participating in and as a bonus/sop the 1966/67 and 1967/68 British Championships doubled-up as qualifying group 8.

Hippies, Carnaby Street, the Kinks – England was swinging whereas Scotland were minging, well at least they were against Northern Ireland in Belfast in October 1967 [qualifying match number 4] when they lost 1-0 to a George Best-inspired home side in front of 55,000 spectators, a result which would prove to be extremely costly.

1967 would be a right mixed bag for although highlights would include a Wembley win, a Scottish club conquering Europe and the introduction of the dessert delicacy Angel Delight, that year would also see the demise of Third Lanark FC, Glasgow trolleybuses and steam passenger trains!

Back to the start however, and Kilmarnock boss Malky MacDonald was Scotland's caretaker manager for the first two games of the qualifying campaign which kicked-off on Saturday 22nd October 1966 with a 1-1 draw with Wales at Ninian Park, Cardiff. Ron Davies had given Wales the lead in the 76th minute before Denis Law equalised with four minutes remaining. Unbelievably, the match took place just the day after the Aberfan disaster when an accumulated rock and shale tip suddenly slid downhill into the south Wales village killing 116 children and 28 adults.

A month later Scotland defeated Northern Ireland 2-1 at Hampden Park but not before the visitors had taken the lead after only nine minutes. Bobby Murdoch got the equaliser with a long-range shot in the 14th minute with his Celtic clubmate and Scotland debutant, Bobby Lennox hitting the winner in the 35th minute. Indeed there were six Parkhead players in the line-up that day and five of them would gain legendary status as part of Jock Stein's 'Lisbon Lions' Celtic team who in May 1967 became the first British side to win the European Champion Clubs' Cup.

In 1967 Bobby Brown left St Johnstone to become Scotland's first full-time manager and in April came the Wembley showdown with the then world champions England who fielded almost their entire 1966 winning line-up, Jimmy Greaves for Roger Hunt being the only change.

Scotland led 1-0 at half-time thanks to a goal from Denis Law but for all Scotland's dominance that's the way the score remained until the final 12 minutes when each team scored two apiece. Bobby Lennox made it 2-0 for Scotland in the 78th minute before Jack Charlton pulled one back for the hosts six minutes later. Three minutes after that, 'new boy' Jim McCalliog of Sheffield Wednesday made it 3-1 for Scotland before Geoff Hurst netted for England with two minutes remaining. Sunderland's Jim Baxter, who had been excellent that day, taunted the English further by playing 'keepie-uppie' with the ball but it might have been better if instead we had pressed for more goals, to try and avenge the 9-3 gubbing from England six years previous.

Scotland's 3-2 victory brought to an end England's unbeaten run of 19 games, however crowning ourselves 'Unofficial World Champions' was only a bit of a laugh – collecting two valuable Euro qualifying points was [or should have been] the real prize, anything else was just a bonus.

So Scotland won the 1966/67 British Championship and at the same time led the qualifying group by one point at the halfway stage – and then it all went horribly wrong at Windsor Park in the same month that Amen Corner charted with 'The world of broken hearts'.

Our penultimate qualifier was against Wales at Hampden in November 1967. Spurs' Alan Gilzean gave Scotland the lead in the 15th minute but Wales hit back through Ron Davies [18th minute] and Alan Durban [49th minute] to give the visitors a shock lead. Gilzean then equalised in the 65th minute with his second headed goal of the game before Rangers' Ronnie McKinnon scored his only Scotland goal ever, 12 minutes from time to give his country a 3-2 victory.

In February 1968 came the Hampden decider. To top the group Scotland needed to defeat England whereas the English only required a draw to make the quarter-finals.

A crowd of 134,000 [a European Championship record] saw Scotland go behind to a Martin Peters goal in the 20th minute. A minute earlier a Bobby Lennox 'goal' for Scotland was disallowed because of a foul on the English keeper, Gordon Banks. Celtic's John Hughes got Scotland an equaliser six minutes before the interval but the game finished 1-1. Despite having taken three points out of a possible four from the English world champions, Scotland were out of the Euros, undone by George Best's Northern Ireland.

In the quarter-finals England edged out Spain over two legs to reach Italy and a finals comprising of just four teams. In the semi-finals England lost 1-0 to Yugoslavia in Florence with Alan Mullery becoming the first England

player to be sent off in a full international. Hosts, Italy won the Henri Delaunay trophy beating Yugoslavia in the final replay whilst England claimed third place by defeating the USSR 2-0.

Scotland Glory, Tears & Souvenirs

MEXICO 1970

Austria, Cyprus and West Germany provided the opposition for Scotland's final set of qualifying matches of the 1960s – a decade in which our club sides performed consistently well in European competition whereas our national team was gloriously inconsistent. This time the prize at stake was a place at the Mexico 1970 World Cup finals.

Bobby Brown's Scotland won their opening qualifier by defeating old 'friends' Austria 2-1 at Hampden Park in November 1968. The attendance was 80,856 and just to make things interesting Scotland went behind after only two minutes. Five minutes later Denis Law headed home the equaliser and fifteen minutes from the end skipper Billy Bremner forced the ball over the line to give Scotland the points.

Two weeks before Christmas 1968, Scotland travelled to the warmth of Nicosia where 5,895 spectators at the GSP Stadium saw the visitors defeat Cyprus 5-0. On a truly dreadful, concrete playground of a pitch, Scotland scored all five goals in the first half thanks to a double from both Spurs' Alan Gilzean and Colin Stein of Rangers. The other goal came from Bobby Murdoch of Celtic whose clubmate Jim Craig was unable to make the trip to the eastern Mediterranean because he was also a dental surgeon who had patients booked for the day of the game!

As a precursor to the tie against Helmut Schon's West Germany, Scotland recorded a major victory in Madrid on 29th March 1969… when Lulu was joint winner of the Eurovision song contest with Boom Bang-a-Bang.

On 16th April 1969 there then arrived at Hampden a West German side which included Franz Beckenbauer, Wolfgang Overath and Hans-Hubert Vogts [none of whom were notable vocalists though] and another big crowd, 95,951 again saw Scotland go behind when the opportunistic Gerd Muller scored six minutes before half-time. Scotland fought back however and two minutes from time Bobby Murdoch slammed home a deserved equaliser.

The following month, Cyprus came to town and Scotland ran riot winning 8-0. Only 39,095 were at Hampden to see Colin Stein hit four of the goals [the next Scotland hat-trick would not come until the 21st century] as well as strikes from Eddie Gray [Leeds United], Willie Henderson [Rangers] and Billy McNeill and Tommy Gemmell [both Celtic]. The Scotland keeper that day was Birmingham City's James Herriot who could possibly have been better employed spending the afternoon writing a story about animals [We know it's not the same one but there is a connection].

In October 1969 [four months after man first set foot on the Moon] Scotland travelled to Planet Hamburg knowing they would have to get a draw to keep their hopes alive [followed by a win in Vienna]. In the Volkspark Stadium and amidst Teutonic pitch invasions Scotland gave it their best shot and went down fighting – in more ways than one. Celtic's Jimmy Johnstone put Scotland in front after only three minutes but the Germans drew level seven minutes before the interval. Scotland then hit the post twice – Tommy Gemmell and Billy Bremner – before Gerd Muller put West Germany in front in the 60th minute. Four minutes later however Alan Gilzean headed in an equaliser. In the 79th minute though Reinhard Libuda got the winning goal for the hosts and in the final minute Tommy Gemmell was red-carded for retaliation – after being tripped by Helmut Haller, the Lisbon Lion then proceeded to chase the German striker before giving him a swift boot up the backside. They don't like it up them, apparently and the Swiss referee was equally unimpressed so off big Tam went.

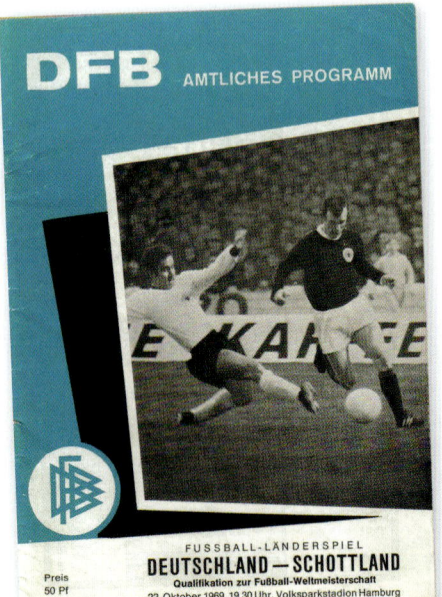

So sadly when Scotland visited the Austrian capital on 5 November 1969 there was nothing at stake. Only 10,091 rattled around the Prater Stadium as Austria won 2-0 against a Scotland side that gave debut caps to Frank Burns [Manchester United not *M.A.S.H.*], Hugh Curran [Wolves] and Peter Lorimer [Leeds United]. For the swinging sixties, for Scotland's World Cup campaign and indeed for Frank Burns' international career it really was a case of Goodnight Vienna.

In the heat, altitude and colour of Mexico, West Germany knocked-out the holders England at the quarter-finals stage. In Leon the Germans came back from being 2-0 down to defeat the English 3-2 but in an amazing semi-final in Mexico City they lost 4-3 to Italy. West Germany clinched third place however by defeating Uruguay whilst Brazil claimed the world crown by dismantling the European champions, Italy in the final at the *Aztec* Stadium. Chocolate bars and free-flowing football have never been so good.

BELGIUM 1972
The 1970-72 European Championships were the fourth such tournament, the second which Scotland had entered but the first in which our qualifying opponents came from mainland Europe, namely Belgium, Denmark and Portugal. For a historical perspective Edward Heath was the Conservative Prime Minister, the pioneering glam-rockers T.Rex enjoyed great chart success at the time and Jon Pertwee was Dr. Who.

Scotland, managed by Bobby Brown, won their opening qualifier in November 1970, 1-0 versus Denmark at Hampden with Derby County's John O'Hare netting in front of a disappointing crowd of 24,618. Between February and June 1971 however it all went 'Pete Tong' as we lost three consecutive away ties – 3-0 against Belgium in a swamp-like

Scotland Glory, Tears & Souvenirs

Stade Sclessin in Liege [with Archie Gemmill making his debut], 2-0 versus Portugal in Lisbon [a Pat Stanton own goal before Eusebio finished us off] and 1-0 against a largely amateur Denmark in Copenhagen [with Kilmarnock's Tommy McLean winning his sixth and final Scotland cap].

We were therefore out of the competition by the time Tommy Docherty had taken charge of the team for the home qualifier against Portugal. On 13th October 1971 Bob Wilson and George Graham [both Arsenal], Eddie Colquhoun [Sheffield United], Alex Cropley [Hibernian] and Martin Buchan [Aberdeen] all made their first appearance for Scotland [as did I, near the top of Hampden's old, uncovered east terracing, if you see what I mean].

58,612 saw John O'Hare give Scotland a first-half lead before Rui Rodrigues equalised in the 57th minute. Less than 60 seconds later however O'Hare's Derby team-mate Archie Gemmill headed the winner. Alex Cropley was my man of the match and if only I didn't have school the next day I could have celebrated the victory properly.

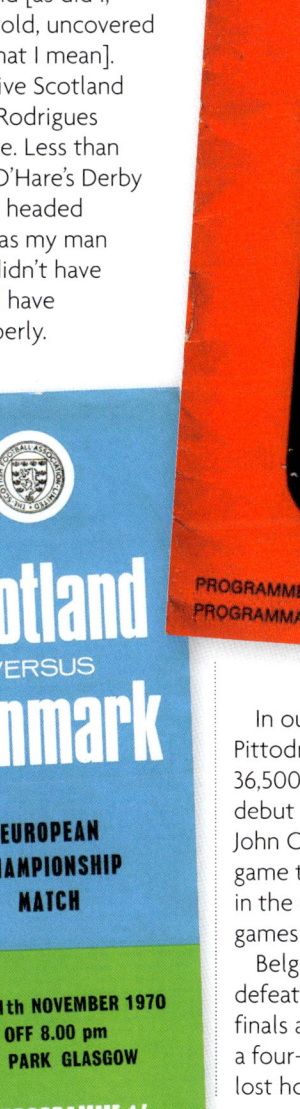

In our final qualifier, which was played at Pittodrie Stadium in November in front of 36,500, Kenny Dalglish made his Scotland debut coming on as a second-half substitute. John O'Hare [again] got the only goal of the game to give Scotland a 100% home record in the qualifiers – shame about the away games – as we finished third in our group.

Belgium topped the group before defeating Italy over two legs in the quarter-finals and then winning the right to host a four-nations finals in June 1972. Belgium lost however to the eventual competition

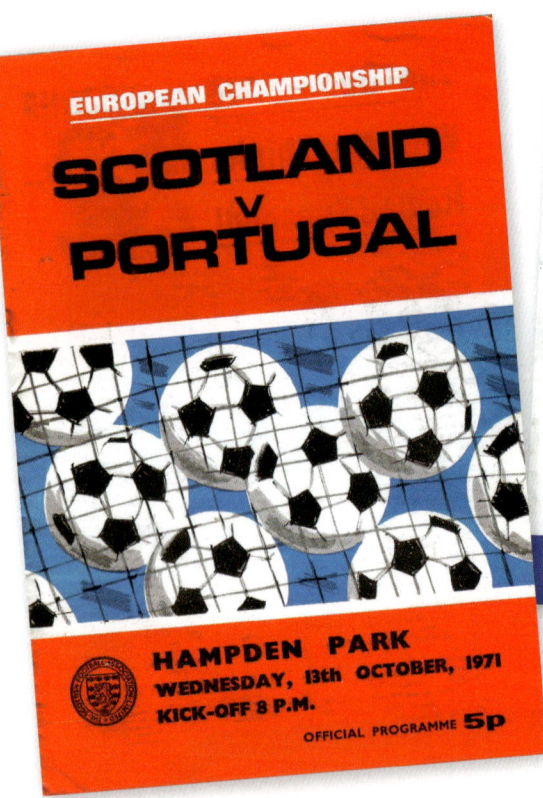

winners West Germany in the semi-finals before clinching third place by beating Hungary in a play-off. So Belgium lost only two matches in the entire competition – 2-1 against the Germans in Antwerp and 1-0 against the Scots in Aberdeen.

A second European trophy did come Scotland's way however in May 1972 when Willie Waddell's Rangers defeated Moscow Dynamo 3-2 in the final of the European Cup-Winners' Cup in Barcelona.

WEST GERMANY 1974

Despite there being 99 entrants for the tenth FIFA World Cup only Czechoslovakia and Denmark stood in front of Scotland and a place at the 1974 finals in West Germany [plus West Berlin]. The upbeat Tommy Docherty was the Scotland manager and the music of Slade and Wizzard added to the feel-good factor.

We felt even better by mid-November 1972 when after a space of just four weeks we had defeated Denmark 4-1 in Copenhagen then 2-0 at Hampden. Lou Macari [Celtic], Jimmy Bone [Norwich City], debutant Joe Harper [Aberdeen] and Willie Morgan [Manchester United] were the marksmen who were on target in the Danish capital whilst Celtic's Kenny Dalglish and Peter Lorimer of Leeds United hit the net at home in front of 47,109.

In May 1973 Czechoslovakia drew 2-2 with Denmark in Copenhagen and that dropped point meant that on the evening of 26th September 1973 'all' Scotland had to do to make it to their first World Cup finals in 16 years was to beat Czechoslovakia at Hampden. It is something of a tradition however with Scotland to let the opposition score first just to make things even more exciting and so it was in the 33rd minute when a saveable shot from Nehoda beat Celtic goalkeeper Ally Hunter. Five minutes from half-time however and a powerful header from Manchester United's Jim Holton meant that Scotland went in at the break on level terms.

Another headed goal – this time from substitute Joe Jordan – 15 minutes from the end would prove sufficient to win the game and get Scotland to Germany. At the conclusion of the match, manager Willie Ormond [who had replaced the Manchester United defector Tommy Docherty in January 1973] was chaired from the pitch by Billy Bremner and Davie Hay to the cheers of 100,000 grateful Scots. We were back in the big time.

Scotland Glory, Tears & Souvenirs

On 16th October there was released the cult Scottish horror movie – *The Wicker Man* - 'Oh Jesus Christ!' and 24 hours later Scotland lost their final qualifying fixture against Czechoslovakia in Bratislava thanks to the award of a spot-kick so dubious it moved the late, great Arthur Montford to comment – 'If the referee thinks that's a penalty he's up a West German gum-tree.' Hear! Hear!

On 14th June 1974 for Scotland's opening match at the finals in West Germany [at Dortmund's Westfalen Stadium] there were no signs of any gum trees, just a potential banana-skin against the so-called minnows of the group, Zaire. Scotland hadn't won a match at either of our two previous World Cup finals so we were understandably nervous as we faced the largely unknown African champions.

Two first-half goals from the Leeds United duo of Peter Lorimer and Joe Jordan helped settle the nerves, however a seemingly more cautious second 45 meant Scotland failed to improve upon our goal difference although Lorimer did hit the bar. Scotland had however achieved their first win at a World Cup finals and 25,800 were there to see Denis Law's international swansong.

Four days later, Scotland took on the defending world champions Brazil in front of 60,000 spectators at the Wald Stadion, Frankfurt and came damn close to beating them with Billy Bremner narrowly missing the target from close range whilst shots from distance from Davie Hay and Peter Lorimer also nearly did the trick. Nil-nil it finished with British Prime Minister Harold Wilson and Scottish world champion racing driver Jackie Stewart looking on from their seats in the stand.

Our third opponents, Yugoslavia had also drawn 0-0 with Brazil but had thrashed Zaire 9-0, so to progress, Scotland had to chase a victory - assuming that Brazil would defeat Zaire by at least three clear goals. In a tight, tense game Scotland [in their unfamiliar white shirts] and Yugoslavia matched one another and cancelled each other out until substitute Karasi put the Slavs in front seven minutes from time. One minute from time, following good work from Tommy Hutchison on the wing, Joe Jordan got Scotland a deserved equaliser – but it was not enough, for Brazil had defeated Zaire 3-0.

Due to an inferior goal-difference four points from three games was not sufficient to see Willie Ormond's boys through to the second stage of the competition and so Scotland became the first undefeated nation to be eliminated from a World Cup.

The Scotland party flew back to a marvellous reception at Glasgow airport where around 10,000 fans had gathered to welcome our heroes home. One can only wonder at what it would have been like if we had won the bloody thing!

Back in West Germany, Yugoslavia lost all three second-stage group matches whilst Brazil lost the third place play-off to Poland – England's conquerors at the initial qualifying stage. In the final

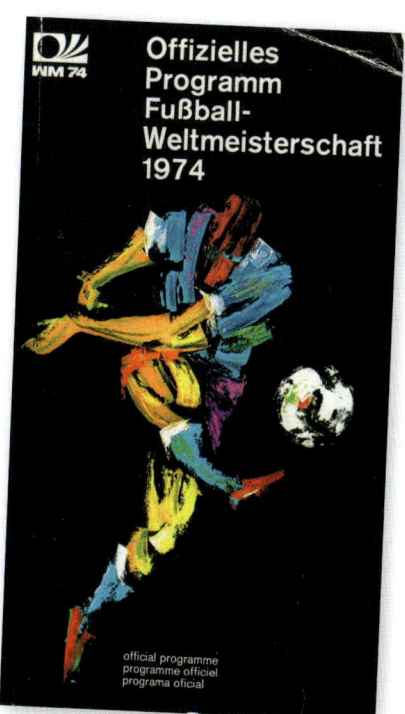

itself the bold Berti Vogts and co helped snuff out the threat of Johan Cruyff and his Total Football teammates as the Germans ran out 2-1 winners.

YUGOSLAVIA 1976

Following on from the 1974 World Cup finals in West Germany from which Willie Ormond's Scotland had returned early, but undefeated, hopes were high that we could progress to the latter stages of the 1976 European Championships and maybe even host the conclusion of the competition.

Scotland's qualifying group opponents were Spain, Romania and Denmark, none of whom had featured at West Germany '74, and so it was that most of the crowd of 94,331 that turned up at Hampden in November for the opening game against the Spanish were in confident mood – and then Scotland fu...messed-up big style.

Billy Bremner had given Scotland the lead in the 11th minute and we should have gone 2-0 in front but Tommy Hutchison's penalty was saved by Jose Iribar and the miss served to give the Spaniards a fillip who then equalised before half-time thanks to Enrique Castro. Castro then got a second half winner for Spain from a shot that I certainly couldn't have stopped but Leeds United's David Harvey perhaps should have saved.

In the return fixture in February 1975 Scotland earned a creditable 1-1 draw in Valencia's Estadio Luis Casanova. Joe Jordan had given Scotland the lead after only two minutes. However, substitute Alfredo Mejido got the equaliser in the 67th minute – barely one minute after coming on to the pitch.

On 1st June 1975 [after having played four games in an eleven-day spell in May which culminated in a 5-1 doing at Wembley] Scotland travelled to the 23 August Stadium in Bucharest and managed another 1-1 draw, this time against Romania. Dudu Georgescu gave the home side a first-half lead before skipper Gordon McQueen [Leeds United] snatched a last-minute equaliser in a game which saw Aberdeen's Willie Miller make his international debut.

On 11th June 1975 the first North Sea oil was pumped ashore at the Sullom Voe terminal in Shetland. 'It's Scotland's oil!' cried the nationalists but I would gladly have swapped some of it for more points on the board.

Back to the football then and on 3rd September a second half goal from Hibernian's Joe Harper gave Scotland two points from Denmark in Copenhagen. Ultimately it proved to be something of a pyrrhic victory for as a result of a 'misunderstanding' in the post-match celebrations in a nightclub in the Danish capital, five Scottish internationalists [including Joe Harper and Billy Bremner] received lifetime bans from the SFA. The bans were eventually lifted although too late to save Bremner's international career. The pocket dynamo from the town of Stirling had played for Scotland on 54 occasions – at that point in time only Denis Law had a greater number of Scotland caps.

The following month Denmark came to Hampden and with Bremner's absence Rangers' John Greig was recalled and given the captaincy. It was Big Bad John's 44th and final appearance for Scotland

Scotland Glory, Tears & Souvenirs

and he skippered his team to a 3-1 victory in front of 48,021. Denmark led 1-0 at half-time but second-half goals from Kenny Dalglish [Celtic], Bruce Rioch [Derby County] and Ted MacDougall [Norwich City] ensured that justice was done.

On 16 November however Spain clinched qualification by drawing 2-2 in Bucharest which goes some way to explaining why there were only 11,375 at Hampden on 17 December for Scotland's final fixture, against Romania. A freezing cold evening only eight days from Christmas didn't help the attendance. I was there of course [with a tartan scarf tied around my wrist], but then again, I'm a numpty. Anyways, Scotland took a first-half lead when Bruce Rioch thumped home a free-kick from just outside the penalty box. The Romanians got an equaliser late on however to ensure that they finished second in the group as well as take the shine off debuts by Johnny Doyle of Ayr United and Andy Gray of Aston Villa. Just to add to the pain and disappointment of that 1974 to 1975 qualifying campaign was the music and the dress-sense [ahem!] of the Bay City Rollers.

In the two-leg quarter-finals Spain were eliminated by world and European champions West Germany whilst an excellent Wales team also went out at the last eight stage to Yugoslavia who then won the right to host a four-nations finals. At the finals, the surprise package was Czechoslovakia who overcame the Netherlands in the semi-finals before going on to lift the trophy by defeating the holders on penalties with Antonin Panenka's cheeky straight-down-the-middle, lofted-chip clinching it. If only Tommy Hutchison had done something similar against Spain.

ARGENTINA 1978

It's generally accepted that the eleventh FIFA World Cup competition [ie Argentina 1978] was a *Disaster for Scotland* – but only because our disappointment was huge following our failure to achieve aspirations which were astronomical bordering on the ridiculous [ie to become the first European team to win the World Cup outwith their own continent and in spite of us being only a Pot 3 team in the seeded draw for the finals].

Tom Baker was Dr. Who at the time, Labour's Jim Callaghan was UK Prime Minister and punk rock slugged it out with disco music for our affections - The Sex Pistols v. Donna Summer, the Stranglers v. Boney M, The Bill Grundy *Today* show v *Saturday Night Fever*, Spittle v White suits.....hopefully you get the picture.

Scotland meanwhile, managed by Willie Ormond then Ally MacLeod, reached their fourth World Cup finals by topping a three-team qualification group which comprised of the then European champions Czechoslovakia and that excellent Wales team [Terry Yorath, John Toshack, Leighton James et al] which had reached the quarter-finals of the same, 1976 European Championships.

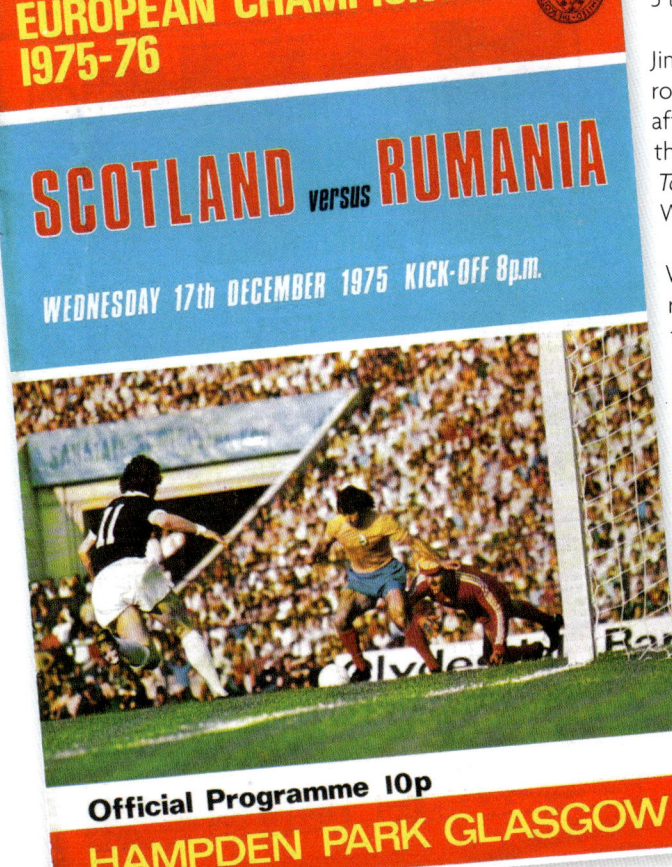

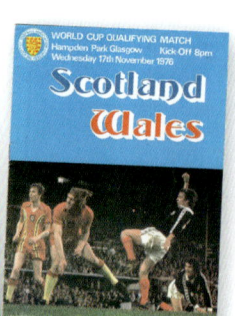

In October 1976 Scotland lost the opening qualifier 2-0 to Czechoslovakia in Prague. However, the following month we scraped a 1-0 win over Wales at Hampden. 63,233 witnessed Ian Evans' own goal.

In September 1977 85,000 were at Hampden when Czechoslovakia were trounced 3-1. Joe Jordan, Asa Hartford and Kenny Dalglish were our scorers. And so to Anfield, Liverpool where on 12th October Scotland beat Wales 2-0 thanks to a dubious penalty award, which Don Masson [QPR] converted and a gem of a goal from Dalglish. Cue wild celebrations, OTT predictions and numerous pubs taking advantage of recent changes to the licensing laws in Scotland to embrace 'all day' opening hours. Ladbrokes eventually offered odds of 8-1 for Scotland to win the trophy and sales of Scotland replica jerseys rocketed like never before. My medium-sized version of that classic Umbro top remains pinned to the ceiling of the spare room.

And then came the finals and Britain's sole representatives lost the opening match at the Estadio Chateau Carreras, Cordoba 1-3 to a supposedly aged but skilful Peru side who were the then South American champions. A crowd of 37,792 saw Joe Jordan, now of Manchester United, give Scotland the lead after only 15 minutes and we all sat back and waited for us to add to it. Those party-poopers Peru hadn't read the script however and Cesar Cueto equalised two minutes before half-time. In the 62nd minute Scotland had the chance to 'sort things' when Hector Chumpitaz was penalised for a clumsy challenge on Bruce Rioch. Don Masson's resultant penalty was saved by the keeper, Teofilo Cubillas then scored in the 70th and 76th minutes and...and I really don't want to say any more as the pain is coming back.

The Scotland camp was not a happy one – inadequate hotel accommodation [eg a swimming pool with no water in it], a rapidly deteriorating relationship with the media, oh yes, and winger Willie Johnston had been sent home in disgrace after failing a drugs test.

Four days after the Peru 'hiccup', in the same stadium but in front of a much smaller crowd of 7.938 Scotland took on Iran, who had won the Asian Football Championship in 1968, 1972 and 1976. Scotland led 1-0 at half-time thanks to an own-goal from Andranik Eskandarian but they were playing without confidence or imagination, like a team who looked like they wanted to be on the same plane home with Johnston.

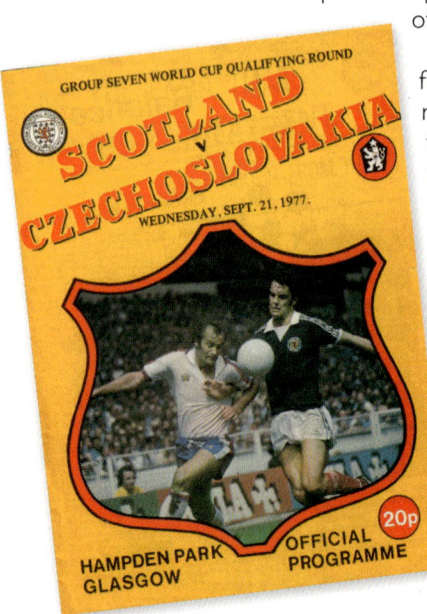

Scotland Glory, Tears & Souvenirs

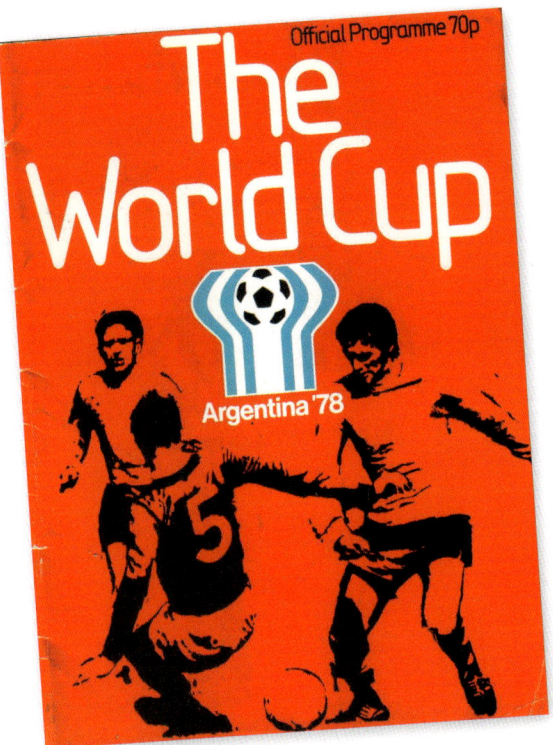

Kenny Dalglish [whose goal at Wembley four weeks previous had given Liverpool the European Champions Clubs' Cup] won his 56th Scotland cap to overtake the previous record holder Denis Law. Dalglish was then substituted in the 73rd minute and four minutes later Iran equalised and a 1-1 draw resulted. Dear oh dear.

Amazingly, Scotland went into their final group game, against the Netherlands, in the Estadio San Martin, Mendoza knowing that a victory by a margin of three goals would still see us through to the second phase of the competition. Fat chance we all said and then in the 68th minute the crowd of 35,130 watched in amazement as Archie Gemmill waltzed past eight or nine Dutch defenders [time may have exaggerated what was a goal of true beauty] to give Scotland a 3-1 lead and send us all into dreamland. A Robbie Rensenbrink spot-kick [which was also the 1,000th goal in World Cup history] had given the Dutch the lead in the 34th minute before Kenny Dalglish and Archie Gemmill [penalty] one minute either side of half-time helped nudge the Scots in front.

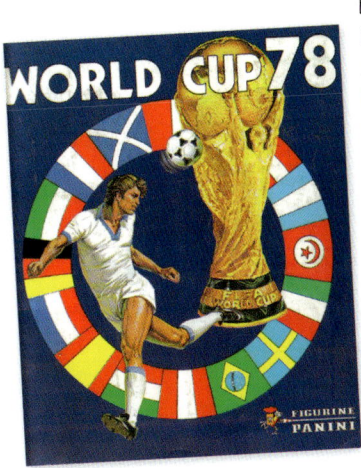

Alas the 'second-stage dream' endured for only about three minutes before Johnny Rep pulled one back for the Netherlands. 3-2 it finished and Scotland were eliminated from the World Cup on goal difference for the second successive time. Cue much wailing and gnashing of teeth. Argentina, probably after having studied a video of Scotland's victory in Mendoza, duly defeated the Netherlands 3-1 in the final to lift the trophy for the first time.

As at 2017, Scotland have appeared at eight World Cup finals and statistically speaking Argentina represents our third-best performance. It was also the last time that there were only sixteen finalists.

These are the bald facts but you would need an entire book to do justice to the hype, the hysterics, the perverse hilarity of it all. We got totally carried away with ourselves and I for one enjoyed much of it. From a purely footballing perspective, I've never felt so alive — well at least until the latter stages of the Peru game. Compared to the seemingly never-ending pain of the 21st century wilderness years, Argentina was but a boot up the arse — albeit a sore one.

ITALY 1980

Ally MacLeod survived the big let-down of the 1978 World Cup finals in Argentina to lead Scotland into the qualifiers for the 1980 European Championship finals which would be held in Italy – the first time a host country was selected before the commencement of the competition. Scotland's four opponents were Austria, Belgium, Norway and Portugal.

As it transpired Ally would only manage Scotland in the opening match – in September 1978 against Austria in Vienna – before resigning to become Ayr United's boss.

In the Prater Stadium, Austria were 3-0 up after 64 minutes before Gordon McQueen and Andy Gray hit back for Scotland and then the ball-boys mysteriously 'disappeared' and the Austrians held on to win 3-2.

The following month, Norway were the visitors to Hampden and new manager Jock Stein chose a starting eleven that all plied their trade in England. No substitutions were made and twice Scotland went behind and twice Kenny Dalglish pulled us level before an Archie Gemmill penalty three minutes from time sent home happy the crowd of 65,372 – give or take the odd Norwegian who probably felt gutted.

In November the Scots lost 1-0 to Portugal in Lisbon's Stadium of Light [Martin Buchan's last game for his country] but the following June, Scotland picked up two points away from home with a convincing 4-0 victory over Norway at the Ulleval Stadium, Oslo. Joe Jordan, Kenny Dalglish, John Robertson [Nottingham Forest] and Gordon McQueen were the scorers.

Into 1979 and in the 1st March Referendum on whether there was support for a Scottish Assembly there was not enough self-confidence around to achieve the sizeable majority required. Some political commentators blamed it on the 'Argentina effect'.

Meanwhile, come October Scotland crucially slipped up at home to Austria, drawing 1-1 in front of a Hampden crowd of 67,895. Hans Krankl had given the Austrians the lead just before half-time following a 'rare' mistake from goalkeeper Alan Rough of Partick Thistle. Late on in the second half skipper Archie Gemmill [now of Birmingham City] scored to give Scotland a share of the points.

There then followed two games against Belgium in which it all went horribly wrong. Personally speaking, I blame the Belgian parody-punk performer Plastic Bertrand of 'Ca plane pour moi' fame. Him, plus Margaret Thatcher becoming UK Prime Minister in May 1979.

Scotland Glory, Tears & Souvenirs

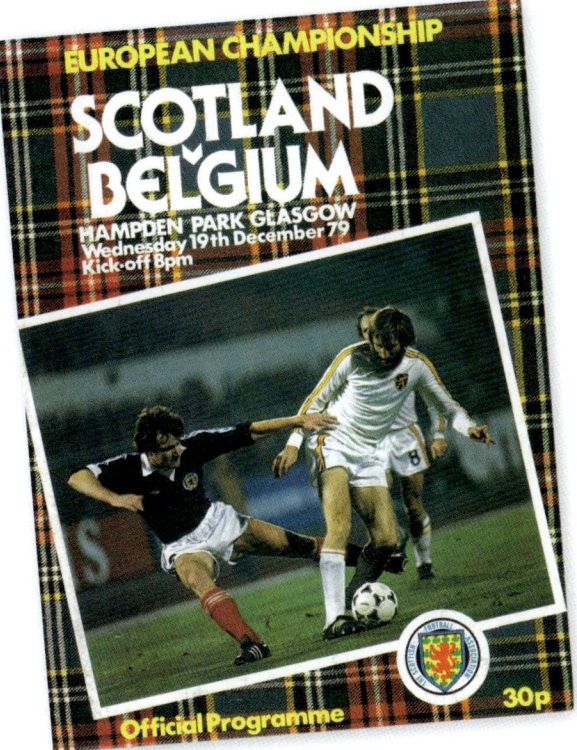

Anyway, in November 1979, only 14,289 turned up at the Heysel Stadium, Brussels to see the home team win 2-0 [Van der Elst and Voordeckers] and thus eliminate the visitors who gave a debut cap to Davie Provan of Celtic.

Six days before Christmas, Belgium then came to Hampden Park needing a win to leapfrog Austria, top the group and therefore qualify for the finals. Guy Thys' classy Belgium team went for the jugular and the real 'Muscles from Brussels' were 3-0 ahead after only 29 minutes [Frankie-boy Van der Elst helping himself to a double this time]. 25,389 [minus those spectators who left at half-time] saw John Robertson net a second-half consolation goal direct from a free-kick. Naturally, it was the best goal of the evening.... Meanwhile, TinTin and Hercule Poirot headed for Sauchiehall Street to celebrate.

In March 1980 20,233 came along to Hampden to see Scotland and Portugal play out the final fixture of the group as well as witness the Aberdeen duo of Alex McLeish and Steve Archibald make their international debuts. Archibald hit the net along with Kenny Dalglish, Andy Gray [Wolves] and Archie Gemmill as Scotland ran out 4-1 winners. Even although the game was technically 'meaningless' it's still enjoyable when you stuff some half-decent opposition.

So Belgium went to Italy 1980 and enjoyed a damn fine tournament topping a group which included the hosts plus England and Spain before eventually succumbing to West Germany in the Final itself.

SPAIN 1982

For many Scotland supporters – myself included- this tournament was the 'Special One,' with the music of Adam and the Ants, Duran Duran, Orchestral Manoeuvres in the Dark, Soft Cell and, er, Sheena Easton adding to the fun. In European qualifying group 6 Scotland had Israel, Northern Ireland, Portugal and Sweden for company with the top two teams making it to the 12th World Cup finals in Spain 1982.

With Scotland having qualified for the 1974 and 1978 finals, the pressure was on manager Jock Stein to make it three in a row and a good start was made in September 1980 when, from a seemingly impossible angle, Aberdeen's Gordon Strachan netted the winner against Sweden in the Rasunda

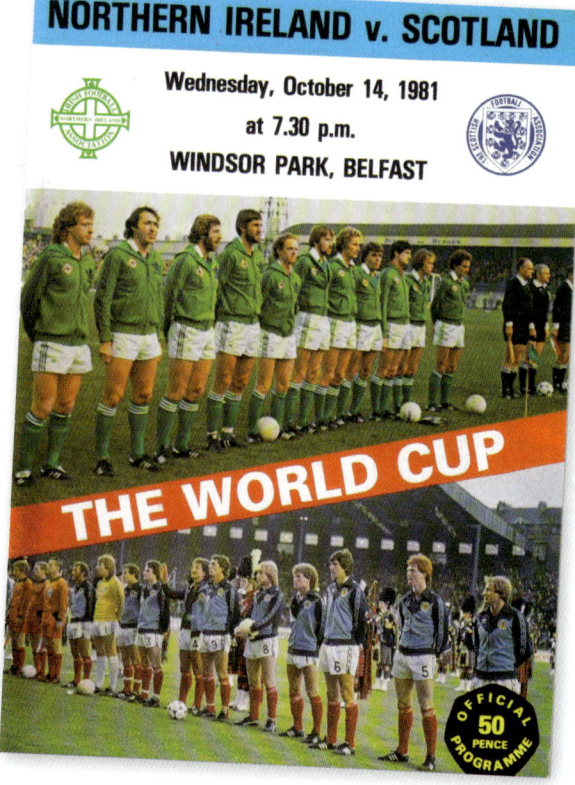

Stadium, Stockholm. The following month however, it was goal-less at Hampden against Portugal with 60,765 looking on.

In a freezing-cold February, Scotland headed for the warmth of Tel Aviv and another hard-fought 1-0 away victory. Kenny Dalglish got the priceless winner for Scotland as no other side would take full points in Israel with both Sweden and the Irish faltering to nil-nil draws and Portugal crashing 4-1.

A month later however Scotland drew again at home – 1-1 with Billy Bingham's Northern Ireland – with Burnley's Billy Hamilton giving the visitors the lead after 70 minutes before Ipswich Town's John Wark equalised five minutes later. There were 78,444 at Hampden Park that evening but Kenny Dalglish was missing through injury and so his run of 43 consecutive internationals came to an end.

In April 1981, Hampden pulled in 61,489 for the visit of Israel. Two successful penalty kicks from Nottingham Forest's John Robertson gave Scotland a 2-0 lead at half-time before Celtic's Davie Provan added a third eight minutes after the re-start with Moshe Sinai nabbing a consolation goal for the visitors.

81,511 packed into Hampden in September for the crunch match against Sweden and it

Scotland Glory, Tears & Souvenirs

was yahoo time after 20 minutes when the head of Joe Jordan [AC Milan] put Scotland in front. Another successful John Robertson penalty sealed it seven minutes from time and Scotland now only required one point from their two remaining games [away to Northern Ireland and Portugal] to qualify.

On 14th October 1981 Scotland travelled to Windsor Park, Belfast and ground out a nil-nil draw to top the group and book a passage to Spain. Our main heroes were Alan Rough in goal and skipper Asa Hartford who had to clear off his own goal-line at one point. I remember complaining at the time that it wasn't the same when qualification was clinched away from home.

In the final fixture at Lisbon's Stadium of Light, Dundee United's Paul Sturrock gave Scotland a ninth-minute lead and for a while it looked like our first-ever victory in Lisbon was a distinct possibility. Manuel Fernandes hit us with the old one-two however to inflict upon Scotland our only defeat of the campaign. Earlier that day Northern Ireland had defeated Israel 1-0 in Belfast to clinch the second qualifying spot.

It was good to see two British teams make it to the finals, but you had to spare a thought for Portugal who, like Scotland in 1966, remained at home whilst their big, noisy neighbour held a big, noisy party.

At the 24-team finals Scotland were drawn in group 6 along with Brazil, New Zealand and the USSR. Scotland would play two matches in Malaga and one in Seville so the Tartan Army were able to set up camp all along the Costa del Sol. My brother Allan and I were based in Torremolinos and it was feckin magic, man. Two weeks of super-soccer, sun, sea and sangria – attractions that Russia 2018 is unlikely to offer – and yet, all against a seemingly surreal backdrop of the ten-week Falklands conflict coming to an end.

Tickets for the three matches which would be played at Malaga's Estadio La Rosaleda [ie two Scotland games plus New Zealand v USSR] were obtained simply by queuing outside the stadium [in 90 degrees afternoon heat] on 14th June, the day before Scotland's opener against New Zealand.

Mercifully, the game against the Kiwis kicked-off at 9.00pm local time and by

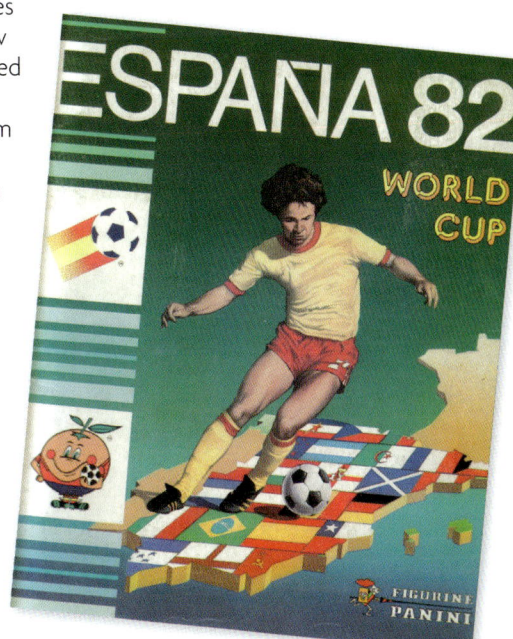

33

9.32pm Scotland were 3-0 in front [Kenny Dalglish plus two from John Wark]. Twenty minutes into the second half however New Zealand pulled it back to 3-2 and it was brown trousers time for the Tartan Army. Blushes were spared though thanks to goals from John Robertson and Steve Archibald and non-stop running from Gordon Strachan. 5-2 it finished for what is still Scotland's biggest victory at a World Cup finals and 20,000 were in the stadium to witness the goalfest.

Three days later over the mountains to Seville we went for a baking-hot 9.00pm kick-off against Tele Santana's Brazil in the Estadio Benito Villamarin in front of a crowd of 47,379. A magnificent strike from Dundee United's David Narey in the 18th minute put Scotland in front and convinced me that we could go on and win the competition [alcohol and high temperatures can be a heady mix]. Zico spoiled things somewhat by netting an equaliser before half-time and in the second half Oscar, Eder and Falcao all pissed on my tapas as an admittedly impressive Brazil ran out 4-1 winners. Both Alan Rough and Asa Hartford won their 50th Scotland caps that day but I don't suppose either of them felt much like celebrating.

On 22nd June Scotland faced the USSR in Malaga knowing we would have to beat the Soviets to reach the second stage [along with Brazil] and fifteen minutes in, Joe Jordan [our footballing James Bond] put us one-up against the evil red empire [or so the BBC and the Americans said it was]. We went in at the break only 45 minutes away from the second round and all our 'Miss Moneypennies' getting a celebratory vodka-martini, shoogled but not stirred.

Of course it wasn't to be and in the 60th minute Alexandr Chivadze equalised whilst six minutes from time Alan Hansen and Willie Miller morphed into Laurel and Hardy before colliding and allowing another Georgian, Ramaz Shengelia to run in on goal and beat Alan Rough. Two minutes from the end skipper Graeme Souness powered through to shoot home an equaliser but it was not enough. The game, which was played in front of 45,000, finished 2-2 and so for the third successive World Cup finals, Scotland were eliminated at the group stage on goal difference. What were the chances of that happening, eh?

It was Poland who had the pleasure of eliminating the USSR at the second round stage; however, it is still something of a mystery as to how the sublime Socrates and co did not go on to win the cup for Brazil. Instead, they were hustled out in the second round by a Rossi-inspired Italy who went on to lift the trophy by defeating West Germany 3-1 in the final.

Scotland Glory, Tears & Souvenirs

FRANCE 1984

Scotland's fifth attempt at reaching the finals of the European Championships saw us placed in a four team group alongside old foes, Belgium plus East Germany and Switzerland but our hopes were high after a good[ish] Spain '82 World Cup.

Scotland got off to a bright start in October 1982 when we defeated East Germany 2-0 at Hampden. 40,355 saw two second half goals from John Wark [Ipswich Town] and Paul Sturrock [Dundee United] as well as Aberdeen goalkeeper Jim Leighton make his international debut.

After defeating the Soviet Sector, sorry, I mean the German Democratic Republic, Scotland then failed to win any of the five remaining qualifiers and finished bottom of the group. Sacre Bleu! Wtf? etc etc.

In November and in the driving sleet, Scotland went down 2-0 to Switzerland in the Wankdorf Stadium, Berne. [I wonder if the Swiss titter at any of our words?] A much improved [though ultimately fruitless] performance by Scotland ten days before Christmas ended in a 3-2 defeat against Belgium at the Heysel Stadium in Brussels. Twice Kenny Dalglish gave Scotland the lead [with two of his finest goals for his country] and twice Belgium equalised before eventually going in front themselves. Twelve minutes from time however Scotland should have earned the draw they deserved but Frank Gray's penalty kick was saved by Jean-Marie Pfaff. From a personal perspective this was the first game of football I ever taped – using my state of the art Betamax video recorder.

Switzerland visited Hampden in the spring of 1983 but only 36,923 were there to see the visitors lead 2-0 with 58 minutes gone. John Wark pulled one back in the 70th minute and then six minutes later came a superb equaliser from Celtic's Charlie Nicholas who was making his debut. 2-2 it finished and another point of note was the debut of Dundee United's Richard Gough.

In May 1983 Alex Ferguson's Aberdeen lifted our spirits however when they won the European Cup-Winners' Cup after defeating Real Madrid 2-1 in

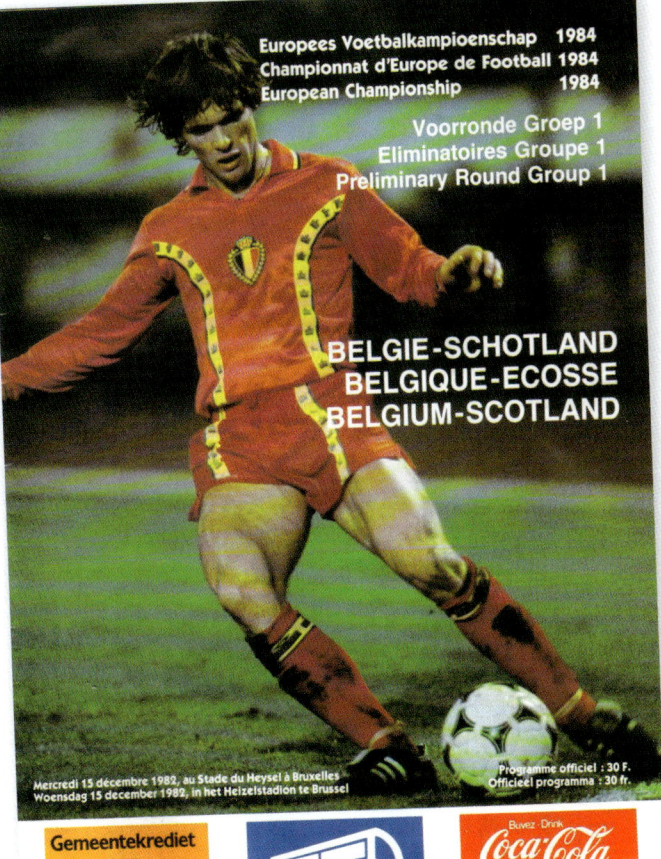

the final in Gothenburg with yet another all-Scottish line-up.

By the time Belgium came to Hampden in October though, the national team were out of the running for Euro '84 whereas our visitors just needed a point to confirm their qualification. The Belgians duly got what they required – Frank Vercauteren scored a first-half goal before Charlie Nicholas netted four minutes after the re-start to ultimately ensure that the game finished 1-1. Meanwhile, manager Jock Stein continued to blood new players with Celtic's Paul McStay picking up his second cap whilst both Arthur Albiston [Manchester United] and Jim Bett [Lokeren] collected their third. Just 23,475 were there to see it all.

Scotland's final dead rubber [I'm not sure I like that expression] took place in November behind the Iron Curtain in the city of Halle. In the Kurt Wabbel Stadium, Scotland lost 2-1 to East Germany – Eamonn Bannon of Dundee United netted Scotland's goal whilst the second German goal was scored by the legendary Joachim Streich [53 goals in 98 international appearances between 1969 and 1984]. Gaun yersel Joachy!

As it transpired, no British or Irish side made it to the eight-team France '84 finals which was won by a Michel Platini inspired host nation. At the group stage, Belgium defeated Yugoslavia before losing to France and Denmark. British television coverage of the event was extremely limited whilst it seemed like there was saturation coverage of the 1984/85 UK miners' strike.

On a lighter note we had the music of Culture Club, Frankie Goes to Hollywood and Wham! plus the unique method-acting of the cast of Taggart to enjoy.

MEXICO 1986

Scotland would ultimately qualify for their fourth successive World Cup finals but it would be a qualifying campaign tinged with sadness as we lost Jock Stein at the end of the game against Wales in Cardiff.

As well as the Welsh, Scotland also had to contend with Spain [runners-up at Euro 1984] and Iceland with the group winners going to the finals and the runners-up facing a play-off against the winner of the Oceania group.

Scotland made the essential good start with home wins against Iceland and Spain in October and November 1984 respectively. Against the Icelanders 52,829 at Hampden saw a 3-0 victory thanks to two goals from Celtic's Paul McStay and one from Charlie Nicholas, then of Arsenal. Against the mighty Spanish 74,299 witnessed a superb 3-1 Tartan triumph starting with two first-half headed goals from Celtic's Maurice Johnston. Spain hit back with a goal from Andoni Goicoechea [aka the Butcher from Bilbao] before Kenny Dalglish scored the third and in so doing equalled Denis Law's record number of goals for Scotland – 30.

A trip to Spain in February 1985 sounded good and for 48 minutes it looked good too until Fernando Clos netted what would prove to be the winner for the hosts in Seville's Estadio Sanchez Pizjuan. I seem to

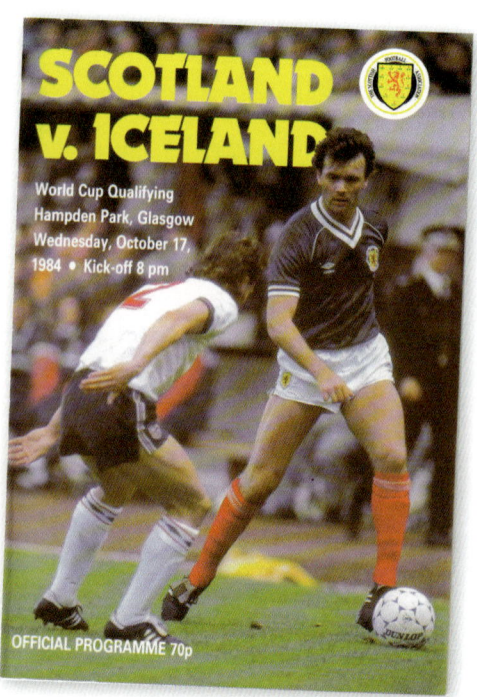

Scotland Glory, Tears & Souvenirs

recall Jim Leighton in the Scotland goal being pelted with oranges throughout.

In March there then followed a somewhat surprising defeat at home to Wales with Ian Rush's first-half goal upsetting most of the Hampden crowd of 62,424. This was Wales' first win in Scotland for 34 years. In June however, Scotland got back on track defeating Iceland 1-0 in Reykjavik – Jim Bett got the winner four minutes from time whilst in the first half Jim Leighton had brilliantly saved a penalty. That qualifier was played just three days after Scotland had defeated England to win the inaugural Rous Cup competition.

And so to that fateful September evening at Ninian Park, Cardiff. A victory in Wales and Scotland would qualify, a draw would give us at least second place whilst a defeat and it would almost certainly be adios. Graeme Souness was suspended for this match whilst Alan Hansen, Kenny Dalglish and Maurice Johnston were all unavailable due to injury.

At half-time things did not look good with Wales leading 1-0 thanks to a 13th minute strike from Mark Hughes. Alan Rough also had to replace Jim Leighton in goal after the Aberdeen keeper lost a contact lens following a collision with Ian Rush. Davie Cooper replaced Gordon Strachan after 61 minutes and 20 minutes later the Rangers winger converted a soft-looking penalty award. Scotland held on to get the required draw but manager Jock Stein collapsed and died shortly after the game. I remember our coach journey from Cardiff back home to Glasgow was made in stunned silence – celebrations would be for another day.

Under the caretaker management of Alex Ferguson, success in the play-offs against Australia did eventually allow for celebrations. The first leg was played at Hampden on 20 November and a crowd of 61,920 saw Scotland grab a two-goal advantage. Both goals came in the second half – a Davie Cooper free-kick followed by a lift-over-the-advancing-keeper by debutant Frank McAvennie [aka the Milton Maestro]. In the second leg at the Olympic Park, Melbourne on 4 December Graeme Souness [then of Sampdoria] won his 50th cap and skippered Scotland to a nil-nil draw which meant his country would go to the Mexico finals.

In September 1985 an earthquake had caused widespread death, injury and damage in and around Mexico City but the World Cup finals went ahead as

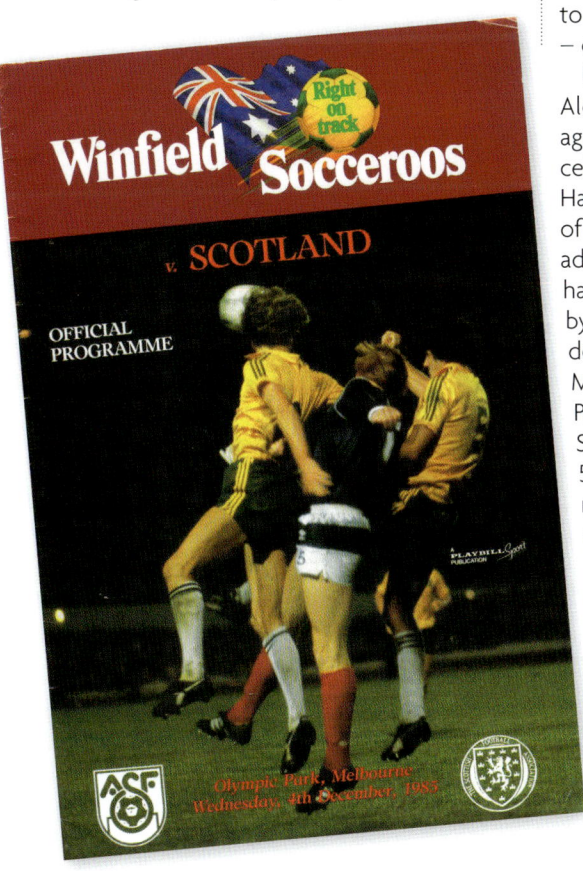

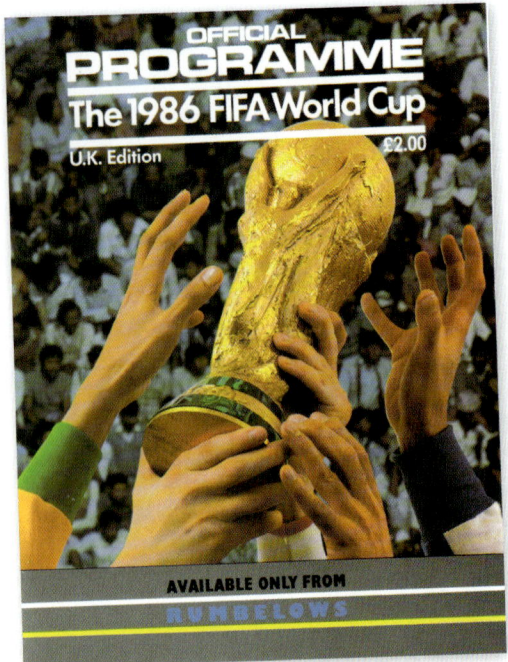

planned. On a much lighter note, 1986 would see the release of movies such as *Highlander* [with Sean Connery playing a 2,500-year-old Shhhpaniard] and *Howard the Duck* [surreal, sci-fi tosh, it won several worst movie and worst screenplay awards but it's still more plausible than *Escape to Victory* —John Wark excepted]. Also in 1986 Edinburgh would host its second Commonwealth Games — it's just a pity these Games included the likes of archery and fencing instead of a winnable football competition.

Back to the World Cup and Scotland were drawn in the so-called 'Group of Death' alongside West Germany, Uruguay and Denmark who had improved considerably from the early 1970s when we considered them to be 'easy meat'. Surprise omissions from Alex Ferguson's squad included Alan Hansen and Maurice Johnston whilst Kenny Dalglish [who hit the 100 cap mark in March 1986] withdrew with a knee injury.

On 4th June 1986 however the former 'easy meat' beat Scotland 1-0 thanks to a 57th minute goal from Preben Elkjaer-Larsen in front of 18,000 in the Estadio Neza, Nezahualcoyotl. [Give me the Wankdorf any day]. Charlie Nicholas went close for Scotland on three occasions, Richard Gough hit a shot just over and Roy Aitken had a 'goal' disallowed for offside. It was all enough to make me stop buying Lego.

Scotland's second match, against West Germany, was played four days later at the Estadio Corregidora in Queretaro and this time some 25,000 were in attendance to see a cracking game of football in which Aberdeen's Willie Miller won his 50th cap. Under the mid-day sun Gordon Strachan gave Scotland the lead in the 18th minute — a shot from the corner of the six yard box beating that pantomime villain, Harald Schumacher in the German goal.

Unfortunately, the lead only lasted for four minutes before Rudi Voller equalised for the Federal Republic of Germany — to give them their Sunday name. Four minutes into the second half and Klaus Allofs made it 2-1 for WG/FRG/Them. Scotland fought hard for an equaliser with Gough and Strachan going close but again it wasn't to be and 2-1 it finished.

Two narrow defeats in a row normally equated to a meaningless third game but this time a re-jigged format for the

Scotland Glory, Tears & Souvenirs

24 finalists meant that four of the six third-placed teams would progress to the second stage. If Scotland could defeat Uruguay that would be enough to get us through to the last sixteen.

On Friday 13th June it was back to Nezahualcoyotl to take on the reigning South American champions and this time 20,000 spectators showed up hoping to see a good game of football – they were to be disappointed big style. After only one minute of play Uruguay were reduced to ten men when Jose Batista was red-carded for a vicious tackle on Strachan from behind. Uruguay then relied heavily on fouling, time wasting and the occasional breakaway to get them through the remainder of the game. Scotland had their chances but failed to take any of them with the most vivid miss belonging to Liverpool's Steve Nicol whose shot at a vacant goal was so gentle it allowed the keeper to make a recovery save. It finished nil-nil and allowed the bad guys to progress [Uruguay were subsequently fined 25,000 Swiss Francs by FIFA – but I don't think they were too bothered]. Once again, Scotland were left to rue the day.

In the second round Denmark lost to Spain [Shame!] and Uruguay lost to Argentina [Hurrah!]. West Germany reached the final but lost 3-2 to Diego 'Hand of God' Maradona and co.

WEST GERMANY 1988
Yet again, Scotland had Belgium for company in a Euro qualifying group along with Bulgaria, Luxembourg and the Republic of Ireland.

There was no flying start though for Scotland and their new manager Andy Roxburgh [Andy Who? said the Scottish press] with 35,070 'treated' to a goal-less draw against Bulgaria at Hampden in September 1986 which was followed up in October with a nil-nil against the Republic of Ireland at Lansdowne Road, Dublin.

In November there were only 35,078 at Hampden to see a 3-0 victory over Luxembourg in which Kenny Dalglish played his 102nd and final game for Scotland with the goals coming from Rangers' Davie Cooper [2] and Maurice Johnston of Celtic.

The following February, Scotland

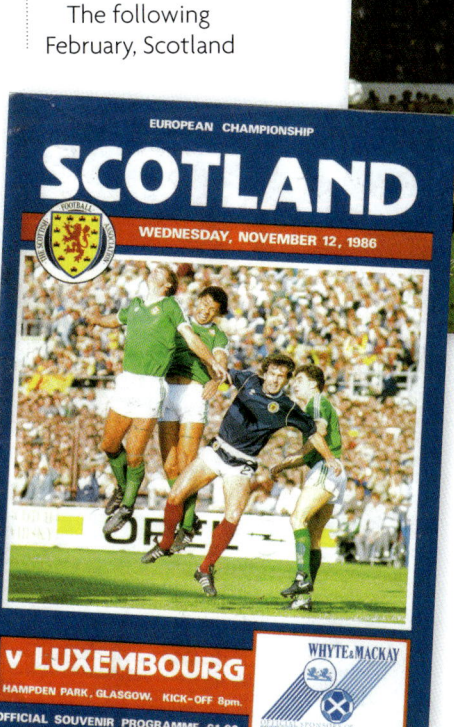

crucially slipped up at home and lost 1-0 to Jack Charlton's Republic of Ireland. A Hampden crowd of 45,081 saw the hosts lose to an eighth-minute goal by Mark Lawrenson – that's right, a goal by Mark Lawrenson – what an embarrassment!

On April Fool's day 1987 Scotland lost 4-1 to Belgium in Anderlecht's Constant Vanden [laughing] Stock stadium. Paul McStay hit a 14th minute equaliser before a second half collapse in which Nico Claesen completed his hat-trick.

In October however it was our turn to laugh as we beat Belgium 2-0 at Hampden. We didn't laugh too loudly however because we were already out of the running for qualification which probably explains why there was a crowd of only 20,052 but boy did we cheer when Ally McCoist and Paul McStay put the ball in the back of the bi-linguals' net.

11th November 1987 was a great day for the Republic of Ireland for it was the day that thanks to a goal from debutant Gary MacKay of Hearts, Bulgaria were defeated by Scotland in Sofia and the Boysingreen 'won' a place at a major finals for the first time in their history.

Scotland had still to play one more dead rubber – there must be a filthy joke in there somewhere – away to Luxembourg in December. Only 1,999 spectators turned up to see Aberdeen's Alex McLeish help ensure that Scotland kept a clean sheet on the occasion of his 50th cap. Unfortunately the Luxembourg defence weren't breached either. Nil-nil it finished, 'nuff said.

Trying hard to say something positive about 1987 from a Scottish perspective, it was the year that Dunoon-born Sylvester McCoy became the seventh Doctor Who...until the entire series, in its original run was cancelled in 1989. Also, in November 1987, the first McDonald's hamburger fast food restaurant in Scotland opened, in Dundee, although I'm more of a KFC man myself – by that, this pie-lover means, Kilmarnock's Fabulous Cuisine.

Anyway, so the Republic of Ireland went to the eight-team 1988 Euro finals in West Germany where they beat England 1-0, drew 1-1 with the USSR and lost 1-0 to the Netherlands coming within seven minutes of a draw and a place in the semi-finals. The Netherlands would go on to win their first major trophy by defeating the Soviets 2-0 in the final.

ITALY 1990

This was the last World Cup qualifying campaign for cold war Europe. In the 1990s the Communist states would come apart at the seams but in the meantime Cyprus, France, Norway and Yugoslavia stood between Scotland and a place at our fifth successive World Cup finals.

In September 1988 and with the UK still under the Thatcher Jackboot, Andy Roxburgh's Scotland travelled to Oslo and defeated Norway 2-1 with goals from Celtic's Paul McStay and Maurice Johnston, then of Nantes. At Hampden in October however we could only draw 1-1 with Yugoslavia in front of 42,771. Maurice Johnston gave Scotland an early lead but it was cancelled out by Srecko Katanec – who would become one of Slovenia's all-time greats.

In February 1989 there was fun in the sun again when Scotland defeated Cyprus 3-2 in

Scotland Glory, Tears & Souvenirs

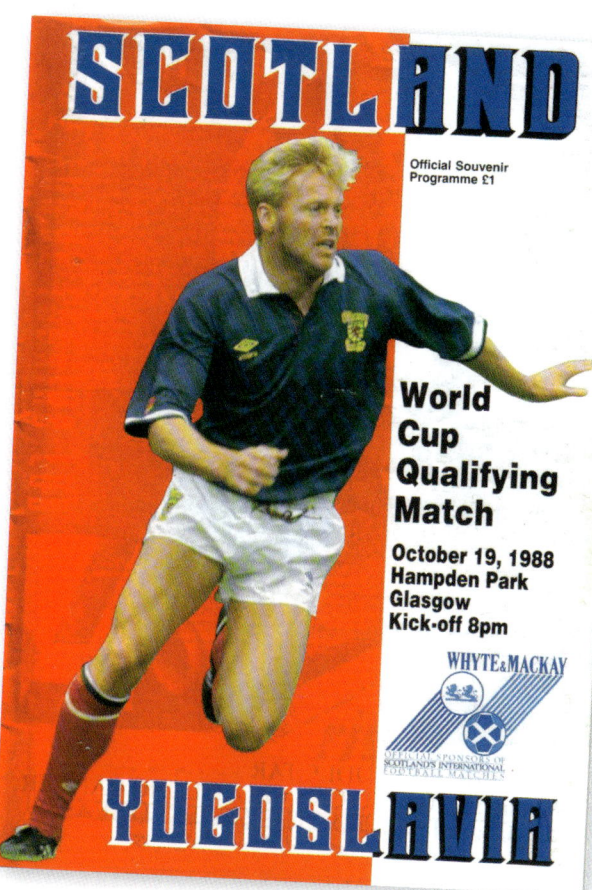

capital of Croatia]. Scotland led 1-0 at half-time thanks to a goal from Gordon 'Jukebox' Durie but were over-run in the second 45. In October Scotland again shipped three goals [without reply] – this time to France at the Parc des Princes, Paris. NB: James McFadden was only six at the time but vengeance would be his.

The final game of the qualifiers was in November at home to Norway and Scotland only required one point to finish second behind the undefeated Yugoslavia but still qualify for Italy. 63,987 turned up for the Hampden hoedown and to say well done to skipper Roy Aitken on winning his 50th cap.

Ally McCoist lobbed the Norwegian keeper one minute before half-time and we all started to party like it was 1989 but when Norway equalised one minute from time the Scottish anal nerves were a-twitching. Eventually the final whistle sounded, numerous pairs of underpants were discarded and Scotland supporters

Limassol with Richard Gough's winner coming deep into injury time, as it was then called. Yet another goal from Maurice Johnston had given Scotland an early advantage but the Cypriots fought back to take a 2-1 lead and scare the brown stuff out of Scotland. Richard Gough then nabbed an equaliser before using his 'Get out of jail free' card in the 96th minute – or thereabouts.

In March a French side which included Laurent Blanc, Frank Sauzee and Jean-Pierre Papin came to Hampden on a wet Wednesday evening and got their soggy derrieres felt. Two goals from Mo-Mo-Super Mo, Super Maurice Johnston did le trick in front of a crowd of 65,204.

The following month however Scotland struggled to beat Cyprus at Hampden, but beat them we did by two goals to one. Maurice Johnston [who else?] got the opener with Super-Ally [McCoist] hitting the second-half winner 60 seconds after Cyprus had equalised. 50,081 saw yet another escape against the supposed Mediterranean minnows.

Come September 1989 however Scotland lost 3-1 to Yugoslavia in Zagreb [the future

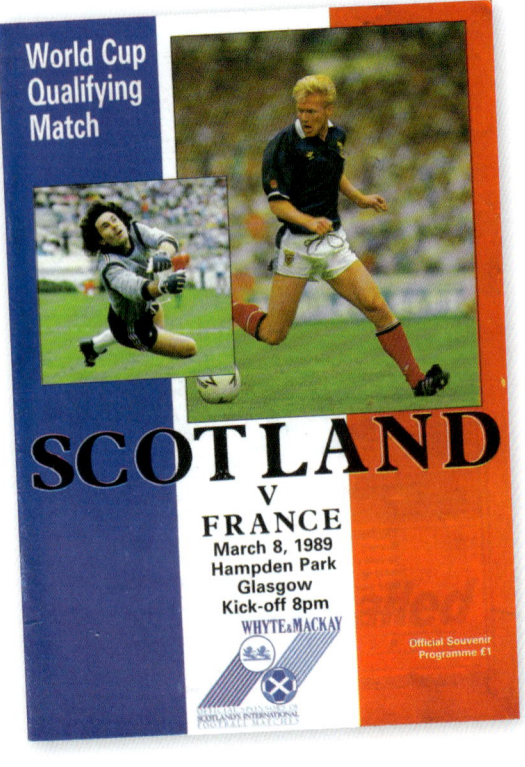

everywhere proceeded to enjoy a dry sherry or two. Qualification came at a cost however, for an injury to Willie Miller effectively ended the Aberdeen defender's international career after 65 games for Scotland.

Two months prior to Italia 90 Scotland nabbed a world title when Hearts-supporting Stephen Hendry, 21, became the youngest ever winner of the World Snooker Championship. Scotsman Hendry would win seven world titles between 1990 and 1999 – are you reading this in Argentina, Brazil and Germany?

At the Italia 90 finals as well as Scotland there were 23 other teams including our group opponents Costa Rica, Sweden and Brazil. On 11th June 1990 [two days before the official demolition of the Berlin Wall commenced] and in the magnificent setting of Genoa's Stadio Luigi Ferraris Scotland lost 1-0 to Costa Rica. I was one of the crowd of 30,867 so I can confirm that it did happen. Scotland did concede a goal to Juan Cayasso in the 49th minute and neither Super Ally, Super Mo, Alan 'Rambo' McInally or anyone else were able to equalise.

Five days later at the same stadium Scotland got their act together and defeated Sweden 2-1 in front of 31,823. The first goal came from Everton midfielder Stuart McCall [his only goal in 40 appearances for Scotland] after ten minutes and nine minutes from time Maurice Johnston [now of Rangers] made it 2-0 from the penalty spot. Glenn Stromberg pulled one back for Sweden four minutes later but Scotland held on to record only our fourth [and most recent!] victory at a World Cup finals.

On 20th June Scotland went over the mountains to the Stadio Delle Alpi, Turin where a crowd of 62,502 saw us take on Brazil. Scotland survived periods of intense pressure before almost taking the lead in the 78th minute when a Roy Aitken header was cleared off the Brazilian goal-line. Three minutes later however came the sucker-punch when Muller forced the ball into an empty goal following some comic defensive capers involving Jim Leighton and Gary Gillespie.

A 1-0 defeat was harsh luck on Scotland, and it got even harsher when it emerged that Scotland were one of the two third-placed teams that would not make it through to the next round – Austria were the other unfortunates.

In the Round of 16 Costa Rica [who had also defeated Sweden] lost 4-1 to Czechoslovakia whilst Brazil lost 1-0 to Argentina. [Brazil's turn for a sore one.] In the actual final West Germany [conquerors of England

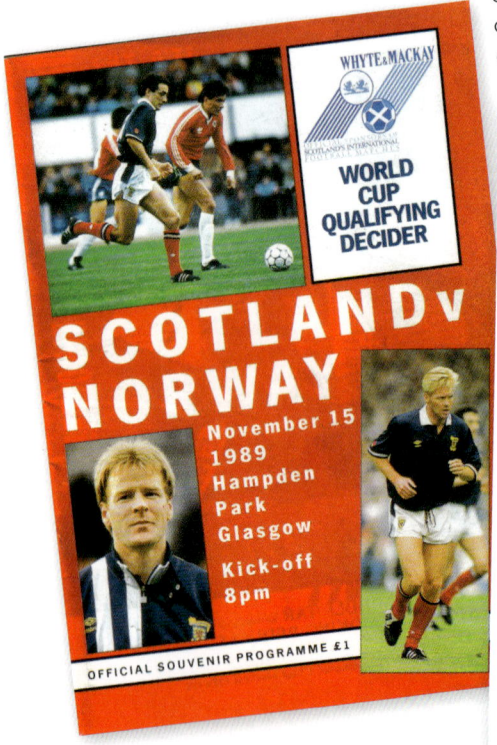

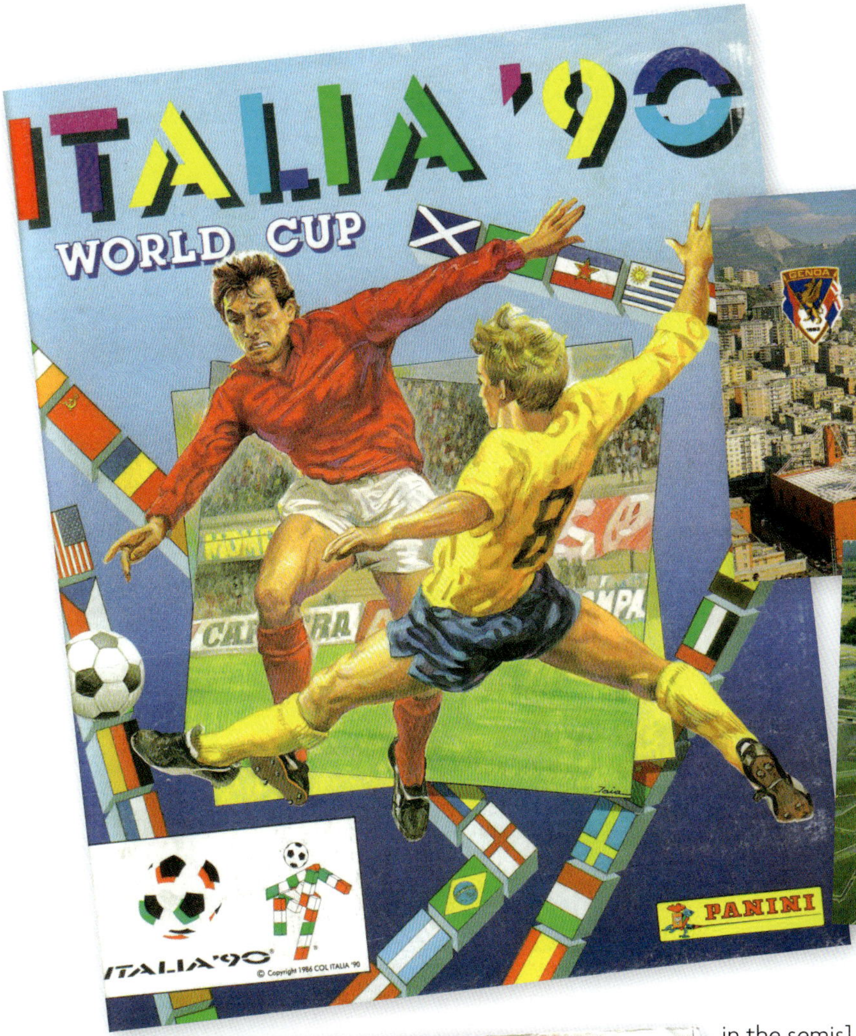

Scotland Glory, Tears & Souvenirs

in the semis] beat Maradona and his mates 1-0 to lift the trophy for the third [and final] time before unification with East Germany.

BBC television's wonderful melodic backdrop to this tournament was the aria 'Nessun Dorma' [None shall sleep] from Puccini's opera *Turandot*. For those of us of a certain vintage, that piece of classical music is now right up there with Rossini's 'William Tell Overture' – which also doubled as the theme music for the 1960s animated TV series *The Lone Ranger*. How's that for culture? This book has got everything...

SWEDEN 1992

Eureka! Europa! At the seventh time of asking, Scotland, managed by Andy 'I used to play for Partick Thistle' Roxburgh, made it to the finals [nay, the last eight] of the European Championships. Bulgaria, Romania, San Marino and Switzerland were overcome as eastern Europe fragmented and the tenth anniversary of the dissolution of Abba approached.

Scotland's first match after appearing at the Italia 90 World Cup finals was our opening Euro qualifier against Romania in September and only 12,801 made the effort to go along to Hampden to see Brian Irvine [Aberdeen], John Robertson [Hearts] and Tom Boyd [Motherwell] make their debuts in a 2-1 home win. Romania took the lead after 13 minutes but the aforementioned Robertson got us an equaliser before half-time. Rangers' Ally McCoist netted the winner in the 75th minute.

The following month at Hampden, Switzerland were beaten by the same scoreline with John Robertson again scoring [a penalty] and Gary McAllister of Leeds United grabbing the second. This time 27,740 turned up. In November, Scotland then went behind an Iron Curtain that was now well-torn to earn a 1-1 draw with Bulgaria in Sofia. Ally McCoist gave Scotland a ninth-minute lead before substitute Nikolai Todorov equalised in the second half.

Scotland Glory, Tears & Souvenirs

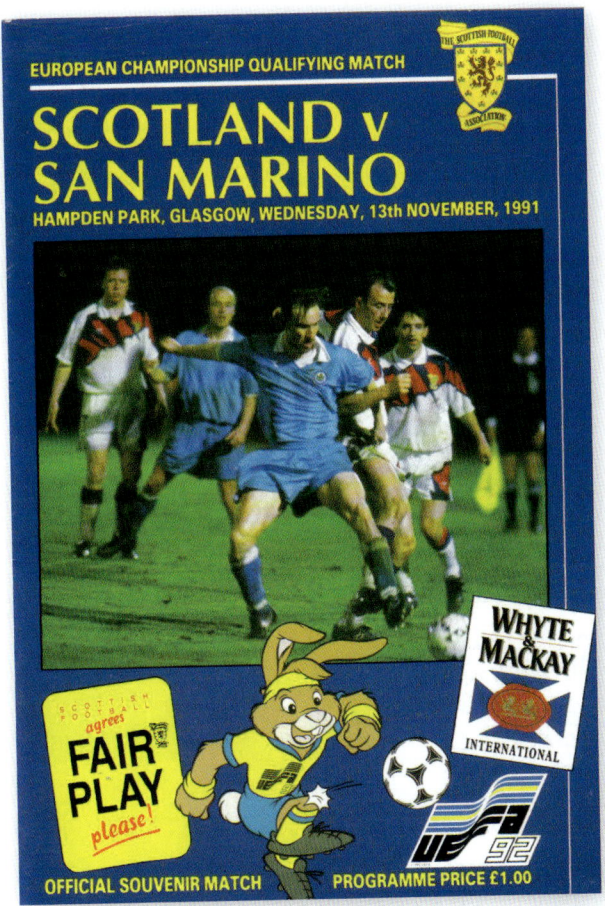

with their destiny not in their own hands. Sure enough Scotland got the victory necessary to keep us in contention – 4-0 with goals from Paul McStay, Richard Gough, Gordon Durie and Ally McCoist – the so-called Maradona of the Campsies [ok so I made that one up]. However, there was no big celebration for the crowd of 35,170 who then headed home and waited for events to unfold.

That same day, Switzerland could have clinched top spot and qualification if they had won in Bucharest but instead they lost 1-0 to Romania which in turn meant that the 'Sons of Vlad' could make the finals if they won their final match [scoring at least two goals] a week later in Sofia.

On 20 November 1991 in the same Vasil Levski Stadium in which Scotland won four years previous to send the Republic of Ireland to the 1988 Euro finals, Bulgaria held their neighbours Romania to a 1-1 draw to send Scotland to the 1992 Euro

In March 1991 it was then Bulgaria's turn to visit Hampden. Again Scotland took the lead [John Collins seven minutes from time] but again we couldn't hold it and Emil Kostadinov equalised with one minute remaining.

For Scotland's first ever visit to San Marino [Italy's answer to Clackmannanshire], in May, we had to rely on second-half goals from skipper Gordon Strachan [a 63rd minute penalty] and from Chelsea's Gordon Durie three minutes later to seal a 2-0 victory. We were still on course however.

In September this Scotland team showed what they were made of and in the Wankdorf Stadium, Berne came back from being 2-0 down at half-time to draw 2-2. Gordon Durie and Ally McCoist were the second half scorers. In October however there was a blip when Scotland lost 1-0 to Romania in Bucherest – a penalty converted by Gheorghe Hagi, the so-called Maradona of the Carpathians.

On 13 November, Scotland went into their final qualifier, against San Marino

finals. Hagi missed a penalty kick before Popescu gave Romania a half-time lead. In the second half however Nasko Sirakov equalised for the home side and I polished off a bottle of Bulgarian red in under 30 minutes as my way of saying thank you.

In Sweden, the eight Euro finalists were split into two groups of four with Scotland being placed in group 2 alongside the Netherlands, a now re-unified Germany and the Commonwealth of Independent States [CIS]. The USSR had topped their qualifying group [ahead of Italy] but on 25/26 December 1991 outgoing President Mikhail Gorbachev oversaw the dissolution of the Union. The CIS was a short-term stopgap until each member of the CIS began competing separately in the world of sport.

And so to the Ullevi Stadium, Gothenburg on 12th June 1992 where 35,720 saw a star-studded Dutch side which included the likes of Frank Rijkaard, Ruud Gullit and Marco Van Basten struggle to overcome Scotland, however the holders came good some thirteen minutes from time with a goal from Dennis Bergkamp. Earlier Richard Gough and Paul McStay had both come close to scoring for Scotland but close doesn't count. 1-0 to the Netherlands it finished.

Three days later at the much smaller Idrottsparken in Norrkoping a crowd of 17,638 saw Scotland and Germany [managed by Berti Vogts] serve up an excellent, free-flowing, attacking game of football in which the German keeper Bodo Illgner was forced to make three fine saves in the first ten minutes. Several other chances for Scotland to get on the scoresheet came and went and so the inevitable happened – twice. First Karl-Heinz Riedle scored with a thunderous shot [let's not call it a howitzer] then a minute after the restart came the fluke-goal of the tournament. A cross from that effin Stefan Effenberg was deflected by Maurice Malpas over the stranded Andy Goram who had lost his footing.

Scotland kept attacking but couldn't take any of their chances and so despite playing some great stuff somehow contrived to lose 2-0 and end their hopes of making it through to the semi-finals.

Scotland's third game on 18th June was far from meaningless as far as the CIS were concerned – a victory would have given them a place in the last four. However this time the 14,660 in the Idrottsparken got to see some Scottish goals as strikes from Paul McStay, Brian McClair [his first Scotland goal in 26 appearances] and Gary McAllister helped deliver a 3-0 victory against a team that would disappear overnight.

Denmark, a late replacement for the violently fragmenting Yugoslavia, defeated the Netherlands in the semi-finals and then Germany in the final – and all on Swedish soil! I wonder if the Danes still mention that glorious achievement to their big neighbour? Can you imagine what it would have been like if Scotland had done something similar in 1966 – I know I regularly dream about it.

USA. 1994

For the first time ever, the World Cup tournament finals moved away from its traditional territories of Europe and Latin America and headed for President Bill Clinton's United States of America. Standing in the way of an Atlantic crossing for Scotland were Estonia, Italy, Malta, Portugal and Switzerland whilst Hampden Park would be unavailable due to a major redevelopment programme.

Scotland's opening qualifier in September 1992, our first match since appearing at the Euro 92 finals, was at Berne's Wankdorf

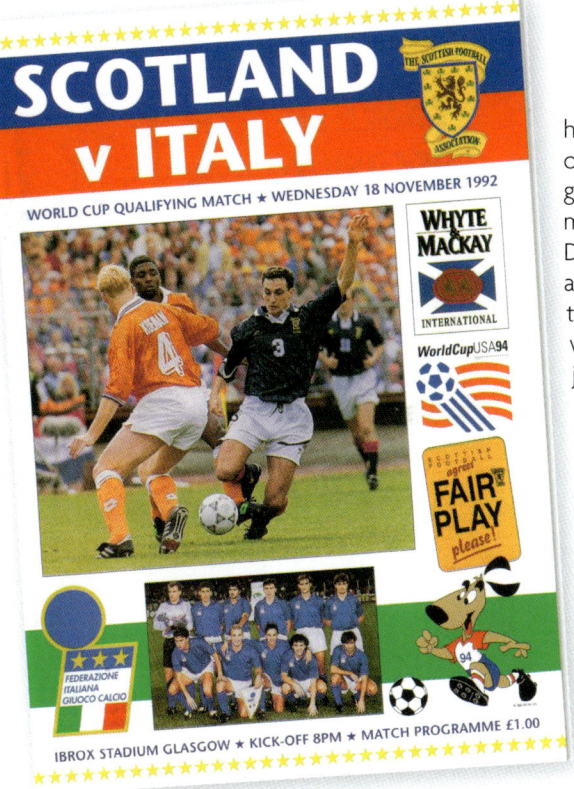

Stadium where things went badly wrong with a 3-1 defeat and a red card for skipper Richard Gough on the occasion of his 60th appearance for his country. The villain of the piece was a water sprinkler on the pitch which apparently had caused an awkward bounce and the subsequent handball offence six minutes from time. Switzerland had taken the lead in the very first minute athough an equaliser 12 minutes later from Rangers' Ally McCoist had given us false hope.

Things improved slightly the following month when Scotland drew nil-nil with Portugal at Ibrox Stadium with only 22,583 paying customers looking on. In November it was goal-less at Ibrox again with Italy the opposition and another disappointing attendance of 33,029.

Malta probably didn't fancy visiting Glasgow in February but they duly turned up and in front of a marginally improved Ibrox crowd of 35,490 [free tickets to hundreds of schoolkids helped] they were unable to prevent Scotland from recording their first victory of the campaign – 3-0 with goals from Ally McCoist [2] and Pat Nevin of Tranmere Rovers.

28th April 1983 has been cited as the day a team died in that Scotland were humped 5-0 by Portugal in Lisbon's Stadium of Light. Certainly it was the last Scotland game for Richard Gough and his Ibrox team-mate Dave McPherson plus Jim McInally of Dundee United. Ally McCoist also suffered a leg break but thankfully would make a winning return to the team just over two years later.

Three weeks after the Lisbon debacle Scotland recorded a convincing 3-0 victory away to a former Soviet Socialist Republic – not something we would make a regular habit of doing in years to come. The other team in Tallinn that day was Estonia who were breached by Blackburn's Kevin Gallacher, John Collins of Celtic and Aberdeen's Scott Booth. Gallacher's clubmate, Colin Hendry made his debut. A fortnight later Estonia visited Pittodrie Stadium, Aberdeen and got more of the

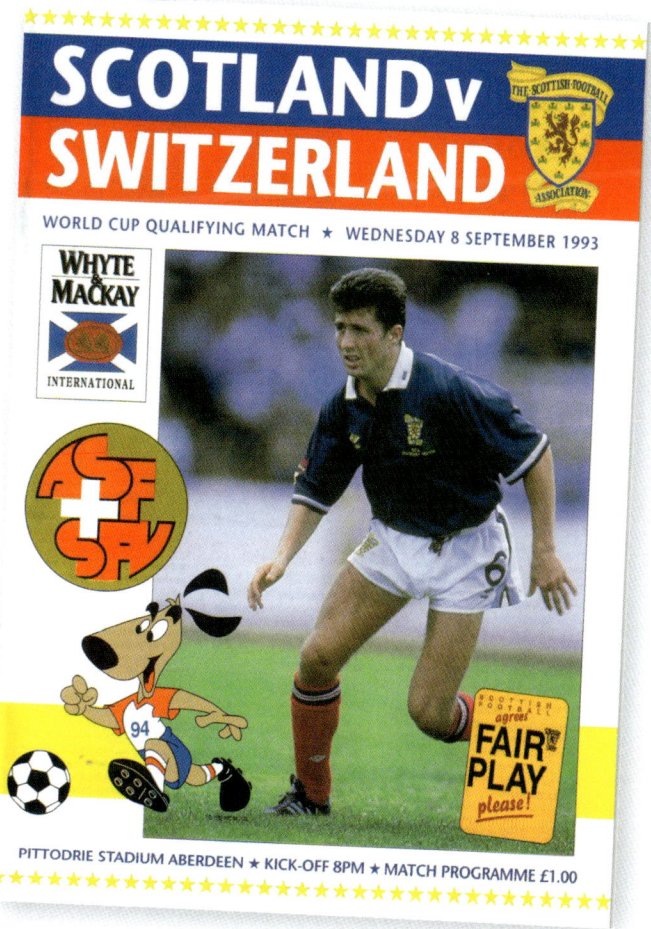

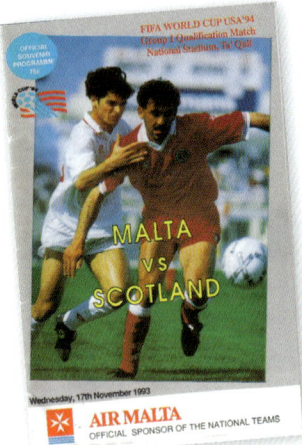

same. With the new Richard Donald stand incomplete, only 14,307 watched Scotland win 3-1 thanks to a goal from Manchester United's Brian McClair plus two from Pat Nevin which included a penalty.

In September it was the turn of Roy Hodgson's group leaders Switzerland to visit Pittodrie and 21,500 saw John Collins score for Scotland in a 1-1 draw – the visitors getting the point they desired to virtually seal qualification. This effectively condemned Scotland and their supporters to spend the summer of 1994 listening to Clydebank's Wet Wet Wet who were at number one for fifteen consecutive weeks with their cover version of 'Love Is All Around' or the Republic of Ireland's World Cup single 'Watch Your House For Ireland!'

Anyway, Andy Roxburgh then chose to resign and Craig Brown was appointed caretaker manager for the two remaining qualifiers. In October, in Rome's Olympic Stadium Scotland lost 3-1 as Italy [featuring Zola, Baresi and the Baggio boys] began a late push which would see them head for the US along with the Swiss. Kevin 'Spartacus' Gallacher netted Scotland's consolation goal.

Scotland travelled to Malta in November for their final qualifier and did a professional job winning 2-0 with goals from Dundee United's Billy McKinlay [on his debut] and Colin Hendry. Craig Brown formally accepted the poisoned chalice soon thereafter.

Six months later in Na-na-na-na-na-na – mer-ee-ka Switzerland reached the second round stage where they lost 3-1 to Spain. Italy went all the way to the actual final where they lost 3-2 on penalties to Brazil who lifted the trophy for a fourth time. For US TV audiences however the summer highlight was the highway pursuit and arrest of murder suspect and former American football hero O.J. Simpson.

ENGLAND 1996

With UEFA membership expanding to more than 40 in the early 1990s it was agreed that the finals of the Euros should expand also to comprise of 16 teams. Furthermore it was now three points for a win. Thirty years after England successfully hosted a World Cup finals, football 'came home' again to the green and pleasant land and this time Scotland managed to get an invite to the gig by battling past the Faroe Islands, Finland, Greece and San Marino to join Russia at Euro 96.

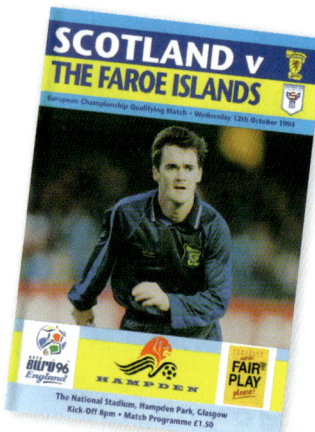

A good start was made in September 1994 when Craig Brown's Scotland defeated Finland 2-0 in Helsinki with goals from Duncan Shearer [Aberdeen] and Celtic's John Collins. This was followed up in October at Hampden with a 5-1 thrashing of the Faroe Islands. 20,885 saw John McGinlay [Bolton Wanderers], Billy McKinlay [Dundee United], Scott Booth [Aberdeen] and John Collins [twice] get the Scottish goals.

A month later Russia [Andrei Kanchelskis included] visited Hampden and took a point home with them as a result of a 1-1 draw. Early in the first half Scott Booth gave Scotland the lead which we held for all of six minutes. 31,254 attended. A week before Christmas Scotland then swapped Mount Florida for Mount Olympus – sort of – and in Athens' Olympic Stadium the gods smiled on Greece and gave them an undeserved 1-0 victory courtesy of a first-half penalty.

Into 1995 and in March Scotland braved a trip to Moscow where with the aid of two debutants – Colin Calderwood [Tottenham Hotspur] and Darren Jackson

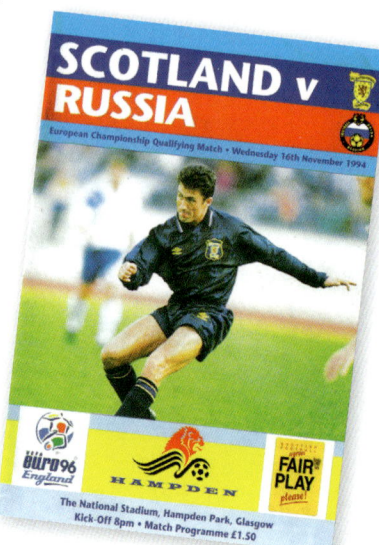

Scotland Glory, Tears & Souvenirs

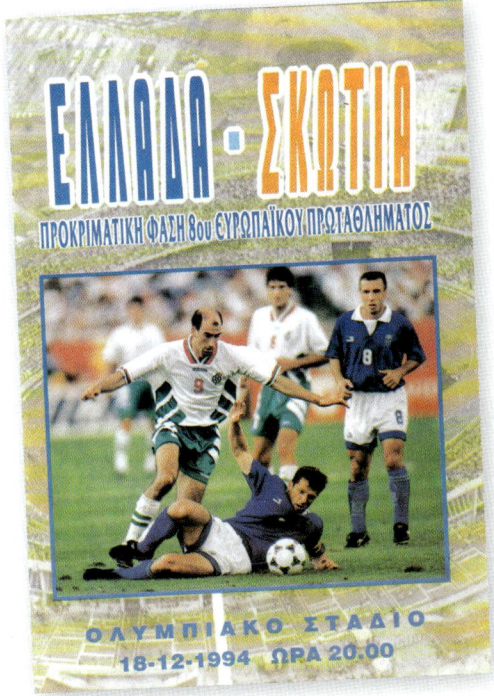

Hibernian] – we ground out a nil-nil draw thank you very much. In April it was sunny San Marino and a 2-0 away win – John Collins and Colin Calderwood doing the necessary. Another 2-0 away win then followed in June against the mighty Faroe Islands and this time it was Billy McKinlay and John McGinlay who took care of business.

Greece turned up at the gates of Hampden in August but didn't bear any gifts. Instead Scotland had to work hard to earn a valuable 1-0 win. Eighteen minutes from time a headed goal from substitute Ally McCoist [his first cap since his leg break against Portugal in April 1993] had the crowd of 34,910 in raptures. There was no slip-up in our penultimate qualifier in September against Finland at Hampden although a 1-0 victory [Scott Booth in the tenth minute] made for some nervous moments. It was watched by 35,505, Scotland's highest home gate of the qualifiers in a national stadium with a reduced capacity of 38,000.

In October Russia defeated Greece 2-1 in Moscow to win the group with one game remaining. The result also ensured that Scotland would finish a 'good enough' second to avoid a play-off and so qualify directly for Euro 96. On 15 November 30,306 attended Hampden to say 'Well done Scotland' as well as to cheer them to a 5-0 victory against San Marino. The celebratory goals were evenly spread – Eoin Jess [Aberdeen], Scott Booth, Ally McCoist and Pat Nevin [Tranmere Rovers] with San Marino's Fabio Francini joining in with a 90th minute own goal.

1995 also saw the release of the Academy Award-winning movie *Braveheart* starring Mel Gibson as William Wallace [the 13th century freedom fighter not the inside forward who won seven Scotland caps in the 1960s]. Meanwhile in the culinary

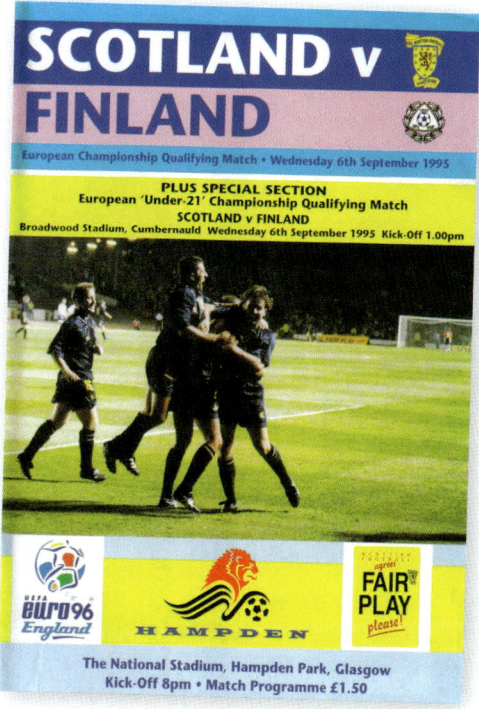

world, a Stonehaven fish and chip shop introduced the deep-fried Mars Bar – allegedly. Back to the fitba and the draw for the finals grouped Scotland along with the Netherlands, Switzerland and Terry Venables' England. Cue 'Battle of Britain' and 'Braveheart Mark II' hype.

Scotland opened however against the Netherlands at Villa Park, Birmingham and from my £35 seat in the Holte End Upper I enjoyed my most exciting goal-less draw ever. John Collins, Gary McAllister and John Spencer all went close for Scotland.

Collins also handled a shot from Ronald de Boer on the goal-line but got away with it whilst Clarence Seedorf and Dennis Begkamp should perhaps have scored for the Netherlands. A point against a Dutch side which also included Jordi Cruyff, Edgar Davids and Patrick Kluivert was celebrated like a victory. A chicken balti has never tasted so good.

And so to Judgement Day – 15th June 1996 – where at Wembley Stadium, Scotland were found guilty of giving too much space to Alan Shearer [in the 52nd minute] and Paul Gascoigne [78th minute]. To make matters worse, Gascoigne's wondergoal came as a direct result of Gary McAllister's penalty miss [or David Seaman's save depending on your point of view]. There is some suggestion that the ball bobbled just before Gary struck it. However, my mate Steph still frets that it was the flash from his camera that put the Scotland skipper off his stride. 2-0 for England it finished.

To reach the last eight Scotland would be required to beat Switzerland at Villa Park; England to beat the Netherlands; and for there to be a 'five goal swing' in the process.... and it so nearly happened. With 12 minutes remaining Scotland were leading Switzerland 1-0 [Ally McCoist 37th minute] whilst a sublime England were beating the Netherlands 4-0. The quarter-finals were in sight – and then Kluivert scored for the Netherlands. Scotland only had themselves to blame though as several good goalscoring chances were spurned. Another glorious failure/unlucky near miss/feckin sore one – call it what you will.

In the quarter-finals the Netherlands were eliminated by France on penalties whilst England went the same way in the semi-finals to Berti Vogts'

Scotland Glory, Tears & Souvenirs

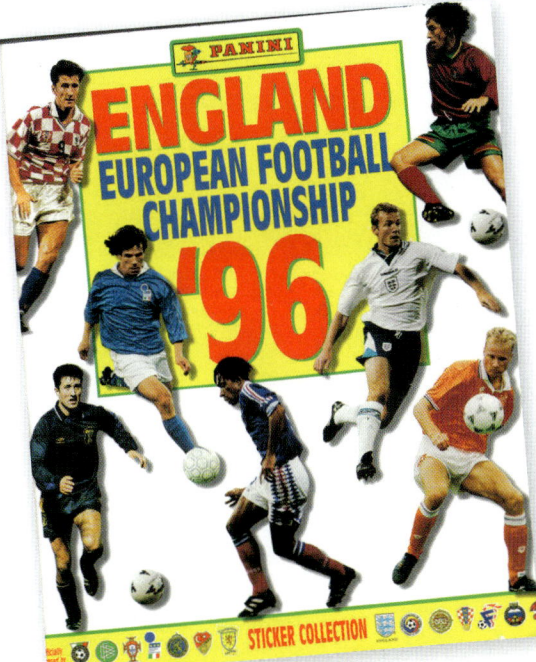

Our first home qualifier was against Sweden in November at Ibrox Stadium, Glasgow – 'New' Hampden was still in the process of being built. The truth is that in front of 46,738 witnesses Scotland mugged Sweden 1-0. Sweden did most of the attacking and Scotland's man of the match was goalkeeper Jim Leighton, now with Hibernian. Special thanks were also due to Bolton's John McGinlay who scored the winner after only eight minutes.

In February 1997 Scotland travelled to neutral Monaco for the re-arranged away game against Estonia. The game should have been played on 9th October in Tallinn but Estonia failed to turn up! [see Abandoned and postponed matches]. In the attractive surroundings of the Stade Louis II justice was not done however and Scotland laboured to a goal-less draw.

The following month Estonia were 'summonsed' to appear at Rugby Park, Kilmarnock where 17,996 saw them punished with a 2-0 defeat. Tom Boyd of Celtic 'cast the first stone' in 26 minutes before Janek Meet did the 'decent' thing and added an own goal in the 52nd minute.

In April, Scotland managed another 'big' win – 2-0 against Austria at Celtic Park, Glasgow. This was my 100th Scotland game [my medal from the SFA is still awaited] and as part of a crowd of 43,295 I savoured an attacking display by Scotland which brought two goals from Kevin Gallacher of Blackburn Rovers. Four weeks later however in Gothenburg, Sweden avenged their Ibrox defeat with a 2-1 win. Kennet Andersson got both of Sweden's goals whilst Kevin Gallacher again netted for Scotland.

In June and September there were back to back matches against Belarus which began with a 1-0 penalty kick win in Minsk. Skipper Gary McAllister

Germany who in turn went on to lift the trophy by defeating the Czech Republic in the final. Five days after the final, Dolly the Sheep [the first mammal to have been successfully cloned from an adult cell] was born at the Roslin Institute in Scotland. Why didn't we clone Denis Law instead?

FRANCE 1998
The 1998 World Cup finals in France was Scotland's last 'success' before we trooped through the door at the back of the SFA Chief Executive's wardrobe and entered the wilderness years.

172 nations were involved in the qualifying campaign [for an extended tournament involving 32 teams]; however, Craig Brown's Scotland only had to face five of them – Austria, Belarus, Estonia, Latvia and Sweden.

A good start was made on 31 August 1996 by way of a nil-nil draw against Herbert Prohaska's Austria in Vienna. In October another fine performance away from home resulted in a 2-0 victory against Latvia in Riga. John Collins [Monaco] and Darren Jackson [Hibernian] were the scorers.

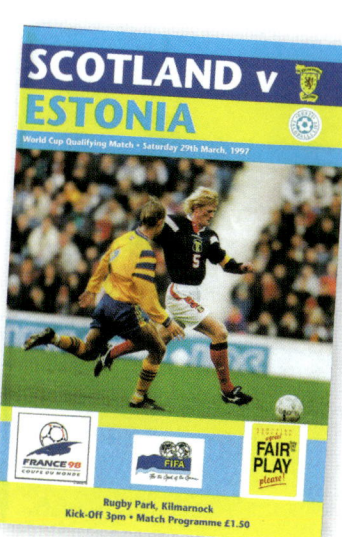

Scotland's Don Hutchison turns to celebrate his goal in a 2000 UEFA European Championship play-off, second leg match against England.

Scotland Glory, Tears & Souvenirs

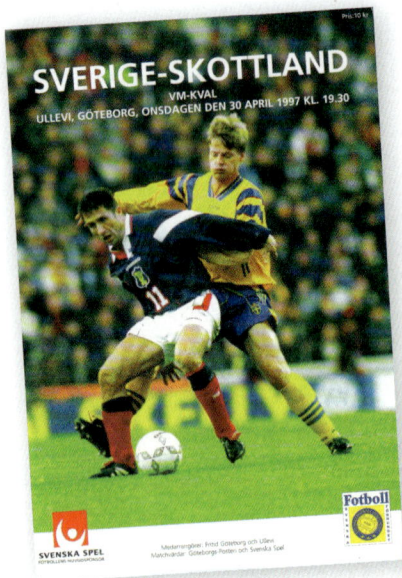

[then at Coventry City] had the balls to take it and score it. The return match took place at Pittodrie Stadium, Aberdeen on Sunday 7th September 1997 having been postponed for 24 hours due to the funeral of Diana, Princess of Wales [again see Abandoned and postponed matches]. Scotland turned in a polished, professional performance and won 4-1 in front of 20,160. On fire Kevin Gallacher got two of the goals as did relative new boy, David Hopkin of Leeds United.

Four days later 75% of the turnout of 60% voted Yes in a Referendum on whether Scotland should have a devolved Parliament.

And so to Celtic Park on 11th October for our final qualifier, against Latvia. Scotland knew in advance that a win would almost certainly see us through as the best of the second-placed teams, finishing behind group winners Austria. 47,613 saw Scotland do what was required — a 2-0 victory with goals from that man Gallacher just before half-time and Gordon Durie ten minutes from the end to calm the nerves. Celebratory pints were then supped, purchased at prices considerably cheaper from those we'll pay whenever we get to do it again.

Scotland were then drawn to meet Brazil, Norway and Morocco with the game against the holders, Brazil being the tournament opener. Ya dancer you!

On 10th June 1998 about 70,000 football supporters and 10,000 hangers-on packed into the brand new, shiny Stade de France in the Parisian suburb of Saint-Denis.[I like the way they give the Lawman due deference.] Cesar Sampaio headed Brazil into the lead after only four minutes and with the original [and best] Ronaldo well up for it Scotland were in danger of being taken apart. Scotland regained their composure, their shape and their self-belief however and in the 38th minute were rewarded with a penalty which John Collins duly converted. Scotland stuck to the task and in the 73rd minute Celtic's Tom Boyd netted the winner...unfortunately it was a winner for Brazil. Jim Leighton had blocked Cafu's shot but the rebound struck Boyd and trickled over the line. D'oh! Merde! Shit!

Six days later Scotland and Norway met at the Parc Lescure, Bordeaux. A crowd of 30,236 took their seats in that reinforced concrete masterpiece of a structure which successfully fuses neoclassicism with contemporary art deco. The Bordeaux blanc

Scotland Glory, Tears & Souvenirs

assisted me in appreciating its monumental archway entrance, Olympic tower, ribbed roofing and Venetian-style bridges acting as stairways to the upper tier. Er, anyway, the game finished 1-1. Haavard Flo gave Norway the lead one minute after the re-start before Celtic's Craig Burley lobbed the keeper to give the yellow-shirted Scotland a deserved equaliser 20 minutes later.

On 23rd June Scotland then travelled to the Stade Geoffroy Guichard in Saint Etienne to face Morocco knowing that a draw might be enough to progress whilst conversely a victory might not be sufficient! As things turned out both Morocco and Scotland were losers for despite the North Africans' comprehensive 3-0 victory it was rendered academic due to Norway's surprise 2-1 win against Brazil. In short, Scotland were run ragged by their more pacy opponents with two of the goals being scored by Salaheddine Bassir who was also involved in the incident which led to [a now peroxide-blonde] Craig Burley being shown the red card. Au revoir grand estrade...when will we see your likes again?

For the record, Norway lost 1-0 to Italy at the Round of 16 stage however Brazil made it to the final before succumbing 3-0 to a Zinidine Zidane-inspired France.

55

BELGIUM AND THE NETHERLANDS 2000

In 2000 the Millennium Bug failed to materialise, the world didn't end and so the 11th European Football Championships was hosted jointly by Belgium and the Netherlands. Scotland were going for three Euro finals in a row as well as three major tournament finals in a row but this time Craig Brown's boys would come up just short.

Scotland were drawn in group 9 along with Bosnia-Herzegovina, the Czech Republic, Estonia, the Faroe Islands and Lithuania and in September 1998 we began with our first ever match against Lithuania, in Vilnius. A nil-nil draw resulted and Barry Ferguson [Rangers], Callum Davidson [Blackburn Rovers] and Neil McCann [Hearts] all come on in the second half to win their debut caps.

In October and with the rebuilding of Hampden still ongoing, Scotland played their next qualifier, against Estonia, at Tynecastle Stadium, Edinburgh. A crowd of 16,930 watched, cheered and fretted as Scotland twice came from behind to win 3-2 – two Billy Dodds goals sandwiching an own goal from Hohlov-Simson. It was the last occasion on which Jim Leighton [91 caps] and Ally McCoist [61 caps and 19 goals] would play for Scotland.

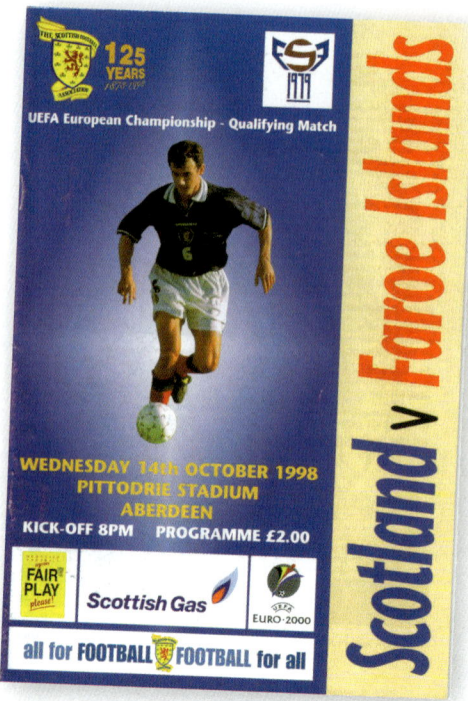

Four days later Scotland moved up the east coast to Pittodrie Stadium, Aberdeen and a 2-1 win against the Faroe Islands. Craig Burley [Celtic] and Billy Dodds [Dundee United] got the first half goals for Scotland, however a converted penalty by the visitors in the 86th minute meant at least four minutes of squeaky-bum time for the bulk of the 18,517 crowd.

In March 1999, at Celtic Park, Glasgow Scotland lost 2-1 to the Czech Republic in front of 44,513 and afterwards skipper Gary McAllister, who during the match was barracked by some of the Scotland support [but not by me, honest], announced his retirement after winning 57 caps.

Scotland Glory, Tears & Souvenirs

In May a devolved Scottish Parliament in Edinburgh finally came into existence but it has yet to host a 'civic reception' for a successful Scotland team...

On 5th June it was fun-time in the Faroes however when the home side scored in the last minute to earn themselves a 1-1 draw. Sunderland's Allan Johnston had given Scotland the lead in the 38th minute before Wandsworth-born Matt Elliott [he had a Scottish granny] got himself sent off.

Four days later it was painful in Prague when Scotland went 2-0 up in the Sparta Stadion after 62 minutes [Paul Ritchie of Hearts and Allan Johnston netting] but ultimately came home with nothing as the Czechs hit back to put three past Wimbledon's Neil Sullivan in the space of 22 minutes.

Still on our travels, we managed to defeat Bosnia-Herzegovina 2-1 in Sarajevo on 4 September [Everton's Don Hutchison got the opener, Billy Dodds netted the winner] and then we had another goal-less draw in the Baltics, this time against Estonia in Tallinn.

On 5th October Bosnia-Herzegovina and 30,000 spectators came to Ibrox Stadium, Glasgow [the Kosovo conflict had caused the postponement of its original March date] where Scotland ground out a 1-0 win [a John Collins penalty] and thus clinched second spot in the group and a place in the play-offs. The Czech Republic were the runaway winners of the group, triumphing in all ten qualifiers. Another four days later and only 22,059 turned up at Hampden for the concluding qualifier against Lithuania which Scotland won 3-0. Don Hutchison plus Gary McSwegan and Colin Cameron [both Hearts] got the goals.

Scotland were then drawn against Kevin Keegan's England in the November two-leg play-offs and as expected the hype went into overdrive. The first leg was at Hampden where the sizeable England support amongst the crowd of 50,132 had two

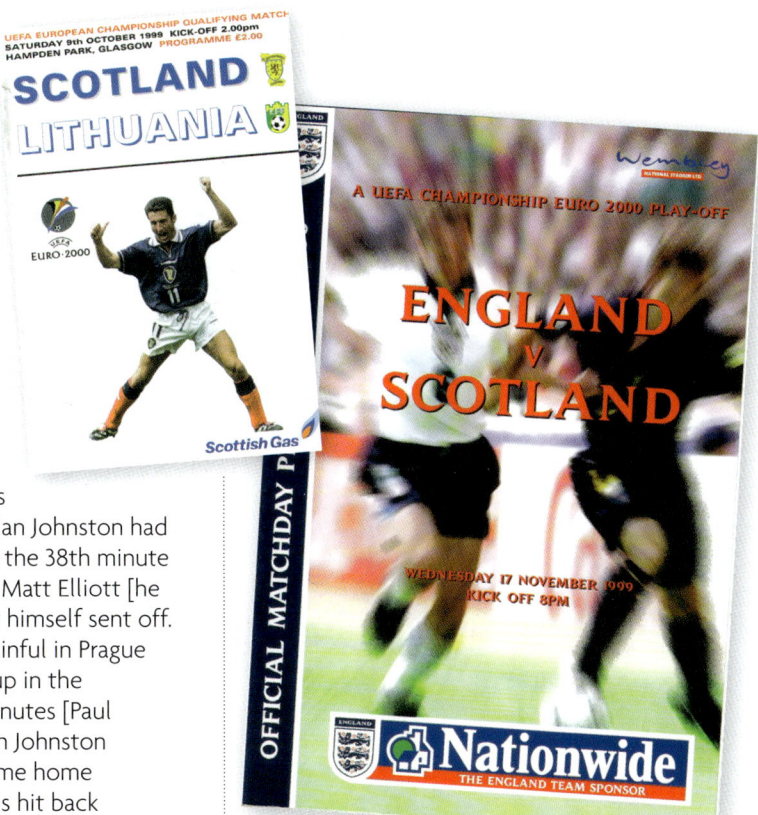

headed first-half goals from the diminutive Paul Scholes to savour. We had Rockall.

Yet another four-day gap and off we went to 'Old' Wembley [for what would be the last time], not with any great enthusiasm it has to be said, however Scotland played really well and won 1-0 thanks to a goal from Don Hutchison. Unfortunately the England keeper David Seaman also played really well and it was largely thanks to the Arsenal man that the tie didn't go to extra-time or penalties. Yet another one for the 'Glorious failures' collection. Sigh...

At the finals both the Czech Republic and England were eliminated at the group stages as France went on to win the competition and add its trophy to the FIFA World Cup that they had won on home soil two years earlier. Sadly for Scotland though, Euro 2000 and a bright, new millennium signalled the arrival of a long-running football famine.

As an aside I travelled to the Euro 2000 finals, to Bruges to see France v Denmark and Amsterdam to take in Spain v Slovenia. Two excellent games of football but it just wasn't the same. I felt like I had gatecrashed a party only to have my bird pinched...

JAPAN/SOUTH KOREA 2002

Only four nations – Belgium, Croatia, Latvia and San Marino – stood between Scotland and a groundbreaking trip to the Far East for the 2002 World Cup finals. Even if we finished second in our qualifying group we had another opportunity via the play-offs. Spoiler alert! – Scotland finished third.

Scotland actually got off to a good start in the Far East [of Europe] by defeating Latvia 1-0 in Riga in September 2000 with Rangers' Neil McCann grabbing the winner two minutes from time. The good work continued on 7 October with a 2-0 win in San Marino's Stadio Olimpico! Matt Elliott of Leicester City and Sunderland's Don Hutchison got the goals late in the second half. Four days later yet another fine result was achieved when Scotland battled back from being 1-0 down to get a draw with Croatia in Zagreb. Kevin Gallacher of Newcastle United cancelled out Alen Boksic's opener.

On 24 March 2001 came what would ultimately prove to be a fatal slip-up against Belgium at 'new' Hampden. A crowd of 37,480 saw Scotland go 2-0 ahead after 29 minutes when Rangers' Billy Dodds slotted home a penalty to add to his earlier goal. The penalty came about when a Colin Hendry header was stopped on the line by Eric Deflandre's arm and the Belgian defender was subsequently red-carded.

Scotland were cruising, Belgium were down to ten men and the Danish referee's middle name was 'Milton' – what could possibly go wrong? Well, in 58 minutes Eric Wilmots headed past Neil Sullivan to bring Belgium back into the game and in the 92nd minute another headed goal – from Daniel Van Buyten – gave Belgium a point. [Guuuu-ted!!!] Four days later there were only 27,313

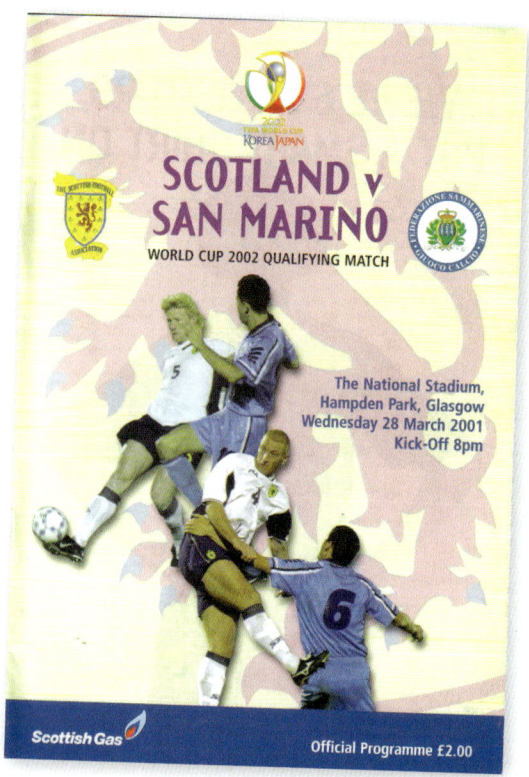

of us back at Hampden to see San Marino skelped 4-0 [Colin Hendry – two goals in his 51st and final Scotland match, Billy Dodds and Colin Cameron.] [Still gutted!]

It was however two fixtures in early September which effectively put paid to our qualification hopes. On 1st September Croatia came to Hampden where 47,400 saw a goal-less draw that suited the visitors. Four days later a sizeable travelling support saw Scotland crash 2-0 to Belgium in Brussels. Same old. Same old.

We then went into our final qualifier 'not quite dead' but we needed Belgium to win in Croatia and for Scotland to deliver a sizeable victory against Latvia at Hampden. In the end we got neither – Croatia won 1-0 in Zagreb whilst Scotland struggled to a 2-1 win – debutant Dougie Freedman [Crystal Palace] and Davie Weir [Everton] were our scorers. Only 23,228 witnessed what was the final match for Craig Brown, Scotland's longest serving

Scotland Glory, Tears & Souvenirs

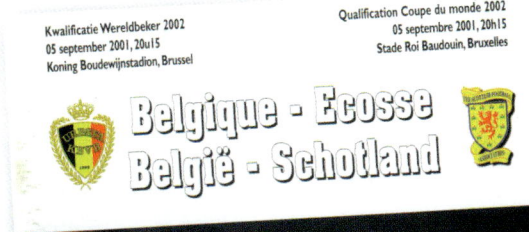

international manager, who resigned shortly after the final whistle. It really was the end of an era – we just didn't know it yet.

And so the Tartan Army were denied the delights of a whole range of different cultural attractions and experiences – from Jeju Island and Gyeongbokgung Palace to the Bullet Train and an overnight stay in a 'Love Hotel'. I really wanted to dress up as Aneka and sing *You're my Japanese Boy* to Billy Dodds. Never mind, we could always take out our frustrations on the groundbreaking video game Grand Theft Auto III which was developed by DMA Design of Dundee. As far as sporting successes go, an all-Scottish ladies curling team won a gold medal for Britain at the Winter Olympics in Salt Lake City in February 2002.

Meanwhile, on the Pacific rim in the summer of 2002 Croatia were eliminated at the group stage whilst in the Round of 16 Belgium lost 2-0 to Brazil who went on to lift the trophy for the fifth time by beating Germany 2-0 in the final in Yokohama. The referee at the final was the renowned Pierluigi Collina of Italy whilst our very own Shugmeister [aka Hugh Dallas from North Lanarkshire] was the fourth official. That's got to count for something...

PORTUGAL 2004

Portugal in the summer of 2004 was going to make for a marvellous family and friends holiday. Here's the background to why it didn't happen, starting with our group 5 qualifying opponents – Faroe Islands, Germany, Iceland and Lithuania.

Scotland had a new boss in the shape of Berti Vogts – a winner with West Germany/Germany as both a player and a manager, however we could devote a whole book/series of therapy sessions as to why things didn't work out between us although Euro 2004 was almost a success story.

The first qualifier in September 2002 was almost a 'Disaster for Scotland!' and a big one at that when, in Toftir, the Faroe Islands went 2-0 in front after just 13 minutes. Indeed the Faroes should have went 3-0 ahead with John Petersen getting his hat-trick but the ball hit a 'trench' just before he struck his shot over with only Rab Douglas to beat [again]. Mercifully, second half goals from Paul Lambert [Celtic] and Barry Ferguson [Rangers] helped reduce the red-face factor.

The following month Scotland again headed North by Northwest, to Reykjavik, to record a 2-0 win over Iceland. Christian 'Cary Grant' Dailly and Gary 'Eva Marie Saint' Naysmith were the scorers. The following March, Iceland made the return trip to Hampden where 37,938 watched Scotland battle to a 2-1 victory – Kenny Miller [Wolves] hit the opener, Eidur Gudjohnsen [Chelsea] got the equaliser, Dundee's Lee Wilkie netted the winner.

Two games in April and June 2003 saw five points dropped, beginning with a 1-0 defeat by Lithuania in Kaunas. Jackie McNamara [Celtic] clipped the heels of

59

Maciulevicius [allegedly] and Razanauskas slammed the resultant penalty past Dundee United's Paul Gallacher. In June, Rudi Voller's Germany visited Hampden and went home with a point. 48,037 saw a Fredi Bobic header give an ordinary looking Deutschland a first half lead before Kenny Miller equalised in the 69th minute. 1-1 it finished.

In September, the Faroe Islands came to Hampden and gave us problems again by having the audacity to equalise Southampton winger Neil McCann's opening goal for Scotland. Eventually goals from Paul Dickov [Leicester City] and James McFadden [Everton] gave the home side a 3-1 victory in front of 40,901. Four days later in the penultimate qualifier in Dortmund, Germany won 2-1 to leave Scotland chasing the play-offs via a runners-up spot. Bobic and Ballack put Germany two in front before Neil McCann pulled one back for the Scots. Maurice Ross [Rangers] being red-carded didn't exactly help the cause although the biggest talking point was the overhearing of Christian Dailly's use of 'industrial language' to describe his disappointment at the result whilst his boss was being interviewed live on television.

On 11th October Scotland had to beat Lithuania at Hampden [and hope Germany didn't lose at home to Iceland] in order to make the play-offs. Germany cruised to a 3-0 victory but Scotland scraped it 1-0. Manchester United's Darren Fletcher did the needful with 20 minutes remaining much to the relief of almost all of the crowd of 50,343.

Into the two-leg play-offs and an unseeded draw pitted Scotland against the Netherlands who were managed by Dick Dastardly, aka Dick Advocaat. The first leg was at Hampden on 15th November 2003 and 50,670 witnessed a hard-fought 1-0 victory for Scotland thanks to a 22nd minute goal from James McFadden – our answer to Quidditch sensation Harry Potter. Scotland had one foot in the Algarve.

Four days later however when we visited the Amsterdam Arena for the second leg it felt as though the retractable roof had fallen in on us as the Netherlands dished out a 6-0 thrashing which included a hat-trick from Ruud Van Nistelrooy. A further three days on England won the Rugby Union World Cup – it wasn't the end of the world but it certainly felt like it.

At the finals the following summer, Germany failed to impress and were eliminated at the group stage whilst the Netherlands lost in the semi-finals to

Scotland Glory, Tears & Souvenirs

host nation, Portugal. In the actual final, Portugal were surprisingly beaten by rank outsiders Greece who were coached by Otto Rehhagel. Maybe Scotland just had the wrong German as our manager.

GERMANY 2006

Germany calling! Germany calling! Regrettably however manager Berti Vogts [and his successor Walter Smith] were unable to steer us to the Fatherland and so for Scotland the 21st century continued like a footballing equivalent of author Lemony Snicket's *A Series of Unfortunate Events*....

Belarus, Italy, Moldova, Norway and Slovenia were our qualifying opponents and whilst, as expected, the Italians proved to be the clear winners, Scotland finished a poor third behind an average Norway and so missed out on the play-offs.

On paper the opening schedule of matches in late 2004 looked good – two home games plus an away trip to the 'minnows' of Moldova. In actual fact we picked up only two points from a possible nine beginning with a goal-less draw against Slovenia at Hampden in September in front of 38,278. It got worse the following month when we lost 1-0 to Norway at Hampden with a larger crowd of 48,882 looking on. Early in the second half Everton's James McFadden was red-carded for deliberate handball on the goal-line and Steffen Iversen netted the resultant penalty. Four days later, the end for 'Der Terrier' came on the eastern front – an embarrassing 1-1 draw with Moldova in Chisinau. Actually it was embarrassing for Moldova – they should have won, with Rangers' Steven Thompson grabbing an equaliser for Scotland. Berti resigned in November citing 'disgraceful abuse'. Dark days indeed.

Former Rangers and Everton manager Walter Smith was in charge for our next dropping of the points – all three away to Italy in March 2005 following a 2-0 defeat. Scotland were undone by two free-kicks from the peerless Andrea Pirlo which over 10,000 Scots in Milan's San Siro Stadium were forced to applaud.

In June Scotland eventually recorded their first win of the campaign – 2-0 versus Moldova at Hampden. An impressive 45,317 turned up to see second-half goals from Christian Dailly [West Ham United] and James McFadden. We were unable to string two victories together however when four days later we drew 0-0 with Belarus in Minsk.

On 3rd September Marcello Lippi's Italy came to town and that would have been a notable scalp if we had managed it – but we didn't and had to make do with a 1-1 draw instead. A headed goal from Wolves' Kenny Miller had given Scotland a first half lead but substitute Fabio Grosso grabbed an equaliser 15 minutes from time. 50,185 got their money's worth.

Another four-day gap later and Scotland proceeded to tease their supporters by beating Norway 2-1 in the Ulleval Stadium, Oslo and in so doing raise our hopes of making the play-offs. Kenny Miller got both Scotland goals in the first half-hour.

On 8th October 51,105 were at Hampden to see Belarus cause an upset [well they

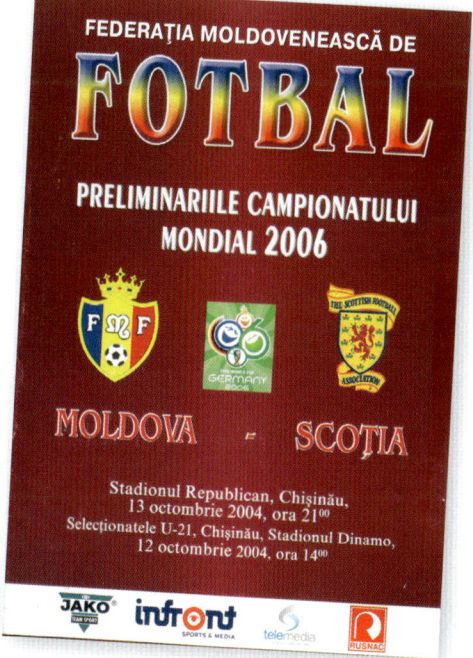

AUSTRIA/SWITZERLAND 2008

In the summer of 2008 Austria and Switzerland were joint hosts of UEFA's 13th European Championship – and guess what, Scotland weren't there. As such the Tartan Army never got to go on its very own 'Sound of Music' tour and sing Doh a deer ad nauseam. Indeed there was no British or Irish representation amongst the sixteen finalists but it could have been oh so different if Scotland hadn't imploded in their two final qualifying matches. Gordon Brown succeeded Tony Blair as UK Prime Minister in June 2007 and fellow Scot David Tennant was Dr. Who at the time, and yet we still blew it! The global financial crisis of 2007-08 was also a bit of a pisser.

To be fair, Scotland had a tough qualifying group which included both the winners and the runners-up from the 2006 World Cup Final [Italy and France], Ukraine [quarter-finalists at the 2006 World Cup] plus Lithuania, Georgia and the Faroe Islands. No less than 12 qualifying matches – it would never have happened under Stalin.

It had all started so well, with manager Walter Smith overseeing three successive victories – 6-0

upset me and the rest of the Scotland support] by winning 1-0 and making Norway uncatchable with one qualifier to go. With nothing to play for, Scotland then turned in their best performance of the campaign – a 3-0 win over Slovenia in Celje courtesy of goals from Darren Fletcher [Manchester United], James McFadden and Paul Hartley [Hearts].

2005 was not a complete disaster however as *Doctor Who* was revived as a TV series by the BBC after a fifteen year absence whilst the UK music charts featured class acts such as The Pussycat Dolls and The Sugababes.

Back to the football and Norway lost to the Czech Republic in the play-offs; however, Italy used what they learned from having to cope with the likes of Lee McCulloch and Nigel Quashie to go on and lift the trophy, beating France in the final in Berlin in July 2006.

against the Faroes at Celtic Park in September 2006 [Hampden was unavailable due to a Robbie Williams concert but Darren Fletcher, James McFadden, Kris Boyd [twice], Kenny Miller and Gary O'Connor hit the net anyway in front of 50,059 real music lovers], 2-1 away to Lithuania [Christian Dailly and Kenny Miller] and 1-0 against France at Hampden in October [52,500 witnessing defender Gary Caldwell netting the winner to avenge a 5-0 friendly match gubbing versus France in his 2002 debut].

We then had a couple of blips on the road when we lost 2-0 to the Ukraine in Kiev [Steven Pressley got himself a red card] and 2-0 to Italy in Bari although sandwiched in between them was a 2-1 win over Georgia at Hampden in March 2007 – Kris Boyd got the opener with Craig Beattie netting the winner in the 89th minute to put a big smile on the face of new Scotland manager Alex McLeish and most of the crowd of 50,850.

There followed four successive victories which had us all dreaming of an Alpine adventure. 2-0 v the Faroes in Toftir in June [Shaun Maloney and Gary O'Connor], 3-1 v Lithuania at Hampden on 8th September [51,349 plus Kris Boyd, Stephen McManus and James McFadden], 1-0 v France in Paris on 12th September [James McFaddennnnn!] and 3-1 v Ukraine back at Hampden on 13th October [Kenny Miller, Lee McCulloch and James McFadden in front of 51,366].

The wheels came off the bogie however in Tbilisi on 17th October when Scotland crashed 2-0 to Georgia. The bogie then slewed over a cliff on 17th November when Italy came to a rain-sodden Hampden and pinched all three points. Luca Toni gave the visitors the lead after only two minutes but Barry Ferguson got Scotland level midway through the second half. In the 91st minute Scotland were well and truly robbed though when Christian Panucci headed home a hotly disputed Pirlo free-kick.

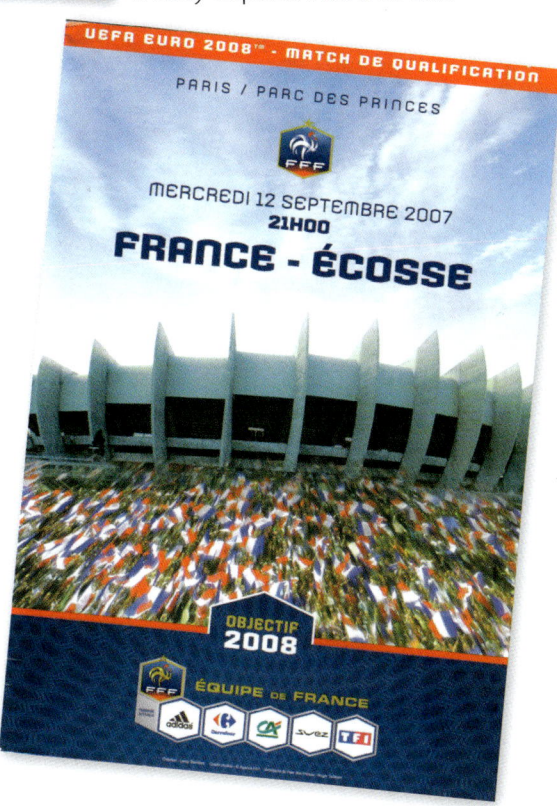

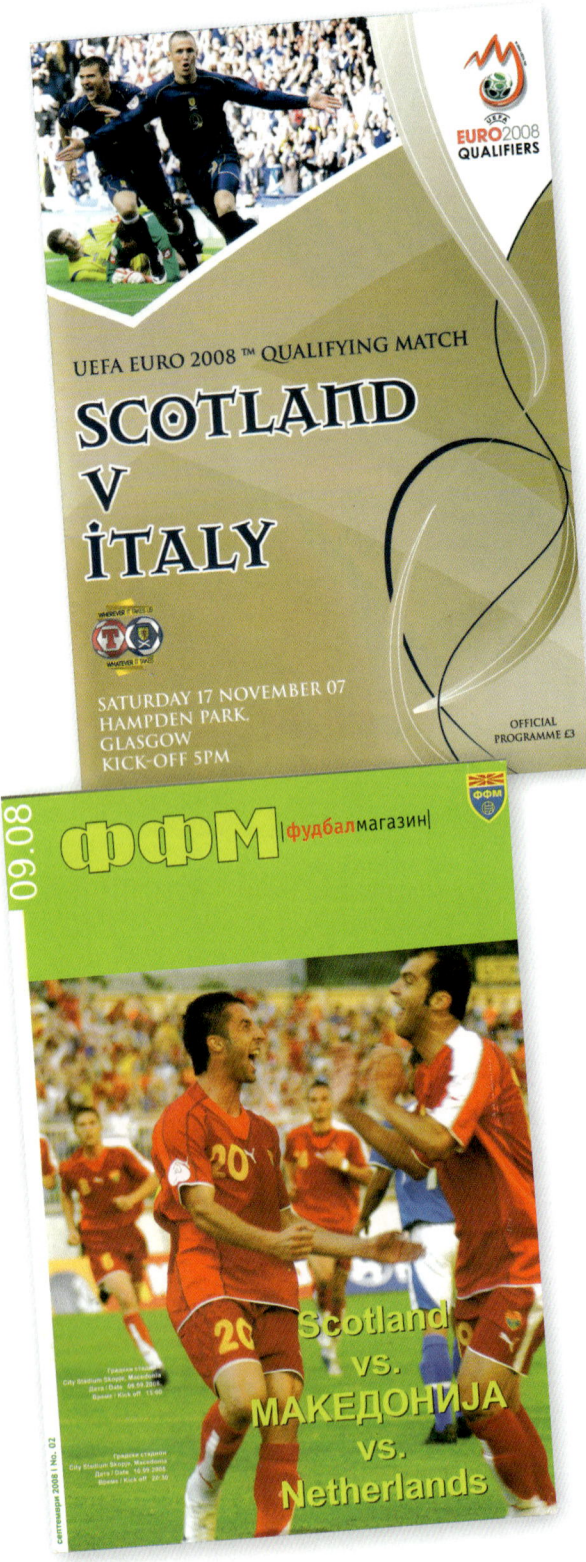

Alan Hutton had been fouled I tell you as would most of the crowd of 51,301!

Only Scotland could take maximum points from a France side that included the likes of Lilian Thuram, Patrick Vieira, Franck Ribery and Thierry Henry and then screw up against Georgia. If Scotland had won their last two qualifiers we would have topped the group and if we had won one of them [or even drawn both] we would have finished second and still progressed to the finals. Aaaaaargh!

At the finals in 2008 Italy reached the last eight whilst France were knocked out at the group stage. In the final itself, the emergent Spain beat Germany 1-0 in Vienna. I spent most of the tournament however fantasising about Julie Andrews on a motorbike – I quite often get her and Steve McQueen confused....

SOUTH AFRICA 2010

Scotland's inability to do well in a World Cup qualifying group which included Iceland, Macedonia, Netherlands and Norway meant we were out of Africa before we were even in it.

Scotland's first four qualifiers yielded only four points out of a possible twelve. The first three points were lost in Skopje on 6th September 2008 when George Burley's boys lost 1-0 to FYR Macedonia. Our excuses? It was a baking hot afternoon, their goal came from a soft free-kick award and in the second half Scotland were denied a penalty when Birmingham City's James McFadden was clipped inside the box.

Four days after being sunk in Skopje there was some sort of redemption in Reykjavik with a 2-1 win over Iceland. Rangers' Kirk Broadfoot opened the scoring on his debut before James McFadden made it 2-0. Eider Gudjohnsen pulled one back from the penalty spot after skipper Stephen McManus was red-carded for handball but ten-man Scotland held out.

On 11th October Scotland and Norway played out a goal-less draw at Hampden Park in front of 50,205. Another Scottish debutant, Chris Iwelumo of Wolves, made a name for himself [but sadly not a good name] when he came on as a second half substitute for McFadden and missed an absolute sitter from just three yards. Unused substitute striker Kris Boyd of Rangers announced his 'retirement' from international football soon thereafter. He'd return three years later.

In March 2009 Scotland returned to the Amsterdam Arena – the venue for a 6-0 mauling in 2003. This time

Scotland Glory, Tears & Souvenirs

we lost only 3-0 so mark that down as some sort of improvement.

Scotland then collected six points from their final four qualifiers beginning with another hard fought 2-1 win over Iceland at Hampden in April. 42,259 watched as Cardiff City's Ross McCormack slammed home the first goal before defender Indridi Sigurdsson equalised for the visitors. Hibernian's Steven Fletcher then got the winner with a close-range header. Skipper Barry Ferguson missed the match having been dropped for his role in a late-night drinking session at the team hotel.

The 12 of August 2009 was anything but glorious however as Scotland crashed 4-0 to Norway in Oslo. The collapse started in the 33rd minute when Gary Caldwell got himself sent off and John Arne Riise scored from the resultant free-kick. The result meant that Scotland would need to win their two remaining matches – both at Hampden – to have a chance of making the play-offs.

On 5th September we managed the first win when the Former Yugoslav Republic of Macedonia on their first visit to the Former Independent Kingdom of Scotland were defeated 2-0. Celtic's Scott Brown and James McFadden got the goals with a crowd of 50,214 looking on.

Four days later, the dream of boarding the David Livingstone supporters' bus bound for South Africa [yes I know I'm stretching it a bit] came to an end when Eljero Elia hit the winner for the Netherlands eight minutes from time. Earlier Kenny Miller had fired against the underside of the crossbar and a Steven Naismith shot had struck the post. Naismith also had a 'goal' disallowed for offside. 51,230 could see that it was not to be.

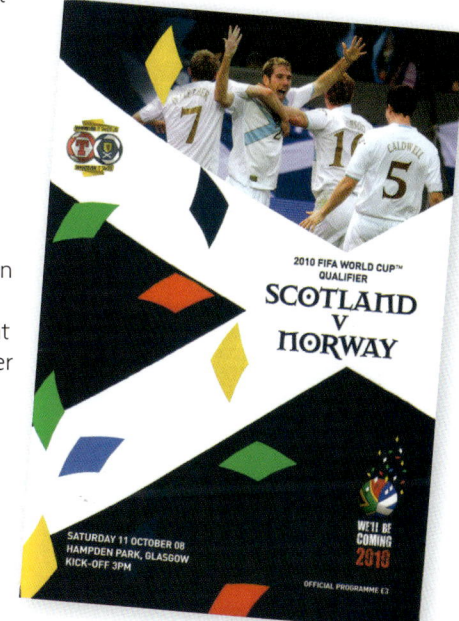

It was also not to be for Norway whose record was the worst of all the runners-up and so they failed to make the play-offs. On the other hand, the Netherlands who had won all eight of their qualifiers went all the way to the actual final in Johannesburg before losing to the new football superpower that was Spain.

Back in Scotland every second summer was now more painful than the previous one and in 2010 the options included watching England making an arse of themselves in South Africa or taking in some classic movies such as *Toy Story 3* or *Hot Tub Time Machine*....

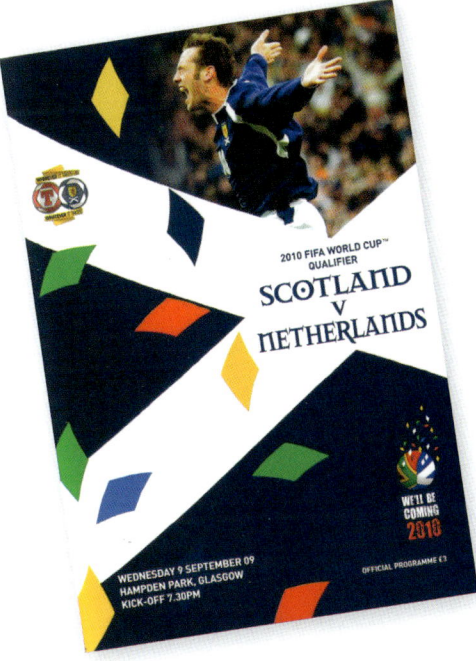

65

POLAND/UKRAINE 2012

When Scotland commenced their group I Euro-qualifiers [which included the Czech Republic, Liechtenstein, Lithuania – for the fourth successive Euros – and world and European champions Spain], Craig Levein was team manager.

The qualifiers began on 3rd September 2010 with a goal-less draw against Lithuania in Kaunas. Kenny Miller and Steven Naismith both missed good chances whilst Barry Robson twice came close.

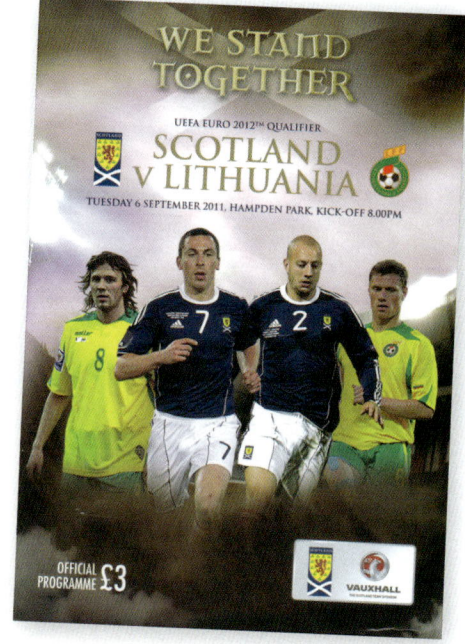

Four days later could, and perhaps should have been the most embarrassing day in the history of Scottish international football. Liechtenstein visited Hampden for the first time, 37,050 went along to see them [and Scotland I suppose] and in the 46th minute a curling shot from Mario Frick gave the visitors a shock lead. Scotland managed to get back up off the canvas and in the 62nd minute an equaliser/tranquiliser arrived when a Kenny Miller shot went in off the underside of the bar. Complete salvation was not achieved however until the 97th minute when Stephen McManus headed in from a Barry Robson corner. Scotland talisman James McFadden won his 48th cap that evening but was substituted at half-time. Sadly, Faddy never played for Scotland again.

On 8th October Scotland travelled to Prague where the manager tried out his 'steam locomotive' formation of 4-6-0. Call Mr Levein brave or call him foolish but playing without any strikers whatsoever didn't work out. Not surprisingly goalkeeper Allan McGregor had a busy evening and played well but was unable to prevent Hubnik from netting in the 69th minute. I don't know about the dressing room, but at this juncture Craig Levein was certainly losing the Tartan Army.

Another four-day gap and Vicente del Bosque's all-conquering Spain came to Hampden and duly demonstrated to the crowd of 51,322 why they were the best team on the planet. That said, Scotland played some good football themselves and made a right game of it. Goals from David Villa and Andres Iniesta had given La Roja a two goal advantage but Scotland fought back to draw level thanks to a Steven Naismith diving header and a Gerard Pique own goal. Eleven minutes from time however a Stephen McManus error allowed Fernando Llorente to tap in the winner. Bugger....

It was on 3rd September the following year that the qualifiers resumed for Scotland with a game against the Czech Republic at Hampden and a crowd of 51,564. Scotland really should have won this match but had to settle for a damaging 2-2 draw. Twice Scotland led [through goals from Kenny Miller and Darren Fletcher] and twice we were pegged back with the seering pain coming in stoppage

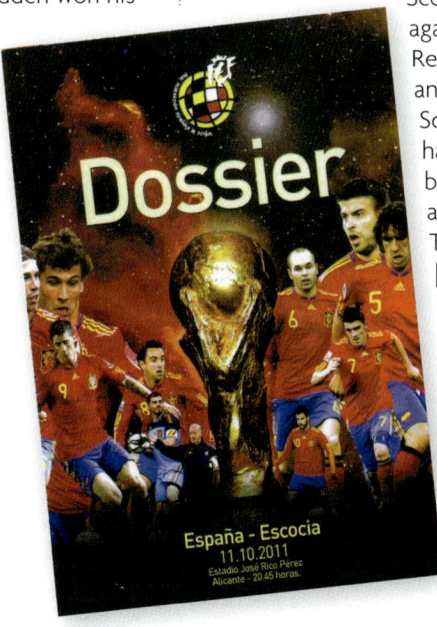

Scotland Glory, Tears & Souvenirs

time when Jan Rezek appeared to dive and the resultant penalty put the sides level. Moments later Christophe Berra was denied a stonewall penalty at the other end and instead was booked for his troubles. As Sir Alex meant to say – 'Football? Fucking hell!'

Scotland then recorded two successive 1-0 victories. At Hampden on 6th September a second-half goal from Steven Naismith was enough to overcome Lithuania in front of a crowd of 34,071. Earlier in the game Darren Fletcher had missed a penalty. In Vaduz on 8th October a looping header from Craig Mackail-Smith allowed Scotland to 'take' another three points from Liechtenstein.

On 11th October 2011 Scotland went into their final qualifier, against Spain in Alicante, knowing that to make the play-offs we would probably have to match the Czech Republic's result in Lithuania that same evening. The Czechs won 4-1, Scotland lost 3-1 [David Goodwillie with the consolation goal]. Competition over, time to reflect, time to say 'if only' yet again.

The Czech Republic defeated Montenegro in the play-offs, but at the finals in 2012 a goal from Portugal's Ronaldo put the Czechs out at the quarter-final stage. The imperious Spain won their third successive major however by destroying Italy 4-0 in the final in Kiev.

For Scottish stay-at-homers the summer blockbusters were *The Amazing Spiderman* and *Abraham Lincoln:Vampire Hunter*....plus Andy Murray winning the US Open Tennis Championships.

BRAZIL 2014

For many of us Baby-boomers this was the 'bucket-list' tournament to attend. The Tartan Army in Rio de Janeiro for the 20th FIFA World Cup finals – there would have been no topping that. Unfortunately, there was no topping our qualifying group either – we finished fourth and so didn't even make the play-offs.

Dry your eyes, I hear you say, so for the record here's how Andy, Hamish, Boab and Tarquin [there's bound to be one] missed out on a Brazilian. Scotland were drawn in group A along with Belgium, Croatia, Macedonia, Serbia and Wales and we failed to win any of our first six qualifiers – two dour draws followed by four painful defeats.

The opening two draws were both at Hampden and were watched by 47,369 and 32,430 respectively. On 8th September 2012 we drew 0-0 with Serbia and three days later we came from behind to draw 1-1 with Macedonia – Kenny Miller cancelling out an opening goal that was clearly offside. Honest.

On 12th October at the Cardiff City Stadium two goals from Gareth Bale in the last ten minutes gave Wales a 2-1 victory after a first half goal from West Bromwich Albion's James Morrison had given Scotland the lead.

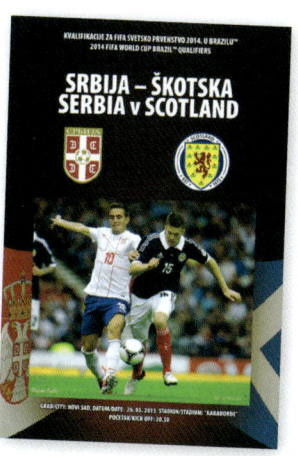

Four days after that mugging Scotland lost 2-0 against Belgium in Brussels – Christian Benteke and Vincent Kompany were the second half scorers for the original Red Devils.

On 5th November Craig Levein was relieved of his Scotland managerial duties but at least he escaped the fate that befell Guy Fawkes. Gordon Strachan was the new manager when Scotland played Wales at Hampden on 22nd March 2013 and with 39,365 paying customers looking on things looked good when Grant Hanley headed Scotland into the lead on the stroke of half-time. Unfortunately Wales repeated their 'Cardiff comeback' trick to win 2-1 thanks to goals from Aaron Ramsey and Hal Robson-Kanu. In the falling snow both Robert Snodgrass [Norwich City] and Ramsey were red-carded and so it wasn't the best wedding anniversary evening out my wife Marion and I have ever enjoyed.

On 26 March 2013 Scotland then lost 2-0 to Serbia in Novi Sad — a game that only went ahead because a number of Scotland supporters helped clear snow from the pitch beforehand. How's that for irony?

In June Scotland finally recorded their first victory of the campaign — in Zagreb of all places. A Robert Snodgrass goal in the 26th minute was enough to defeat Croatia who were fourth in the world rankings at the time. However, by then qualification was no longer possible for the Scots.

A win at Hampden continued to prove elusive when on 6th September Belgium won 2-0. 40,284 were at the National Stadium for a fixture which only meant something to the visitors. Scotland achieved a second away win four days later however when Macedonia were defeated 2-1 in Skopje. Ikechi Anya [Watford] and Shaun Maloney [Wigan Athletic] were the scorers.

A largely wretched campaign came to an end on 15th October when Scotland managed a home win against Croatia in front of 30,172. 2-0 it finished with goals from Robert Snodgrass and Steven Naismith [Everton] ensuring that we did the double against a side who would defeat Iceland in the play-offs and head for Brazil.

At the finals Croatia would be eliminated at the group stages whilst Belgium made it to the quarter-finals before losing to Argentina. Germany defeated Argentina 1-0 in the final.

Ten days after Germany's triumph, the city of Glasgow commenced hosting the 20th Commonwealth Games and Scotland went on to win a record haul of 53 medals — 19 gold, 15 silver and 19 bronze. Add tennis heroes Andy and Jamie Murray into the mix and you can see that Scotland is successful in the world of sport — but just not at football.

FRANCE 2016

Twenty-four of UEFA's [then] 54 member associations had teams at the 2016 European Championship finals. That 'success' figure represents 44% and it included England, Northern Ireland, the Republic of Ireland and Wales.

You can set fire to this book or bury it in your back garden if you like but the testicle-squashing, painful fact remains that Scotland were amongst the 56% losers — and yet at one point it had all looked

Scotland Glory, Tears & Souvenirs

so promising in a qualifying group which included Georgia, world champions Germany, Gibraltar, Poland and the Republic of Ireland.

On 7th September 2014 Scotland opened with one of our 'glorious defeats' – losing 2-1 to Germany in Dortmund. A beautiful curling shot from Watford's Ikechi Anya had drawn Scotland level after 66 minutes. However, a mere four minutes later Thomas Muller got his second goal of the evening and that was that save for Celtic's Charlie Mulgrew getting sent off in stoppage time.

On 18th September 55% of the voters said 'No' in a referendum on Scottish independence. I was one of the 45% that said 'Yes' but if I was somehow given the choice of full independence OR a successful national football team then I would be in a bit of a quandary.

Anyway, with Hampden still being converted back from its Commonwealth Games manifestation Scotland's qualifier, against Georgia on 11th October was played at Ibrox Stadium, Glasgow and attracted 34,719. Scotland got the three points thanks to a first-half own goal from Khubutia. Three days later Scotland played their part in an exciting 2-2 draw with Poland in Warsaw. Shaun Maloney [Wigan Athletic] got us back on level terms after 18 minutes and then Steven Naismith [Everton] put Scotland 2-1 in front early in the second half. Poland equalised with fourteen minutes remaining however to ensure a fair result.

The following month Shaun Maloney scored the only goal of the game to give Scotland a hard fought victory against Martin O'Neill's Republic of Ireland. 59,239 watched the match at Celtic Park that evening.

On 29th March 2015 Gibraltar – UEFA's controversial Team 54 – plus 34,255 spectators, came to Hampden where they witnessed a little bit of history. With Scotland leading 1-0 thanks to an 18th minute penalty from Chicago Fire's Shaun Maloney, Lee Casciaro scored Gibraltar's first ever competitive goal in the 19th minute. "Well done sir!/Holy shit!" Further goals from Shaun Maloney, Steven Naismith and a hat-trick from Sunderland's Steven Fletcher [our first hat-trick since 1969] made sure that history did not become infamy.

In June Scotland then visited Dublin and in a bruising encounter earned a 1-1 draw thanks to John O'Shea deflecting a Shaun Maloney shot into his own net. Earlier, Jonathan Walters had given the Irish a half-time lead. It was an enjoyable summer and fair stood the wind for France.

On 4th September however in Tbilisi, Georgia the 'Scotland Express' was de-railed [figuratively speaking] when we went down

1-0 and tamely at that. What's the Georgian for déjà vu? Kazaishvili scored the only goal of the game after 38 minutes and incredibly Scotland didn't manage a single shot on target in the entire match. What's the Gaelic for – You've blown it you stupid buggers!

Actually Scotland still had two home matches [and an away game against Gibraltar] to redress matters. Alas, we only took one point from six in the Hampden encounters. On 7th September we battled back twice to draw level against Germany – a Mats Hummels og and a strike from James McArthur [Crystal Palace] meant parity at half-time. A second-half, in-off-the-post shot from Ilkay Gundogan however gave the world champs a 3-2 victory. 50,753 was the official, mostly disappointed, attendance.

On 8th October France was lost, when in front of 49,359 Scotland drew 2-2 with Poland and the Republic of Ireland defeated Germany 1-0 in Dublin. The prolific Robert Lewandowski opened the scoring in the third minute but Scotland fought back to lead 2-1 with goals from Matt Ritchie [Bournemouth] and Steven Fletcher. The final boot in the chuckies came in the 94th minute when Lewandowski snatched an equaliser for Poland although the Dublin result was enough in itself to give the Irish the third spot play-off place.

Three days later more than 10,000 Scots were in the Estadio Algarve for the party that never was although we did see a 6-0 away win which included another Steven Fletcher hat-trick. Chris Martin [Derby County], Shaun Maloney [Hull City] and Steven Naismith got the other goals but the inflatable crocodile was my man of the match.

The Republic of Ireland overcame Bosnia and Herzegovina in the play-offs and at the finals in France reached the Round of 16 stage before bowing out to the host nation. Poland lost to Portugal in the quarter-finals. Germany lost in the semi-finals to France who in turn were beaten by Portugal in the actual final. And to think that just a few months previous, Scotland had recorded a 6-0 win on Portuguese soil. OK, so it was against Gibraltar who had to play their home games in neighbouring Portugal whilst their national stadium was being brought up to UEFA standards, but I'm now beyond desperate...

Oh yes, and right in the middle of the 2016 European Championships a referendum was held in the UK and Gibraltar on our membership of the European Union. Scotland, Northern Ireland and Gibraltar voted to remain but the aggregate result was that we all say Au Revoir to Brussels although football skelpings from Belgium will no doubt continue as before.

RUSSIA 2018

At the point that this book went to print, Scotland had played six of their ten World Cup qualifiers and we were still hanging in there. Arithmetically Scotland could still make it to President Putin's funhouse, Gordon Strachan could still be Jeff Tracy of International Rescue in disguise.

A winning start is always a good thing and in September 2016 we managed it with a somewhat fortuitous, though comfortable-sounding, 5-1 victory away to Malta. A Robert Snodgrass hat-trick began with a cross-come-looping-shot and was followed by a penalty and a tap-in for the Hull City man. Chris Martin [Derby County] and Steven Fletcher

Scotland Glory, Tears & Souvenirs

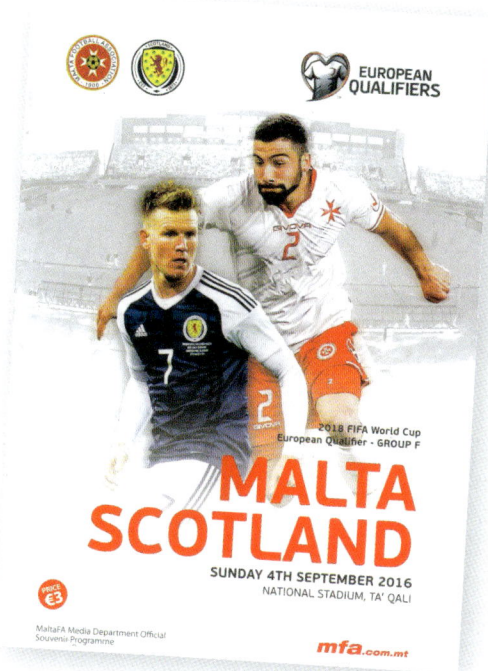

Raheem Sterling missed a sitter to make it 4-0!

26th March 2017 was Mothers' Day and this time those 'Mothers' in the dark blue jerseys turned in an impressive performance at Hampden against Slovenia which should have resulted in an emphatic victory instead of that of a solitary goal which came in the 88th minute from substitute Chris Martin whose initial appearance had resulted in booing from some of the crowd of only 20,435. Aerosols! Incidentally, there were six Celtic players in the starting line-up including Leigh Griffiths who hit the woodwork twice and debutant Stuart Armstrong who was the man of the match.

Two days after the Slovenia win the Scottish Parliament voted to seek a second referendum on independence and on Saturday 10th June England sent north [Sheffield Wednesday] got the other goals whilst Malta had two men red-carded.

On 8th October, Lithuania came to Hampden having lost at the national stadium on all four previous occasions. This time however, they went home with a 1-1 draw. Indeed our visitors nearly won the game as Scotland had to rely on a last-minute equaliser from Crystal Palace's James McArthur. The vast majority of the crowd of 35,966 were not amused.

Three days later Scotland travelled to Trnava to play Slovakia for the first time. We've had better 'first-nighters'. Skippered by 'Mad' Martin Skrtel, Slovakia trounced Scotland 3-0. A month after being turned over by 'new' opposition, Scotland then suffered a 3-0 doing from our oldest adversary, England. Long before the end the Three Lions roamed about Wembley like it was Blair Drummond Safari Park – it could have been worse I suppose,

71

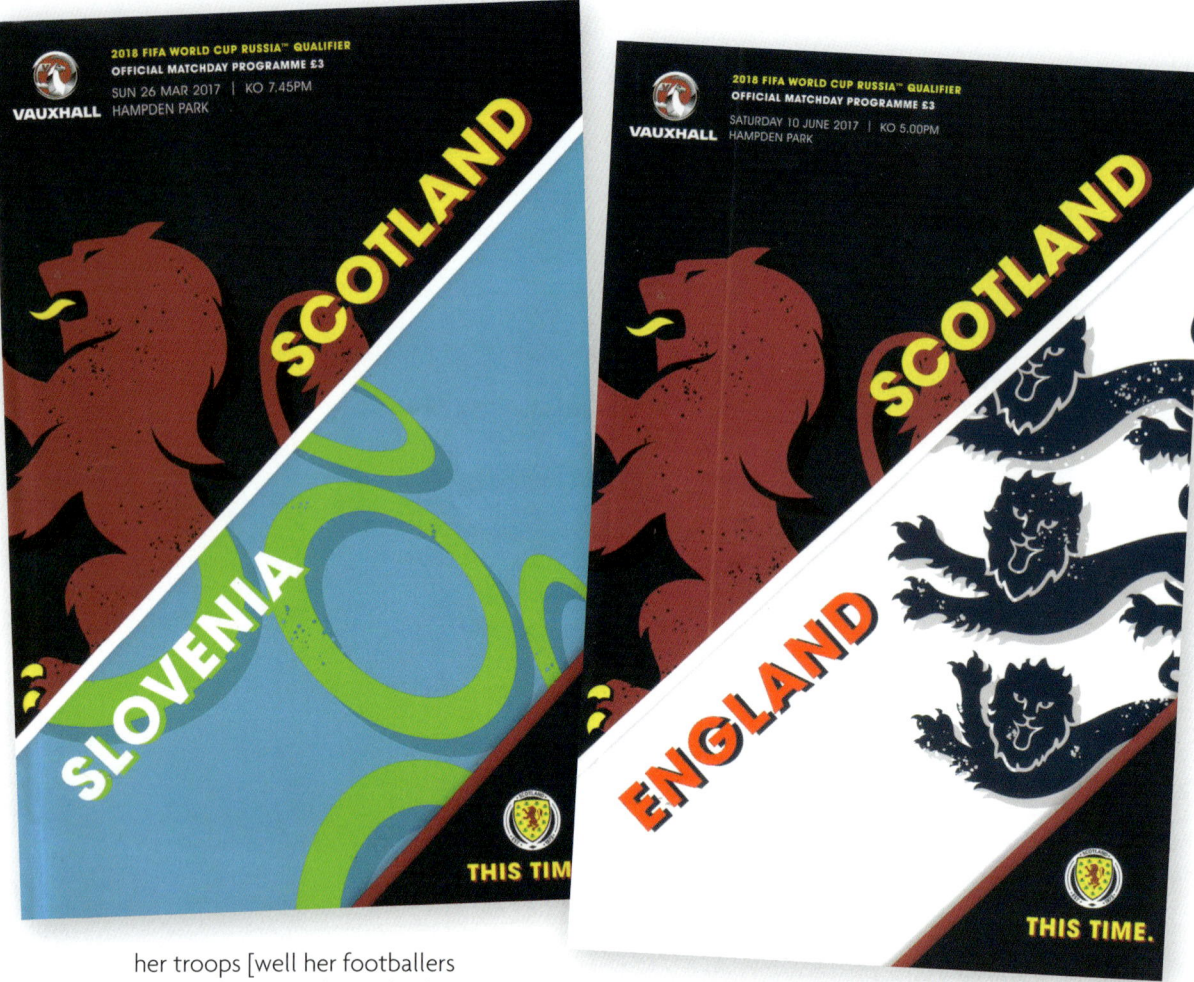

her troops [well her footballers anyway] to Hampden Park where 48,520 witnessed a quite astonishing 2-2 draw.

England took the lead after 70 minutes thanks to a left-foot shot from Alex Oxlade-Chamberlain that perhaps goalkeeper Craig Gordon should have kept out and the visitors looked to have won the tie until six crazy minutes right at the end. Two spectacular goals from Leigh Griffiths – direct from free-kicks – put Scotland right on the cusp of a legendary victory. It was multiple orgasms for the Mount Florida faithful but before you could say 'How was it for you?' Scotland gifted Harry Kane an equaliser and it was cold showers all round.

A draw has never been so painful. On the same day that comic-book hero actor Adam West passed away it really was a case of 'Holy heartbreak, Batman'.

And then this latest campaign was interrupted by the publisher's deadline, so, dependent on the outcome of Scotland's four remaining qualifiers in the latter months of 2017 – Lithuania [away], Malta [home], Slovakia [home] and Slovenia [away] [and any subsequent play-off] please delete the alternative headline as appropriate – **Yippee ki-yay Mother-Russia! Super Scotland defy the odds and return to the big time. Moscow here we come!**
or
Ten successive failures for sad, sorry, Scotland – the wilderness years continue...

EURO 2020

In celebration of 60 years of the European Football Championships, the 2020 finals will be staged in thirteen cities in thirteen different European countries. The lucky thirteen are Amsterdam [Netherlands], Baku [Azerbaijan], Bilbao [Spain], Brussels [Belgium], Bucharest [Romania], Budapest [Hungary], Copenhagen [Denmark], Dublin [Republic of Ireland], London [England], Munich [Germany], Rome [Italy], Saint Petersburg [Russia] and Glasgow [Clap, clap, clap-clap-clap, clap-clap-clap-clap, SCOTLAND!]

Personally speaking I would prefer to have seen the inclusion of Cardiff's magnificent Millennium Stadium [aka the Principality Stadium] at the expense of the trans-

SCOTLAND GLORY, TEARS AND SOUVENIRS

continental and natural gas and oil-rich Baku but what do I know about economics, politics and Machiavellian manoeuvres – I vote SNP!

I suppose Glasgow 2020 will kind of make up for the disappointment of our failed joint bid [with the Republic of Ireland] to stage Euro 2008 which eventually went to Austria and Switzerland – both of whom failed to get beyond the group stage with only one victory between them.

Anyway, there is no automatic qualification for any of the thirteen hosts – we've all got to battle through a complicated and convoluted qualification process that commences in September 2018 involving the new UEFA Nations League. Please Scotland, don't have the unique distinction of being a host nation who failed to make it to their own party!

It will be a proverbial festival of football and even the inevitable associated art and cultural events [and hangers-on] should prove interesting. Pints, poets and posers, all – well almost all – are welcome. And let's not forget about boosting the economy by spending a small fortune on the associated souvenirs and memorabilia – eg books, programmes, posters, badges, trading cards, stickers, t-shirts, chocolate bars and underpants!

Hampden Park is of course the Glasgow venue and it has been allocated three group stage matches and a round of 16 game. If Scottish scientists and bio-chemists can successfully neutralise the 'qualification cock-up virus' which has afflicted our nation for about two decades now, and our national football team makes it to the finals then two of our group games will be at Hampden. The final itself will be just down the road at Wembley. So, come on Scotland! Come on Scotland! Come on Scotland!

73

Scotland's Chris Martin and Lithuania's Georgas Freidgeimas battle for the ball during the 2018 FIFA World Cup qualifying match at Hampden Park, Glasgow.

A to Z ▶

SCOTLAND GLORY, TEARS AND SOUVENIRS

Scotland line up for the 2018 FIFA World Cup, Group F, qualifying match v England at Hampden Park, Glasgow. Back row (from left) Craig Gordon, Leigh Griffiths, Charlie Mulgrew, Christophe Berra, Robert Snodgrass and James Morrison. Front row (from left) Stuart Armstrong, Scott Brown, Andrew Robertson, Kieran Tierney and Ikechi Anya.

A&BC CARDS – THE SCOTTISH CONNECTION

A&BC Company of Romford, Essex, started producing football cards from the late fifties through to the mid-seventies when the company was wound up. I started collecting all sorts of cards in the late 60s and eagerly anticipated each football season as it came with a new set of footballer cards.

A&BC didn't produce their first Scottish set until 1962/63 but had featured many Scots in their sets previous to this and not just those at English clubs. In 1970, they released an International set, but unfortunately it was an England one for the World Cup in Mexico that year. However throughout their sets there have been a few Scots in their national colours as opposed to their club ones; some of which we have highlighted.

Incidentally, the reverse side of these cards contained background information on each player both statistical and descriptive ie birthplace, height, weight, club, no of caps plus the likes of 'a relentless tackler and masterful distributor of the ball'. As a bonus there was also a football quiz question for which you were instructed to rub a coin edge on the blank space to reveal the answer.

Bobby Evans – 1959/60 set

Bobby had featured in the set the year before this but here he is seen in his full Scotland kit with his unmistakeable red 'heid' and just look at the size of that badge. Bobby would play for Scotland 48 times with 45 of them coming as a Celtic player stretching from 1948 through to 1960.

Bobby would be part of two World Cup squads in 1954 and in 1958, however he would not take part in '54 but would play in all three group games of the 1958 World Cup in Sweden. Bobby captained Scotland on 12 occasions.

Andy Weir – 1962/63 Scottish set

In 1962 A&BC released their first set solely for the Scottish market; like their other sets it was based on the English set released at the same time. This first set featured some great Scottish club players and has a mix of portrait and action cards. There are a couple of players in their Scotland colours as such; Pat Crerand is there in his Celtic days with a big cheesy grin and a Scotland blazer and then there is Andy Weir. Andy played for Motherwell and can be seen in his card in his Scotland colours with that mighty badge in full view.

Andy was part of the Motherwell side that was known at the time as Ancell's Babes. Managed by Bobby Ancell from 1955 to '65, Motherwell would produce several players for the national side including Ian St. John, Pat Quinn, Bert McCann, Willie Hunter and among others Andy Weir. Andy would only play six times for Scotland, scoring one goal which came in six minutes of his debut in a 3-2 friendly match victory against West Germany in May 1959 at Hampden in front of 103,415.

Scotland v England – 1964/65 set

In a departure from the English set, this Scottish one had a few action cards and included among them are this card of the annual Scotland and England match from 1964.

SCOTLAND GLORY, TEARS AND SOUVENIRS

Alan Gilzean is shown in the picture and he would be the scorer of the game's only goal to secure victory for Scotland at Hampden making it three wins in a row for Scotland.

A&BC would continue to release sets throughout the sixties and into the seventies but there would be no Scotland kits in their main sets although Willie Callaghan of Dunfermline Athletic can be found resplendent in his Scotland colours in the pin-up set from 1970/71. There was a pin-up within each packet of cards and even though they all have folds these are quite expensive to buy, as are a lot of the early Scottish sets.

With A&BC there was always a mistake or two along the way. In 1969/70 we have the blonde-headed, Swedish Rangers player Orjan Persson represented by dark haired teammate Ronnie McKinnon. The following year there's John Lunn of Dunfermline Athletic in two different cards (I wonder if he got double pay?) and among their Anglo players is English born John Angus of Burnley; despite his fine Scots name, he actually played for England in 1961.

Pat McCluskey – 1973/74 set
This set would see a plethora of players in their Scotland kit, that's if four can be described as a plethora. There would be a Rangers duo of goalkeeper Peter McCloy and Derek Johnstone as well as Celtic and Scotland legend Danny McGrain and then there's the oddity that was Pat McCluskey.

Pat was also a Celtic player but he never made it to full international level. He was capped six times as an Under-23 and was probably feeling good about himself when the night after winning his sixth such cap in Denmark in 1975, he was invited by Scotland captain Billy Bremner out for a drink. A minor fracas in a Copenhagen nightclub and wee prank in the team hotel a few hours later would see McCluskey given a lifetime ban and although it would be lifted in 1976 he never made it back into the international reckoning. As for Billy Bremner that's a different story.

That set was to be the last but one for A&BC as the company would go belly up in 1974 and the Topps Chewing Gum Company would start to produce sets but personally I hanker more for A&BC and those halcyon days of my childhood.

ABANDONED AND POSTPONED MATCHES

It's actually quite rare for Scotland matches to be abandoned or postponed – although there have been numerous games which I would have been delighted to have seen abandoned mainly because Scotland were well on their way to getting their arses felt. Here are seven 'problem' matches from more recent times.

8th May 1963 – Scotland v Austria [Abandoned after 79 minutes]
94, 596 spectators made their way to Hampden that Wednesday evening to see a supposed friendly match which ultimately English referee Jim Finney felt forced to abandon with eleven minutes remaining to prevent anyone from being seriously hurt.

Austria were reduced to eight men at the time [two sendings off plus an injury] and Scotland were leading 4-1. After the second 'red card', Denis Law had to avoid a flying boot from Anton Linhart, Law then retaliated, Linhart went down and the ref said 'No more tears [Enough is enough]' some sixteen years before Barbra Streisand and Donna Summer converted it into a hit single.

The result isn't included in official match statistics although caps were awarded to the Scotland players which included three making their international debuts. The goals scored by Denis Law and Davie Wilson of Rangers are also in the record books.

19th December 1979 – Scotland v Belgium [Postponed from 7th February 1979]

The original match had been postponed as a result of heavy snowfalls. However the SFA announced that the tickets [£2.00 for the covered west terracing] would remain valid for the re-arranged fixture which didn't take place until the following season.

By the time this European Championship qualifying match actually took place Jock Stein's Scotland were no longer able to reach the finals, the Belgians having killed us off in Brussels the month previous. Belgium however required a point to make it to Italy 80 but instead took both with a convincing 3-1 victory.

Dundee United's Eamonn Bannon made his debut for Scotland that evening whilst Sandy Jardine, who skippered the side, made his 38th and final appearance for his country.

26th March 1980 – Scotland v Portugal [Postponed from 6th February 1980]

Scotland's final, and ultimately meaningless fixture from the 1980 European Championships qualifying campaign was also postponed due to snow. It's unclear how much of the wording from the original match programme carried over to the re-scheduled tie but it included this less than diplomatic language – 'In a bid to solve the problem of finding a new date for their postponed game against Belgium, Scotland tried to get the Portuguese to come to Hampden last September. Portugal, then group leaders, refused to bring forward their visit. So now they must shiver in silence!'

Scotland won the re-arranged match 4-1 at a less than tropical Hampden Park so some sort of perceived justice was done. Adeus Amigos!

11th February 1997 – Estonia v Scotland [Re-scheduled from 9th October 1996 when it was 'abandoned' after three seconds]

The original World Cup qualifying match was abandoned because the Estonian team were absent come the supposed re-arranged kick-off time due to a dispute over the quality of the stadium's floodlights. There were around 1,000 [mostly Scottish] supporters in the ground at the time with many giving voice to the chant 'There's only one team in Tallinn'.

Justice would have been done if FIFA had awarded Scotland a walkover victory, but instead it was decreed that the match be 'replayed' on neutral territory which proved to be the Stade Louis II in Monaco and so it was Mediterranean rather than Baltic when the real event started. The real event finished goal-less however but Scotland would still go on to make it to the finals of France 98. So G.I.R.U.Y.

7th September 1997 – Scotland v Belarus [Postponed from 6th September 1997]

Following the death of Diana, Princess of Wales in a car crash on 31 August 1997 her funeral was arranged for Saturday 6th September, coincidentally the date for the scheduled World Cup qualifier between Scotland and Belarus at Pittodrie Stadium, Aberdeen. The SFA considered going ahead with the match as scheduled

and received much criticism as a result with three Rangers players apparently saying they would not play for Scotland that day. The SFA also considered whether the match should go ahead at all that weekend. Eventually, following consultation with the Lord Chamberlain's office at Buckingham Palace, the SFA postponed the game for 24 hours.

Who knows what Belarus thought about the hysteria which engulfed much of the UK at the time but they duly turned up on the Sunday for a game of football and did the decent thing by losing 4-1 to Craig Brown's boys.

8th October 1999 – Scotland v Bosnia and Herzegovina [Postponed from 27th March 1999]

This Euro qualifier was postponed as an unfortunate side-effect of the Kosovo conflict and NATO air strikes in the Balkans. The Bosnians were due to fly into Glasgow from Sarajevo which is close to the Serbian border but NATO had warned that the team's safety could not be guaranteed if they travelled.

Again, the tickets were valid for the re-scheduled match [£15 for the Govan Stand rear] and when the tie took place the following season at Ibrox Stadium, as originally planned, Scotland won 1-0 thanks to a goal from Everton's John Collins.

3rd September 2004 – Spain v Scotland [Abandoned after 59 minutes]

This match in Valencia was another one of manager Berti Vogts' infamous friendlies. However it was abandoned in the second half due to a floodlight failure after a lightning storm caused a power cut. Torrential rain then followed which flooded the ground and left the referee no option but to say 'Stuff this for a game of soldiers'.

The score was 1-1 at the time, Scotland having taken a first-half lead due to an own goal by Ruben Baraja which was then cancelled out by a Raul penalty just two minutes before the lights went out. If memory serves me right, it was dry and sunny in Glasgow that evening...

ADVERTISING & PUBLICITY

It is a capitalist society in which we choose to live and so advertising is just part and parcel of everyday life. With specific regards to football the question is, is advertising more in our face [and in our psyche] now than ever before or is it just that the products and services advertised have changed and some of the associated adverts are much more OTT than yesteryear?

A quick look at some of those adverts contained within Scotland match programmes and adorning stadium trackside hoardings provide an interesting snapshot of our ever-evolving world.

For some strange reason alcohol features prominently and in the 1950s and 1960s there were the likes of Aitken's Falkirk Beer, Drybrough's Burns Strong Ale, Usher's Golden Export, and The Challenge Old Scotch Whisky – delicacies which I believe are sadly no longer with us.

In the 1970s the brewing industry's big boys got in on the act with Scottish Brewers offering up Kestrel and Harp lagers whilst Tennent's tried to seduce us with Hemeling,

Lamot and Charger lagers. Personally speaking I still can't see past McEwan's Export or Younger's Tartan Special – dark beers for those of us not interested in 'sexy but tasteless' continental beers or sexy but tasteless continental football.

Adverts for that other 'evil' – cigarettes – included brands such as Envoy, Rocky Mount, Senior Service and Capstan. Add in adverts for sweet shops and confectionery and you start to understand why this country has had some serious health issues. I don't seem to recall any adverts for salads, health drinks and dental floss or maybe my chocolate-addled brain just blocked them out.

Gone but not forgotten, there were adverts for now defunct airlines [British Caledonian], defunct newspapers [*Evening Citizen*], defunct technology [Betamax video recorders], defunct financial institutions [Leeds [not so] Permanent Building Society] and nearly defunct occupations [caulkers and welders]. Special mentions also for classic cars [eg Chrysler Avenger], trendy tailors [Tom Martin] and naff, portable, outdoor football games [CentaPost].

Regular football related adverts included that for the Thomlinson T football [first produced in 1921] – apparently the sole manufacturer was based in Dumbarton Road, Glasgow and these footballs were regularly used by the SFA right into the 1970s. Come the 1980s Mitre were supplying the match balls although there was also the Dunlop Super Pro and the Derby Star. You can keep your Etrusco Unicos however.

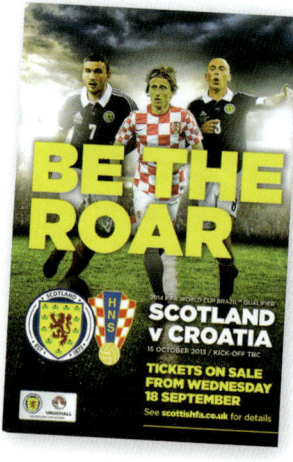

In the 1980s the SFA cottoned on big style to merchandising possibilities with regards to replica Scotland kits and regular 'models' included Graeme Souness, Alan Rough and Ally McCoist. It remains a mystery however as to why the likes of Davie Dodds, Doug Rougvie and John Spencer never got in on the 'Posing like a big haddie' act.

And so to publicity.....

Roll up! Roll up! The greatest show on earth is coming to town – Scotland's national football team are playing at Hampden Park. OK so I may have egged it on a bit there but in recent years the SFA have deemed it necessary to encourage the masses to attend the Hampden Cathedral by way of roadside billboard adverts and 'catchy' campaign slogans.

The 2006 World Cup campaign slogan was 'All eyes on Germany' whilst for the 2010 competition it was 'We'll be coming'.

It continued thus – Euro 2012 [We stand together], World Cup 2014 [Hampden will Roar], Euro 2016 [We are Scotland] and World Cup 2018 [This time].

'We'll be coming' would have been a good choice between 1974 and 1998 when we were regular qualifiers although perhaps with the added suffix of 'But we'll not be staying long.' Gerrintaethem! therefore remains our preferred alternative slogan for the wilderness years of the 21st century.

AGING PROCESS – PLAYERS AND SUPPORTERS

My co-author, David, maintains a Facebook page for the *Scotland Epistles* fanzine and a regular feature which never fails to both amaze and sadden me is his birthday dedications to former Scotland international footballers, many of whom are now over seventy years of age.

The brain can play tricks on you however for in my mind these demi-gods are still in

SCOTLAND GLORY, TEARS AND SOUVENIRS

their twenties or thirties. The aging process comes to us all but surely there could be exceptions made for those dark blue heroes who helped their country stuff England and/or qualify for the World Cup finals?

I'm now several years older than Billy Bremner was when he died in December 1997 just two days before his 55th birthday. Then there was big Jim Holton [15 caps and two goals between 1973 and 1974] who was taken from us in October 1993 aged just 42. To be blunt, it's scary stuff.

Like movie stars however, most of our post-Second World War internationalists are immortalised on celluloid [or whatever it is called now] as well as in print and as such this modest tome

also pays tribute, from Jock Aird of Burnley [four caps] to Tommy Younger of Hibernian and Liverpool [28 caps] and everyone in between.

This book also aims to assist us supporters in our fight against fading grey matter etc by flagging up all sorts of memories, facts, figures and visual images. Everyone will probably have at least one JFK-type Scotland moment. However, I wonder if during his lifetime, the late American President remembered where he was and what he was doing on the 30 of April 1952 when he heard that Scotland had defeated the USA 6-0 in a friendly match at Hampden in front of a crowd of 107,765. Hibernian's Lawrie Reilly grabbed himself a hat-trick that day and I also can't but wonder if the Hibs man thought about saying to the press – "George Washington, Abraham Lincoln, John Wayne, Joe DiMaggio, Al Capone…your boys took one helluva beating!"

Of course there are other areas where this book simply cannot help – like coping with weak bladders, hikes to the stadium and climbing up the stairs when you get there – except perhaps to suggest that you indulge in fewer pints and fewer pies, but hey who are we to lecture anyone especially when we don't practise what we preach and have

missed several goals over the years as a result. There are few things more annoying than standing at the urinal waiting for the flow to ebb when without warning the stadium suddenly reverberates to the unadulterated expressions of joy associated with Scotland scoring a goal – and I have the dry-cleaning bills to prove it!

ANFIELD '77

First things first, I wasn't there so I can't tell you what the atmosphere was like on that magical October evening for Scotland. What I can say is that as a fourteen year old when I heard that the Welsh FA had announced that they were moving the game to Anfield Road, the home of Liverpool FC, I just knew Scotland would win.

For years though, I had thought the game was moved to Anfield for financial reasons as the Welsh hoped to gain a buck or two from the hordes of Scotland fans they would expect to get at the game but no, part of the real reason lay in something that had happened in May 1976.

Unlike the other Home Nations Wales had progressed from their Euro 1976 qualifying group into the quarter-final play-offs and drew eventual finals host-nation Yugoslavia. The first leg had not gone well with Wales going down 2-0 in Zagreb but with players such as John Toshack, Terry Yorath, Leighton James and Brian Flynn, the Welsh were hopeful of turning the tie around at Cardiff's Ninian Park [aka The Bear Pit].

Note to any nation taking part in a play-off; don't piss the referee off before kick-off. Unfortunately for the Welsh they did just that by flying the flag of West Germany rather than East Germany – the home 'nation' of the man in charge. A few ropey decisions later, a goal apiece and the crowd were baying so much for the referee Herr Glockner that

a few fans entered on to the pitch to try and get at him. Although the crowd calmed down and a generous penalty decision was given the Welsh way, which Yorath missed, further pitch invasions at the end saw UEFA hand down a ban on the Welsh playing at Cardiff for a few years.

For the visit of Scotland, consideration was probably given to the Vetch Field, Swansea and the Racecourse Ground, Wrexham but taking cognisance of the restrictions imposed by the 1975 Safety of Sports Grounds Act, the Welsh went for Anfield and all Scotland rejoiced. Anfield, home of many a Scot throughout the years from Alex Raisbeck to Billy Liddell through to the Shankly era of Ian St. John and Ron Yeats and the then current home of King of the Kop Kenny Dalglish. It was home from home for Ally's Tartan Army as thousands upon thousands headed to Liverpool to make up a significant proportion of the crowd of 50,800.

A draw for the Scots would mean the Welsh would have to beat Czechoslovakia away to have any chance of qualifying ahead of us. For Scotland fans, [at the stadium as well as watching on TV] moments in that match are etched upon our souls. Toshack's volley that Alan Rough gets a hand to and puts over the bar and then there's that other Scot using his hand in the penalty area. I have no doubt in my mind that Joe Jordan produced a hand of God moment in the 79th minute but what I love about it was the commentary by well-respected Archie McPherson at the time on the BBC. "Appeals . . . surely . . . penalty kick, it's a penalty kick to Scotland if ever there was one", he then goes on to say "the referee perfectly correct, watch it, up goes the hand and a punch if ever there was one."

What can't be doubted is that Masson put away the penalty with considerable aplomb. [It's just a pity he couldn't do the same in Cordoba against Peru eight months later.] Just like Maradona at Mexico '86 one moment of

gamesmanship was followed by a moment of glory. Kenny Dalglish's goal for Scotland's second doesn't have the individual brilliance of Maradona but it makes up in being a classic breakaway goal with Dalglish's majestic finishing from a pinpoint Martin Buchan cross.

Argentina here we come!

PS: In 1998 and 1999 due to large demand for tickets from visiting supporters, Wales chose to play two home Euro qualifiers, against Italy and Denmark respectively, at Anfield Stadium, Liverpool. Coincidentally both matches were lost 0-2 although Joe Jordan was completely blameless!

ANGLO CONFECTIONERY
One of my favourite football cards sets is the Anglo Confectionery collection of 1968/69, which has players from big clubs such as Denis Law and Willie Morgan of Manchester United, Eddie McCreadie from Chelsea, Billy McNeill and Ronnie Simpson of Celtic and Rangers' John Greig and Colin Stein.

As if that's not enough, this set also comprises only 84 cards are still generally easy to collect but the interesting thing is, it has players from really unfashionable teams such as Chester, Port Vale, Southport and Peterborough

SCOTLAND GLORY, TEARS AND SOUVENIRS

United and it is here there are some gems of Scotland players in perhaps what could be called the twilight of their careers.

Card #27 is of Alex Young. Alex played for Hearts and Everton winning championships with both. However after leaving Everton in 1968 he headed to Stockport County where he would make only 23 appearances. Alex was capped by Scotland on eight occasions scoring five goals.

Next up is card #29, which is of Bobby Collins. Bobby played for Celtic, Everton and Leeds United among others and was capped by Scotland 31 times in a fifteen year period from 1950-1965, scoring ten goals in the process. For this set of cards, Bobby is with Bury but he would go on to turn out for Greenock Morton playing beyond his 40th birthday.

Card #56 is Ralph Brand, well known as a Rangers striker from the early 50s to early 60s winning the Scottish championship six times. Brand would go on to play for Manchester City and then Sunderland where this card is from. Brand won eight Scotland caps, scoring eight goals.

Finally David Herd, card #62 in his Stoke City days. David had played coincidentally at Stockport County before going on to Arsenal and then Manchester United. At Old Trafford he won the First Division twice and also the FA Cup in 1962/63 where he scored two goals in the final. Herd played for Stoke for a couple of seasons and won five Scotland caps scoring three goals.

In terms of Scotland games they have amassed a total of 52 caps and scored 26 goals between them, which works out a goal in every two games. If only we had one player who could do that. One final fact, Herd and Collins played for Scotland on the day that Denis Law made his debut on 18th October, 1958 as the Scots beat Wales 3-0 in Cardiff with Law and Collins among the scorers.

Anglo also released a World Cup / Learn the Game set in 1970 which has illustrations of players displaying different skills; so you can learn to scissor kick like Denis Law or dummy kick like Willie Johnston. However Eddie McCreadie's shows you the art of 'goal by a head' (?) rather than 'high kick to the neck' as he did to Billy Bremner so infamously in the 1970 FA Cup Final replay.

ANNUALS [THE SCOTTISH ANNUAL ANNALS]

Christmas no longer comes with the magic of a new shiny Scottish football annual; sometimes it comes though with an old tattered collectible one from the 60s; the heyday of football annuals as such.

However, long before that, published in 1937 there was Alan Breck's *Book of Scottish Football*. Breck was a journalist with the *Scottish Daily Express* who published this weighty tome, which has just over 190 pages and must have at least 250 photos of players, current to that time. It also doesn't just feature the big teams but fans of the likes of Montrose, East Fife and Albion Rovers will find pictures of heroes past along with players from teams such as St. Bernards and Edinburgh City who were to disappear after the Second World War. The name Edinburgh City has returned to the Scottish Leagues recently but has no connection to the original side.

Further to these inclusions, there is also an extensive section on the Junior (English non-league equivalent) sides of the day and some from the Highland Leagues. As to Scotland itself, there is a photo spread on the recent internationals against England as

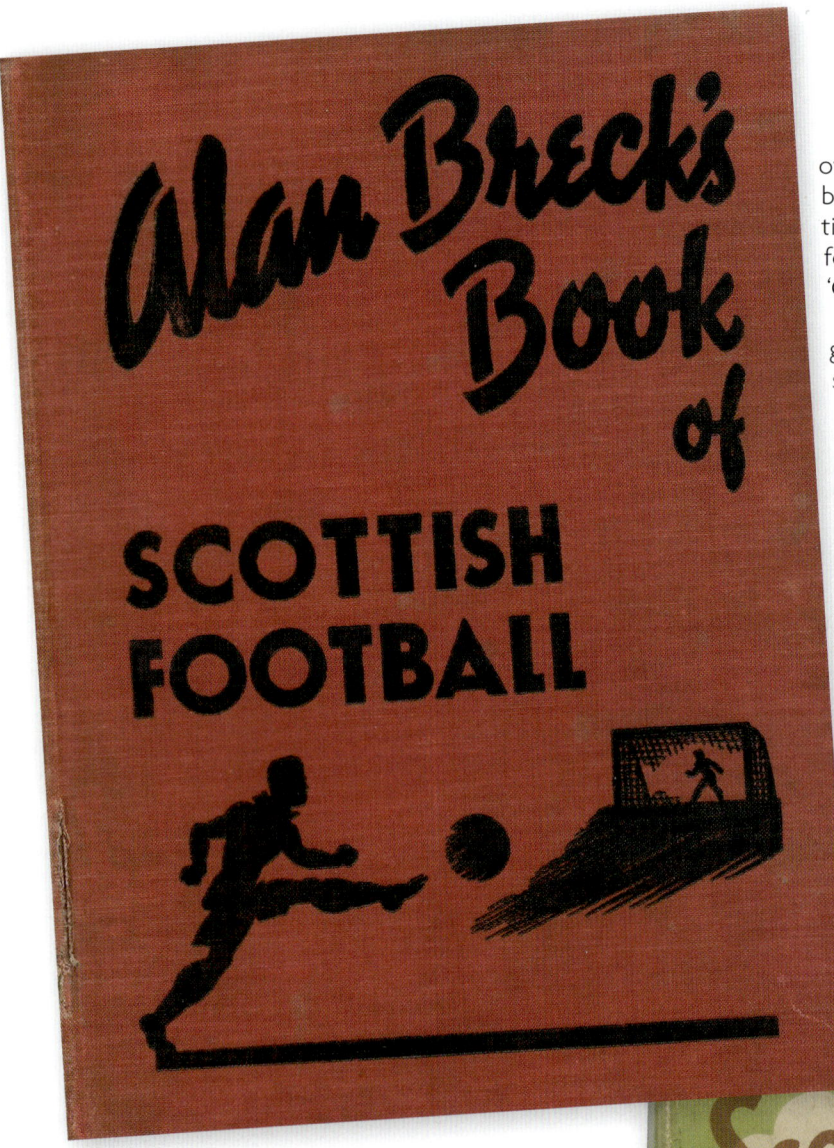
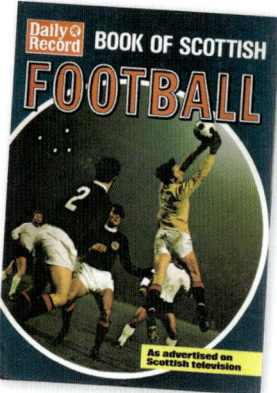

over to fictional boys' stories with titles such as 'Send for Snowdrop' and 'Good Shot, Laddie'. For most boys growing up in the sixties and seventies in Scotland, you would hope for the latest copy of the *Scottish Football Book* edited by Hugh Taylor unless you longed more for *Playing for Rangers* or *Playing for Celtic*. (Somewhat surprisingly *Playing for Partick Thistle* was never an option.) Hugh Taylor's books ran from the mid-fifties to the early eighties when they were no longer the must-have item they once were.

Most had the same comfortable format; a colour picture of Scotland in action on the front, an article on the latest Scottish champions and cup winners, the well as a piece on Scotland's tour of Canada and the USA in 1935. If you only buy one old annual next Christmas, then make it this one, although my copy did cost £30.

Next up, came the *Boys First Book of Scottish Soccer* published in 1949 by Bonar Books. The *Boys Book of Soccer* had been going for a number of years at this time and would continue into the sixties but the Scottish version would be the first and last issue, which is a pity as it does have some great photos in it plus a piece called 'When Scotland outclassed and outplayed England'. Oh, for such days. The only down side is the pages given

SCOTLAND GLORY, TEARS AND SOUVENIRS

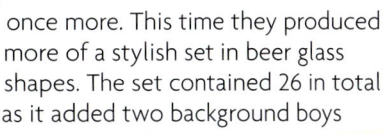

most likely Irn Bru for me but for grown-ups they could go to pubs and drink beer for a few hours and if they were really lucky they could place their drink on a World Cup beermat.

Tennent's Lager released a set of 23 beermats to coincide with the start of the World Cup in West Germany. Unlike the makers of cards and stickers they hung back until the very last minute to produce the mats, so their set is unique in that every player in the final 22 was given a mat as well as manager Willie Ormond.

This included Peter Cormack of Liverpool who was originally named as a squad reserve until Ormond decided not to take Jimmy Smith of Newcastle United just after that year's Home International series. Just prior to the British Championship matches Jimmy had turned up for the squad get-together a few days late without explanation and so Willie axed him.

Also included in the set are some others who, like Cormack, had short Scotland careers such as goalkeepers Thomson Allan and Jim Stewart. Stewart was perhaps unlucky in constantly being the understudy to Alan Rough for a number of years but he did rack up quite a few air miles in doing so. His daughter-in-law Julie Fleeting however has racked up well over 100 caps and 100 goals for the Scotland women's team.

1978, Argentina, Ally MacLeod and all that, unleashed a myriad of footballing souvenirs and pride of place goes to the Tennents Beer

once more. This time they produced more of a stylish set in beer glass shapes. The set contained 26 in total as it added two background boys in Donnie McKinnon and Hugh Allan. Trainer/physio Hugh was brought into the Scotland set up by Willie Ormond and would be present with the Scotland side for six World Cups.

The 23 players were more relaxed in these photos as in the '74 set there seemed to be a rabbit caught in the headlights look to many of them. In the '78 set you had the likes of veteran Aberdeen goalkeeper Bobby Clark wearing an outfield strip whilst Archie Gemmill has a pair of denims on. This set was obviously devised way before MacLeod named his squad as goalkeeper David Stewart of Leeds United is among them instead of Jim Blyth of Coventry City as was the injured Danny McGrain and also winger Arthur Graham of Leeds United with actual Argentine-travellers Kenny Burns and John Robertson omitted. The most controversial player omitted from the squad was Aston Villa's Andy Gray who appears on his own beermat.

You do wonder, did these go missing from pubs up and down the land almost as soon as they were laid out by bar staff and did tegestologists (beermat collectors) moan about getting another Hugh Allan when they were desperate to find a Joe Harper? I wonder on the night of 3rd June 1978 as Don Masson missed that penalty in Cordoba did punters start to tear up his mats in disgust and by the end of the night did they all get thrown around the pub? Did the Ally MacLeod ones get severely damaged by the end of the Iran game? And after Archie Gemmill scored that goal against Holland did people scour the pub for his mat and take it home as a prized possession?

In comparison to the 1978 bandwagon, the 1982 World Cup was a much more sombre occasion without the hullabaloo that MacLeod had whipped up in '78 and so there were to be no more beermats nor would there be for any of the following World Cups. However, in late 2015 DC Thomson, publishers of such titles as *The Dandy*, *The Beano* and *Oor Wullie*, produced for their *Sunday Post* newspaper a set of 11 beermats of Scottish football legends as a dream team. The side named was as follows: Andy Goram, Sandy Jardine, Danny McGrain, Billy Bremner, Alex McLeish, Willie Miller, Kenny Dalglish, Jimmy Johnstone, Denis Law, Jim Baxter and Graeme Souness. Not a bad line up but where's the manager, trainer, physio and the other two goalies?

THE BLAZERS aka THE SUITS

Some organisations are good at leadership and bureaucracy. Sadly however the Scottish Football Association tends not to be one of them, at least not for any length of time. To be fair they have a difficult job to do and it is human nature to always blame someone else so here's a quick look at some of the distinguished SFA Office-bearers/Blazers/Suits who have contributed in their own special way to the glory, the tears and the souvenirs. Some of these appointed officials went by the title Secretary whilst in more recent times Chief Executive is their delusional 'Nom de guerre'. They shouldn't be confused however with the elected office of President which, for some reason, tends to get a smaller share of the blame when things go wrong.

Sir George Graham was 'Heid-Bummer' at the SFA from 1928 to 1957 so he is 'het' as far as the decision goes not to compete at the 1950 World Cup finals in Brazil. Eleven days after our fateful World Cup qualifier against England, Scotland played Switzerland in a friendly match at Hampden Park and in the centre pages of the match programme, the following wording perhaps best sums up our arrogant, so out of touch position at the time – 'If Scotland adheres to its decision not to join the other football countries at Rio – although a World Cup tournament without a Scottish team in it scarcely merits the designation – we shall watch the progress of our Swiss friends with more than passing interest'.

SGG was still in control when Scotland eventually did appear at the World Cup finals in 1954 and what a shambles that turned out to be with the selectors choosing to take only 13 players to the tournament and which included only one goalkeeper.

Willie Allan was in charge from 1957 to 1977 – a term of office which coincided with the decision that Scotland would not take part in both the 1960 and 1964 European Championships although it would be unfair to blame him for you-know-who becoming world champions in 1966. On the plus side we did qualify for the 1958 and 1974 World Cup finals and we eventually viewed the position of Scotland manager in a much more professional, modern way.

Ernie Walker, CBE was the man who would be king between 1977 and 1990 and as such he presided over Scotland's 'Golden Age' with qualification to successive World Cup finals in 1978, 1982, 1986 and 1990 as well as the 'Gentrification?' of the Tartan Army.

SCOTLAND GLORY, TEARS AND SOUVENIRS

After Scotland's infamous match against the 'over-physical' Uruguayans at the 1986 Mexico World Cup saw us eliminated from the competition a somewhat upset Mr. Walker described the South American team as 'Scum'. It was not the most diplomatic of comments but as a result he went up in the estimations of much of the Scotland support.

Ernie has to take some of the organisational blame however for the debacle that was Argentina 78 and perhaps as a 'punishment' he then had to contend with Thatcherism and a National Stadium that was no longer fit for purpose.

The bold Ernesto was followed by Jim Farry – the man who would be God – between 1990 and 1999. In private, Mr. Farry, a former landscape gardener, may have been a really nice person who was also kind to children and animals but in his public persona he came across as an arrogant, egotistical bully. His term of office ended when he was forced to leave the post following a dispute with Celtic Football Club over the registration of Portuguese player Jorge Cadete.

On the credit side, under Jim Farry's watch Scotland qualified for the finals of three major tournaments [the 1992 and 1996 European Championships and the 1998 World Cup] and Hampden Park was completely rebuilt – albeit to a now questionable design – but a design which still merited the hosting of the 2002 Champions League Final and the 2007 UEFA Cup Final as well as a support role in the 2020 European Championship finals.

Next up was David Taylor [1999-2007] who was viewed as a thoroughly decent bloke despite the fact that he was a qualified solicitor as well as being the man in charge when 'Der Terrier' Berti Vogts was appointed national team coach. He brought honesty and integrity to his office and these and other attributes were recognised by his peers and eventually he became Joint General Secretary of UEFA.

Mr. Taylor streamlined and modernised the SFA and apparently he was in favour of Scottish independence saying his experiences travelling to other countries for football had made up his mind.

After David Taylor came Gordon Smith whose short tenure lasted from 2007 to 2010. Gordon Smith was a former footballer who played for Kilmarnock, Rangers, Brighton & Hove Albion, Manchester City and FC Basel amongst others. Despite all his winners' medals he is sometimes best remembered for missing a good goal-scoring opportunity for Brighton against Manchester United in the closing minutes of extra-time in the 1983 FA Cup Final at Wembley – which United won in the replay. 'And Smith must score' goes into the collection of unwelcome Wembley soundbites along with 'They think it's all over... it is now!'

Mr Smith was the driver behind the 2009 Home Nations Agreement whereby players being educated for five years under the age of 18 in a Home Nation became eligible for that nation at full international level. Under that rule, Somali-born Islam Feruz became eligible for Scotland whilst Jamaican-born Raheem Sterling went on to play for England.

In 2010 Stewart Regan assumed command. Durham-born, his background is the brewing industry and Yorkshire cricket. Personally speaking I would have preferred it if someone more akin to *The Sweeney's* Jack Regan had been appointed.

BOBBY BROWN

Bobby Brown who was born in Dunipace, Stirlingshire, both played for and managed Scotland. His caps all came just after the Second World War and are generally a subject of debate due to the authenticity of whether the Victory Internationals were counted as full matches or not. Some places, you will see the Rangers goalkeeper listed as having been capped five times and in others three times. The SFA credit him with five and that's good enough for me.

George Burley with SFA Chief Executive Gordon Smith (left) and SFA President George Peat (right)

Bobby also went on to manage Scotland [our first full-time manager] and had what was arguably the greatest start to any Scotland manager's career with that famous 3-2 win over England at Wembley in 1967. However, in 28 games under Bobby, Scotland only won nine, drew eleven and lost eleven.

To be fair to Bobby, if you look at the '67 team; Jim Baxter who was the star that day only played two more times for Scotland as his career began to wane. Denis Law, due to fitness issues would only play six times for Bobby in total, with three games in '67, one in '68 and two more in '69. Also, at this time English clubs were still reluctant to release players, so at various points you find Billy Bremner and his Leeds United colleagues missing from games among others but even lesser teams would be reluctant to part with players.

Bobby gave debuts to Ronnie Simpson and Jim McCalliog that day in April 1967. The full line up being; Simpson, Tommy Gemmell, Eddie McCreadie, John Greig, Ronnie McKinnon, Billy Bremner, McCalliog, Denis Law, Willie Wallace, Jim Baxter and Bobby Lennox.

Overall, the highs would be far outweighed by the lows including failing to qualify for both the 1968 Euros and the 1970 World Cup in Mexico plus a poor start to the 1972 Euro qualifying campaign.

Four years after that Wembley victory in his third last game Bobby lined up against England with Bobby Clark (Aberdeen), John Greig, Jim Brogan (Celtic), Billy Bremner, Frank McLintock (Arsenal), Bobby Moncur (Newcastle United), Jimmy Johnstone (Celtic), Tony Green (Blackpool), Peter Cormack (Nottingham Forest), Davie Robb (Aberdeen) and Hugh Curran (Wolves). Frank Munro of Wolves and Drew Jarvie of Airdrie would come on as subs. There were some good players in that team but also a few sadly lacking international class particularly compared to the team of '67. England won 3-1 with Hugh Munro scoring for Scotland.

Bobby would quit a month or so later as Scotland lost another two games, making it four in a row with a defeat to Denmark in Copenhagen in a Euro qualifier being particularly galling. Bobby would be succeeded by Tommy Docherty and then Willie Ormond who was Bobby's successor at St Johnstone.

BRITISH HOME INTERNATIONAL CHAMPIONSHIPS

Over thirty years have now passed since the last British Home International Football Championship involving Scotland, England, Northern Ireland and Wales but to many supporters of a certain vintage it is missed in much the same way that we yearn for our youth, unfragmented television and vinyl records. Indeed once upon a time it meant something to be the Best of British.

In season 1883-84 Scotland beat Ireland [all of it] 5-0 in Belfast and then England and Wales 1-0 and 4-1 respectively, at Cathkin Park, Glasgow to win the inaugural British Home International Football Championship.

SCOTLAND GLORY, TEARS AND SOUVENIRS

With no other national associations coming into existence until 1889 [Denmark and Netherlands] and FIFA not being founded until 1904 [UEFA in 1954], technically Scotland were also world and European champions. Surely it's not too late for special medals to be struck. Just for good measure we were also world, sorry, British champions in 1885 and 1887.

Furthermore, the Home Nations provided Scotland with our opposition for our first 143 internationals until we ventured across the North Sea to Bergen to beat Norway 7-3 in May 1929. Indeed we didn't invite any 'foreigners' back to our gaff until November 1933 when Austria drew 2-2 at Hampden in match number 166.

For the official 1950 and 1954 World Cups FIFA allowed the 1949/50 and 1953/54 British Championships to double as qualifying groups with the top two sides going to Brazil and Switzerland respectively. This somewhat lopsided approach meant that both Scotland and Wales were favoured with two home matches to one away tie whilst the reverse applied for England and Northern Ireland [the Emerald Isle having been partitioned in 1921]. On both occasions England topped the 'group' with Scotland finishing second. However the SFA chose not to go to Brazil in 1950.

UEFA went for a more egalitarian approach with the 1966/67 and 1967/68 British Championships doubling as European Championship qualifying group 8 and with only the winner progressing to the quarter-finals. Scotland took three out of a possible four points from England but it was our southern neighbours who qualified for the last eight of the competition – Scotland having been undone by Northern Ireland in Belfast.

From 1969 to 1981 all six British Championship fixtures were scheduled to be played over eight or nine days in April, May or June at the end of the season [as opposed to being spread throughout the season] although the 1981 competition was not finished due to civil unrest in Northern Ireland which caused the cancellation of the visits to Belfast of both England and Wales.

The so-called 'Troubles' in Northern Ireland [1968 to 1998] affected the competition as early as 1972 when Scotland refused to travel to Belfast and the fixture was played at Hampden Park instead. Indeed, Northern Ireland also played their 'home' tie against Scotland at Hampden in 1974, 1976 and 1978.

The record books show that Scotland were British champions on no fewer than 41 occasions which included 17 shared titles. There were 11 'clean sweeps' by the Scots [the last one coming in 1976 and ultimately clinched through Ray Clemence's legs at Hampden] and by comparison, the Scotland rugby union team have won their 'Triple Crown' ten times between 1883 and 2017. Back to the round ball competition and England lead the way with 54 wins [including 20 shared], Wales had 12 wins [including five shared] and Ireland/Northern Ireland had eight wins [including five shared]. Northern Ireland also have the distinction of being the last ever winners of the trophy – in 1984 when they won the title on goal difference with all four nations equal on points. Scotland's last title came about in 1977 when we clinched it with a dramatic 2-1 victory at Wembley and the turf and goalposts screamed 'Take me! Take me!'

The British Championship gave Scotland their record victory – 11-0 versus Ireland at Celtic Park in 1901. We also stuffed the Irish 8-2 in 1885, and 9-1 in 1899; England 7-2 in 1878 and 6-1 in 1881; and Wales 9-0 in 1878 and 8-0 in 1893. If you could ignore issues such as poverty, disease and overcrowding, it must have been great fun to have been a Scotland supporter during Victorian times.

Talking of 'overcrowding' and some of the attendances at these British Championship matches are mind-boggling. On no fewer than 25 occasions between 1906 and 1972 there were 100,000 plus crowds at Hampden Park to see Scotland versus England. In 1937 an incredible 149,547 squeezed into Hampden to see Scotland beat England 3-1 whilst two years later 149,269 saw the English win 2-1.

Games against our 'Celtic cousins' never quite matched that level of popularity although 98,776 were at Hampden in 1946 for the match against the Irish whilst the visit of Wales in 1947 attracted 88,000.

Of Kenny Dalglish's record haul of 102 caps, 26 of them were for British Championship matches. Jim Leighton played 91 times for Scotland but only five of them were in the Home Internationals. That said, he played in all three fixtures in the final, 1983-84 season as did Richard Gough, Alex McLeish and Paul McStay. Our last ever British Championship match – against England at Hampden on 26th May 1984 – finished 1-1 with England's Tony Woodcock cancelling out an earlier goal from Aberdeen's Mark McGhee.

Conversely, Super Ally McCoist's 61 caps [and 19 goals] all came after the 'Brits' as he didn't debut until 1986 whilst Maurice Malpas [55 caps] made his first Scotland appearance against France on 1st June 1984 – a mere six days after the curtain came down on the British Championship. Great games, great memories, great shame that competition isn't still in existence. Maybe after BREXIT...

BROWN, CRAIG
Although not the most charismatic of Scotland bosses perhaps Glasgow-born Craig Brown should be regarded as among the best. In terms of players available to him he certainly had a poorer selection than those before him although it is considerably better than what the Scotland manager has available in 2017.

The one thing Craig did well was to blend his teams and have them playing more as a unit. If you look at the forwards he had available such as Billy Dodds, Kevin Gallacher, Duncan Shearer, Scott Booth, John McGinlay, Darren Jackson etc., none of whom were world beaters but each and every one of them worked their socks off for the team as did the rest of the side.

Taking over from Andy Roxburgh for the final two 'academic' games in the 1994 World Cup qualifiers gave Brown just under a year to get ready for the Euro '96 qualifiers. Scotland were actually seeded third in their group but would qualify as runners-up to Russia. They barely put a foot wrong only losing to Greece in Athens through a disputed penalty. An inspired substitution at home to Greece in August '95 was the pivotal moment as Brown brought back Ally McCoist for the first time following his leg break in April '93.

With his forwards struggling to penetrate the Greek defence he took off Darren Jackson and Duncan Shearer and replaced them with McCoist and John Robertson of Hearts in the 71st minute; McCoist had the ball in the back of the net by the 72nd minute.

Prior to the finals of Euro '96 Brown surprised a lot of people by announcing that Andy Goram would be his first choice goalkeeper for the tournament as Jim Leighton had played between the sticks for the majority of the qualifiers. He would do something similar for France '98 but would reverse it with Leighton being first choice. Andy Goram then withdrew from that squad unwilling to play second fiddle to Leighton and so ended his Scotland career prematurely.

Scotland would be unlucky not to progress at the finals in England and Brown could look back with some pride at their performances there. A blank draw with the Netherlands was followed up with defeat to England in a game that changed fortunes within a couple of minutes to leave England with a 2-0 victory. In the final match against Switzerland, once more McCoist would produce a moment of magic but of course it was tinged with some sadness as Scotland would yet again fail to progress as one goal was not enough with England conceding a late goal to the Dutch in their 4-1 mauling of the men in orange.

However, there were more good times ahead as Scotland once more qualified for a major tournament following some impressive performances to reach France 98. Kevin Gallacher [like Mo Johnston did for Italia 90] found a rich vein of scoring form that produced some golden moments but other forwards also contributed to the goals including Darren Jackson and John McGinlay. McGinlay scored early against Sweden at Ibrox in a match that saw the Swedes pound the Scottish penalty-box time after time only to be defied by Jim Leighton in perhaps his finest Scotland performance. Even Gary McAllister following his miss at Wembley stepped up to the plate to take a penalty in Minsk to give Scotland victory against Belarus. So once more you get a sense of a team effort, rather than down to individuals.

France '98 started well enough for even though the Scots were defeated by Brazil they had performed well and were unlucky to lose to that pantomime of an own-goal by Tom Boyd. The draw with Norway was a good result too but the match against Morocco was as poor as any that a Scotland side has produced at a World Cup finals. Of course, I blame Craig Burley and his peroxide blonde hair for thinking he was a superstar; Brown should have told him to get rid of it. Still, it could have been worse – he could have permed it a la Argentina 78 I suppose.

Brown would continue as Scotland manager for two unsuccessful campaigns both of which saw us miss out by the narrowest of margins. He very quickly lost his captain Gary McAllister in the campaign for Euro 2000 after fans booed the Coventry City man during a game against the Czech Republic at Celtic Park. Truth is, Gary was quite poor that night but booing your own player is pretty low. Gary would quit because of it which, when you consider the excellent spell he had with Liverpool shortly afterwards, was a great pity. It's fair to say in the group that also included Lithuania, Estonia, Bosnia and the Faroes, the Czechs were bouncing and romped through the qualifiers, winning every game and even coming back from two down against Scotland in Prague to win 3-2 in the final minutes.

During the campaign there was also time for a friendly victory over Germany in Bremen when Don Hutchison scored the only goal. In an interview after the match Brown talks about sticking to a 'rigid game plan' and a 'willingness to work' and these are the things he was able to instil in his sides and why they were rarely overwhelmed by greater teams.

So Scotland did end up an easy second in the group and faced Ingerland in a play-off. Scotland were overwhelmed by the occasion more than their English counterparts for the first leg of the tie and Paul Scholes gave the English a comfortable 2-0 lead going into the second leg but boy did we give them a fright at Wembley. Big Don Hutchison once more scored the only goal in the 39th minute and Scotland fought hard for that aggregate equaliser but it was not to be.

The campaign for the 2002 World Cup was lost in one moment. Scotland did what they had to do to progress; they beat the minnows home and away and they drew away and at home to the group winners, a very good Croatia. The misstep was at Hampden in March 2001 having taken a 2-0 lead over Belgium and having a one man advantage perhaps his side didn't follow the 'rigid' plan and so allowed the Belgians back into the game and to equalise with what was almost the last kick of the ball.

Scotland would miss out on a play-off by the two points a victory would have secured. I hate bloody Belgium...

And so Craig's time came to pass as he stepped down from the hot seat feeling he had taken Scotland as far as he could. Although it ended in failing to qualify for two major finals Pa Broon's time with Scotland should be remembered for the highs rather than the lows and after all, there was a whole load of numpties to follow him.

BURLEY, GEORGE

After the resignation of Alex McLeish, the SFA took about six weeks before appointing Cumnock-man George Burley as the next Scotland manager in January 2008. George had been capped 11 times at full-back for Scotland in the late 70s/early 80s and was part of the Ipswich Town side that flourished around that time under Bobby Robson, along with other Scots in John Wark and Alan Brazil.

Burley had been on the management merry-go-round for a few years, taking his first appointment at Ayr United following the departure of Ally MacLeod in his second stint there but in Scotland his stock had risen during a short spell with Hearts where he had led them to the top of the Premier League, winning eight of their first ten games. However, George left this position by mutual agreement with the club due to his deteriorating relationship with chairman Vladimir Romanov. So when GB was appointed Scotland boss there were no real dissenting voices, indeed for most of us there was a curiosity mixed with an optimism that the progress begun under Walter Smith and then Alex McLeish would continue. Sadly it was not to be so.

A creditable draw with Croatia at home was followed by a defeat to the Czech Republic in Prague but he had bled new players in Steven Fletcher, Ross McCormack, James Morrison and Christophe Berra. A blank draw with Northern Ireland at Hampden was not too troubling either and again he had given caps to Kevin Thomson of Hibs, Darren Barr of Falkirk and Kris Commons of Derby County so there was a sense of bringing new players in to expand the squad.

He did though look to the more experienced players for Scotland's opening match in the 2010 World Cup qualifiers away to Macedonia but the team conceded an early goal after five minutes and for much of the match seemed to toil in the heat of Skopje. Scotland never really created any clear-cut chances and so the campaign began with a defeat.

An unlikely hero for Burley would be defender Kirk Broadfoot of Rangers scoring a goal in his debut international a few days later in Reykjavik to give Scotland a lead that was added to in the second half. A few nervous minutes awaited Scotland as Iceland scored late in the game but the team held on for the win.

The Netherlands were hot favourites to top our qualifying group and so despite grumblings over the Macedonia result, the fact that our main rivals for second place, Norway, dropped points at home to Iceland worked in Burley's favour. However, the cracks would really begin to show in his tenure in October 2008.

Scotland were struggling at Hampden against a poor Norwegian side and were looking for goals. The manager decided to make changes to try and achieve this with a double substitution in the 56th minute bringing on Steven Fletcher, and for his first cap, Chris Iwelumo of Wolves leaving proven goalscorer Kris Boyd of Rangers on the bench. This decision stunned a lot of us looking on and when Iwelumo missed an open goal minutes later, the 'Burley Out' brigade was born. It was no surprise when after the match Kris Boyd announced his retirement from international football but things were to go a bit more pear-shaped after the following qualifier, against the Netherlands.

Scotland had been beaten soundly by the Dutch in Amsterdam 3-0, however on their arrival back home to prepare for the next game, a qualifier against Iceland at Hampden, the Rangers pairing of Barry Ferguson and Allan McGregor got involved in a late-night drinking session which resulted in them being banned from taking part in the Icelandic tie. To make matters worse, during the match both players were seen blatantly to give the 'V' sign to the TV cameras and so their Scotland ban was extended further. Very few people came out of this with their credibility intact except perhaps their club manager, ex-Scotland boss Walter Smith who also banned the players, fined them and stripped Ferguson of his captaincy for embarrassing club and country.

However Burley and Gordon Smith, the SFA's Chief Executive at the time, didn't seem to come out of it all that well either with the press having a field day over the whole event, naming it 'Boozegate'. Ferguson was never universally loved by a lot of Scotland fans mainly for his day job of being Rangers captain but he was the darling of the media and quite soon the story was more about Burley's lack of control over matters rather than the actual misdemeanours themselves.

Despite all this, Scotland managed to win the qualifier against Iceland and even with a severe defeat to Norway in Oslo could still manage to grab that second spot with a victory over Macedonia at home and a point against thr Netherlands. The win against Macedonia on 5th September 2009 was achieved pretty much on the back of Scott Brown literally and figuratively with the Celtic man taking the game by the scruff of the neck and opening the scoring in the second half. The match against the Dutch at Hampden four days later was lost however due to an unfortunate slip-up by David Weir allowing Elia to nip in and score.

Scotland had played well in what was perhaps their best performance of the campaign but it was not to be. Ultimately it was not to be for the group runners-up Norway either as they were the worst second-placed team points-wise with a measly ten and so missed out on a play-off. Scotland had also finished on ten points and shortly after it was announced that Burley would continue in his role for the Euro 2012 qualifiers.

If there's a lesson to be learned here; it is never to take your side to Cardiff for a friendly and get pumped 3-0 by the Welsh as Burley did in November 2009. He was dumped the next day and the not-so-glory-days of Craig Levein were soon to be released upon us.

George Burley did move back into club management but you can't help but think that Apollon Limassol got it right when they sacked him after only two matches. Can you imagine all the grief we might have been spared if the SFA had done something similar – but hey, hindsight is a great thing.

CAPTAINS COURAGEOUS AND OTHERWISE

So what makes for a great Scotland captain; is it hard men like Battling Billy Bremner, Graeme Souness or even the current incumbent Scott Brown or should it be a towering centre-half like Billy McNeill or Colin Hendry or should they be more creative like Gary McAllister or Darren Fletcher? Over the years there have been a number and so here is a quick overview.

The very first was goalkeeper Robert Gardner of Queen's Park who also helped arrange that first international against England; so we owe him a very big debt. Interesting to note that Gardner played part of the game up front as well and that tradition has of course been carried on by millions of kids ever since mostly followed by the moan: 'it's no ma turn to go in goals'.

Andrew Watson captained Scotland to a 6-1 victory over England in London in 1881. Watson is credited as being the first black footballer to appear at international level. Andrew was the son of a wealthy Scottish sugar planter and born in Demerara, British Guiana. He studied at Glasgow University where his love of football began and which would lead him to playing for Queen's Park and Scotland.

Next up of note comes John Lambie who at 17 is still the youngest player to be capped for Scotland, score for Scotland and captain the side and he achieved this all in the same game as Scotland beat Ireland 7-2 in 1886. Lambie's brother William would also captain Scotland a few years later as a teenager too. I would mention Bob Smellie who captained the side for two occasions also in the 1880s but only because of his surname. However, I am too mature for that type of indulgence – suffice to say he never had a stinker.

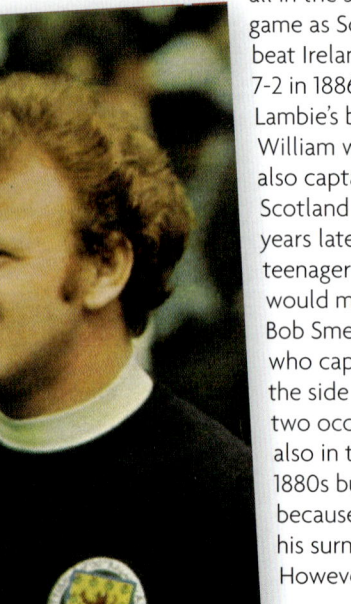

Fast forward to the 1920s and mention must go to Jimmy McMullan of Partick Thistle and Manchester City who captained the side on six occasions and was the man who led the team that would be dubbed the Wembley Wizards to the 5-1 victory over England in 1928.

Also around the same time Celtic legend Willie McStay captained the side on five occasions whilst his great-nephew Paul McStay would lead the team seven times in the 1990s. In the thirties, Jimmy Simpson of Rangers led the side on thirteen occasions whilst his son Ronnie would go on to become one of the Lisbon Lions and of course played for Scotland at Wembley in 1967.

After the Second World War the role of captain clearly becomes defined by George 'Corky' Young. To this date George, who would captain Scotland on 48 occasions, is still the record holder for the position. He would lead the side from 1948 to 1957. George was a giant of a man and was part of the famous Rangers 'Iron Curtain' defence.

Sadly, George was denied a place at the World Cup finals on not one but three occasions. Scotland did qualify for the World Cup in Brazil in 1950 but in a moment of hubris the SFA decided that they would only go as British champions; defeat to England in April that year saw them finish as runners-up and so they did not travel to Brazil. Scotland did qualify and did travel to the 1954 World Cup finals in Switzerland but unfortunately Young's club team Rangers had booked a North American tour at the same time and refused to release any of their players. As for 1958 it came just too late for George and although he played in some of the qualifiers he announced his retirement from the international scene in the summer of '57.

Just before George took up the mantle brief mention should go to the Shaw brothers – Jock of Rangers and Davie of Hibs who captained the side on six and one occasion respectively. It was Willie Cunningham of Preston North End who captained Scotland at the 1954 World Cup finals whilst Liverpool goalie Tommy Younger had that honour in Scotland's first two games at the 1958 finals.

Young was followed by such others as Bobby Evans of Celtic, Dave Mackay of Hearts and Spurs and into the sixties Eric Caldow would lead the side 15 times until the game at Wembley in 1963 where his leg was broken. This would then see three players in this period take over from Eric who were all natural leaders. First up was Billy McNeill of Celtic (eight games) who would be followed by John Greig of Rangers for 15 games in total, both undeniably among the greatest of players for the Glasgow clubs.

They were superseded by the man who many consider to be the epitome of a Scotland captain, Billy Bremner. The Leeds United legend at only 5ft 5in is probably one of the smallest Scotland captains but he was as hard and fiery as they come and with his distinctive ginger hair was hard to miss on the pitch. Billy played hard and in some ways lived hard as he was well known for his boozing that would ultimately be his downfall but who can forget his anguish as that ball slipped past the post against Brazil at the World Cup finals in 1974. Most of the captains that have followed on from Billy are, for the generation that grew up with Bremner as their icon, pale imitations by comparison. Billy has come the closest to George Young's captaincy record with a total of 39 games with the armband.

After the fracas in 1975 when Billy was banned by the SFA, and in an effort to boost attendance and morale at the next home game – a Euro qualifier v Denmark, it is perhaps a measure of both men that manager Willie Ormond chose to recall John Greig for the first time in five years to the side and to the captaincy for just the one game.

Archie Gemmill would take up the mantle of the small, tenacious captain for the late 70s and into the 80s although ironically in his greatest match against the Netherlands at the 1978 World Cup finals he was not captain – Aldershot-born Bruce Rioch was.

Into the 80s and the fearsome Graeme Souness took over and saw us through the 1982 World Cup, taking over from Danny McGrain who was in charge for the opener against New Zealand. Souness would also captain in the first two games of Mexico 1986 but is still irked today by being robbed of the chance to get in among the Uruguayans in the third match after being regarded too unfit due to illness by Alex Ferguson. In among them he certainly would have got!

After Graeme came Roy Aitken who equally liked to get about his opponents and led by example at Italia 90. I do wonder sometimes though, how Souness would have taken to the schoolmasterly regime of Andy Roxburgh. Aitken like Souness was captain on 27 occasions with Aberdeen's Willie Miller deputising eleven times around the same period. It was Richard Gough however who had the honour of captaining Scotland at the Euro 92 finals which took place in the land of his birth, Sweden.

For much of the 90s Gary McAllister takes over the mantle and manages to reach 32 games as Scotland skipper including the

100

SCOTLAND GLORY, TEARS AND SOUVENIRS

Scotland captain Martin Buchan exchanges pennants with Argentina captain Jorge Omar Carrascosa in a friendly, June 1977.

Euro 96 finals but is often second choice to 'Braveheart' Colin Hendry who captained his country at the 1998 World Cup finals in France. If Bremner epitomised the hard midfield man of Scotland it is Hendry who does something similar for the strong centre-half role. He probably is the last great captain Scotland have had; perhaps for many of us it was all those rearguard actions many a Scotland team had to produce with Hendry always seeming to win that header or produce that lunging tackle. He was also quite a striking individual with his long blonde hair and with the hullabaloo that came about for all things Scottish following the release of the *Braveheart* movie he seemed to be a man of his time.

Like Bremner, Hendry's Scotland career ended prematurely when he was retrospectively given a six game ban by UEFA for elbowing an opponent.

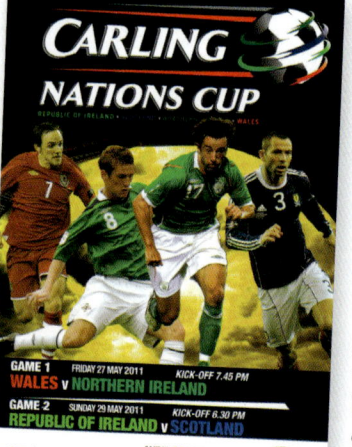

Colin had scored two goals in the match against San Marino in March 2001. It was to be his 51st and final cap for Scotland having worn the captain's armband on 22 occasions.

Since then there have been some good captains of Scotland as opposed to great ones which is perhaps a sign of the times with the likes of Paul Lambert, Christian Dailly and Darren Fletcher all taking up the mantle. Fletcher with 32 at the time of writing is third on the all-time list with McAllister. Barry Ferguson captained Scotland on 29 occasions but his tenure must surely be overshadowed by the manner of his departure following the 'Boozegate' furore in 2009.

Some of the all-time greats did get their shot at the captaincy with the likes of Dalglish with a total of six including on the occasion of his 100th cap, Denis Law for five games and Jim Baxter for four but then there's a couple to note with just one. To commemorate his 50th cap Ally McCoist was given the armband for a friendly with Australia in March 1996 and of course being Super Ally he scored the game's only goal.

Finally however, spare a thought for John Collins who had the honour for mere seconds as it was he who led out the side for the game that never was, against Estonia in Tallinn in October 1996.

CARLING NATIONS CUP

It was a British Isles championship but not as we knew it. In 2011 the Republic of Ireland replaced England and joined Wales, Northern Ireland and Scotland for a four-team tournament played on a league basis. It comprised of six matches that were all played in the one country – the one stadium in fact, namely the new 52,000 capacity Aviva Stadium at Lansdowne Road, Dublin which had officially opened just the previous year. The sponsors were Carling – the Canadian brewing company.

By playing two tournament matches in February then the remaining four games three months later the opportunity was missed to compact the six matches over an eight-day period in the warmth of May or June with perhaps Galway and/or Cork supplementing the Irish capital to create a proper 'Festival of Football' so to speak.

Three double-header souvenir programmes were produced to cover the six games.

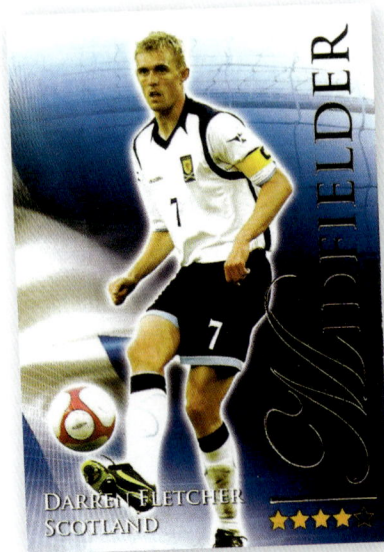

SCOTLAND GLORY, TEARS AND SOUVENIRS

Game 1 Tuesday 8 February
Republic of Ireland 3 Wales 0
[Attendance 20,900]

Game 2 Wednesday 9 February
Scotland 3 N. Ireland 0
[Attendance 18,742]

Game 3 Tuesday 24 May
Republic of Ireland 5 N. Ireland 0
[Attendance 15,092]

Game 4 Wednesday 25 May
Scotland 3 Wales 1
[Attendance 6,036]

Game 5 Friday 27 May
Northern Ireland 0 Wales 2
[Attendance 529]

Game 6 Sunday 29 May
Republic of Ireland 1 Scotland 0
[Attendance 17,064]

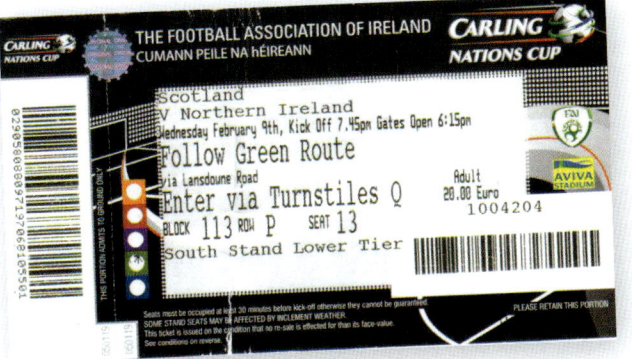

The Republic of Ireland were the outright winners with Scotland second, Wales third and Northern Ireland fourth. The Republic's Robbie Keane was the top scorer with three successes.

Scotland manager Craig Levein [whose tournament counterparts were Nigel Worthington, Gary Speed and Giovanni Trapattoni] used the competition to award debut caps to six players who went on to varying degrees of success at international level. Robert Snodgrass [Leeds United], Chris Maguire [Aberdeen] and Mark Wilson [Celtic] all made it on to the pitch at some point in the game against Northern Ireland. Grant Hanley [Blackburn Rovers] and Russell Martin [Norwich City] came on to face Wales whilst James Forrest [Celtic] got his first full cap against the Republic of Ireland.

It was hoped that the Carling Nations Cup would become a biennial tournament but poor attendances at the inaugural competition would appear to have helped knock that idea on the head. The second tournament was provisionally scheduled to have taken place in Wales in 2013. Apparently Brittany also expressed an interest in taking part and perhaps their inclusion along with Guernsey, Jersey and the Isle of Man might have offered up something different – or at least some nice, new places for us Groundhoppers to get worked up into a lather about.

CENTENARY CELEBRATIONS – 1973

Come 2023 the second-oldest Football Association in the world – The Scottish Football Association – will be celebrating its 150th anniversary. Back in 1973 at a time when Glam-Rock was king, the SFA celebrated its centenary with matches against England, Brazil and the Federal Republic of Germany [aka West Germany] who between them had won the FIFA World Cup on the five previous occasions with the FRG being the host [and future winner] in 1974.

First up were our beloved near-neighbours England who came to Hampden Park on Saint Valentine's day that year and duly massacred their hosts 5-0. 'Roses are red, violets are blue, Clarke Chivers and Channon, all shafted you'. In fact Allan Clarke scored twice

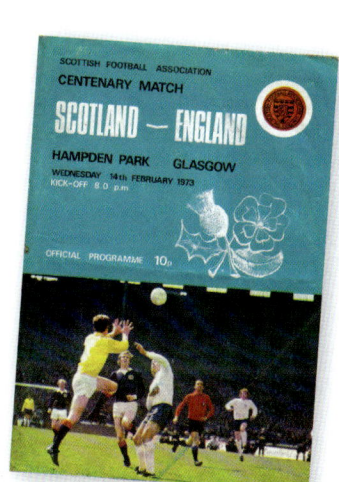

whilst his Leeds United clubmate, Peter Lorimer started the proceedings with an own-goal after just six minutes. It was 3-0 to England at half-time.

48,470 supporters braved the wintry conditions that evening to see a Scotland team which included Aberdeen's Bobby Clark in goal plus Celtic's Kenny Dalglish up front. The other ten players who wore the dark blue that evening were all 'Anglo-Scots' – so if you are looking for scapegoats… On the bright side however, The Sweet were at number one in the UK singles charts with 'Blockbuster'.

Centenary celebration match no.2 came about on 30th June when Brazil [then the reigning world champions and an incredible nine games into a close-season tour of North Africa and Europe] stopped off at Hampden Park.

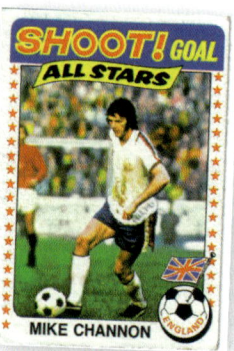

A sizeable proportion of the crowd of 78,181 [which included debutant David Stuart and his Dad] paid at the gate [77 pence for the North Enclosure] to see Rangers' Derek Johnstone score the only goal of the game after 33 minutes – unfortunately for us though it was an own goal.

The Brazil team were going through the proverbial transition at the time but they still had World Cup winners in their ranks such as Piazza, Clodoaldo, Rivelino and Jairzinho. The Scottish team were impressive enough in their own right – seven players from Celtic and Rangers; Jim Holton, Willie Morgan and George Graham from Manchester

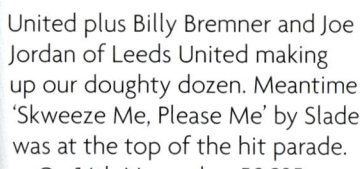

United plus Billy Bremner and Joe Jordan of Leeds United making up our doughty dozen. Meantime 'Skweeze Me, Please Me' by Slade was at the top of the hit parade.

On 14th November 58,235 turned up at Hampden Park to see celebration no.3 against West Germany which was really a double celebration given that Scotland had qualified for the 1974 World Cup finals just two months previous.

Scotland should have won this game but Billy Bremner missed a penalty and in the end we had to settle for a 1-1 draw. Jim Holton had given Scotland the lead after only seven minutes but we were unable to add to that and not long after the penalty miss

Uli Hoeness equalised for the reigning European champions some ten minutes from time. It was an impressive German side that included the likes of Franz Beckenbauer, Gunter Netzer and Berti Vogts. Gary Glitter was at number one in the charts with 'I love, You love, Me love' – er, time to move on….

In summary, an aggregate attendance of 184,886 saw Scotland play three, lose two and draw one, scoring but one goal in the process and conceding seven. Scotland certainly have a unique way of celebrating but I guess that's what happens when you send out invites to three of the best teams in the world and then they have the audacity to turn up and perform!

CHIX

I Love the Chix – Chix Bubblegum Cards that is. From the mid-50s to the early 60s the Chix Confectionary Company released a number of football card sets, most of which had their own albums to place them in. Scottish players did feature in them such as home stars like Lawrie Reilly of Hibs, George 'Corky' Young of Rangers and of course, the obligatory Anglos such as Jackie Mudie of Blackpool and there's an early

SCOTLAND GLORY, TEARS AND SOUVENIRS

Denis Law with Huddersfield Town also.

However, Chix did release two wholly Scottish sets. The first was issued in 1954 and had 24 black and white photos of contemporary Scottish players. I have yet to come across any of these but I loved the way they went about it as the set has only two players each from Rangers and Celtic but seven from Aberdeen, four each from Partick Thistle, Raith Rovers and East Fife and a final one from Hibernian.

I do however, have the complete set from the 1960 Scottish footballers set which is rather wonderful if slightly bizarre. Once more there are 24 in the set with a much more equal division among clubs this time. The cards are drawn portraits which are done quite well but it's just that the strips in some cases are just made up. For Hibs, some of Hearts and Dundee players it seems okay but Willie Telfer seems to be stuck in two camps. He has on a blue top of Rangers but then it has the badge of St Mirren on it, the club he left for Ibrox a few seasons before.

Poetic licence has been taken by the artist as he goes through some of the others such as Bobby Wishart of Aberdeen and the Clyde duo of Harry Haddock and Tommy Ring who appear in red tops complete with an SFA badge emblazoned on them. Duncan Mackay of Celtic has a green top with an SFA badge whilst team-mate Bobby Evans has a green top plus the Scottish League Select badge. Fellow Celt Bertie Peacock has a nice Irish badge on his jersey though. Gordon Smith and John Cumming of Hearts both have maroon tops with Scottish League badges. However my personal favourite is Sammy Baird of Rangers who has a green shirt with the League Select badge.

On the back of the cards is a short biographical piece on each player but in terms of predictions for future caps they seem to have got it way wrong. Given that it's 1960, predicting more caps for Sammy Baird and the Aberdeen pairing of Fred 'I conceded seven against England in 1955 so I did' Martin and Hugh Baird may have been a bit foolhardy to say the least and as for the Dons' Bobby Wishart and Dundee's Bobby Cox, well neither made it to the full Scotland team despite both being on the 'fringes' as such. Overall a great set with some great players.

CIGARETTE CARDS [THE SWEET KIND]

So who remembers back in the 60s and 70s when you could buy sweetie cigarettes before they became the more pc Candy Sticks? It's hard to believe that such a thing existed; they even had a wee red tip so you could pretend you were smoking. Barratt & Co. were the main producers of these and the collectors' cards that went with them and had been releasing sets since the 1920s with football featuring frequently throughout the years. Geo. Bassett & Co. Ltd had taken over the company in the early 70s but still produced sets with the Barratt name.

Back then I was a 20 a day man or rather boy, particularly in the glorious summer of '74 when Scotland had qualified for the World Cup. There had been football sets before this but this was a World Cup one with a fair smattering of great players and of the 50 in the set, 24 were Scottish. Among the world stars there were Gerd Muller, Franz Beckenbauer, Johann Cruyff, Dino Zoff, Rivelino and a few from the Polish team that had qualified ahead of England.

As to the Scots, there were a few oddities among the

great and good. There were of course some players who ranked among the all-time greats for Scotland such as Billy Bremner, Denis Law, Kenny Dalglish, Danny McGrain, etc., but the set was obviously put together well in advance of the World Cup so there was a bit of a guessing game as to who would make manager Willie Ormond's squad that summer, which led to one or two interesting choices.

There were some players who had already played their last games for Scotland in 1973,

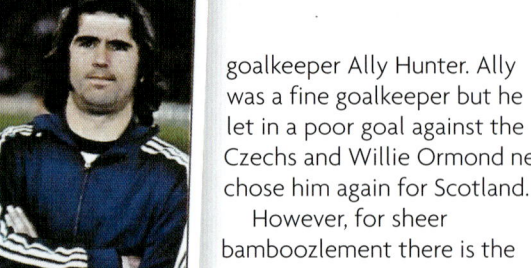

goalkeeper Ally Hunter. Ally was a fine goalkeeper but he let in a poor goal against the Czechs and Willie Ormond never chose him again for Scotland.

However, for sheer bamboozlement there is the inclusion of John Connolly in the set. John started out at St Johnstone but moved to Everton in 1972. An outside-left, John would be capped just once in June 1973 as Scotland faced Switzerland in an end of season friendly. He would be replaced by Joe Jordan at the

among them Colin Stein, then of Coventry City, George Graham from Manchester United and two players who had played on the night that Scotland qualified in October 1973 in the 2-1 win over Czechoslovakia.

George Connelly of Celtic had received the Scottish Football Writers' Player of the Year award for season 1972-73 and made his Scotland debut against the Czechs. A lot was expected of Connelly who had bountiful talent and was able to play in midfield or in the heart of the defence. Sadly the expectation placed on George was too much for him and he was lost to the game a few years later due to mental health issues. George only ever gained two Scotland caps.

The other player from that game in 1973 that didn't make the squad was Celtic

start of the second half but his 45 minutes of fame as a Scotland player are forever remembered thanks to the guys at Bassetts.

I also loved the matter-of-fact wording on the reverse side of the card for Rangers striker Derek Parlane [another player who didn't make the squad] – 'He too has won just about everything in Scottish football and is eager to add a World Cup winner's medal to his collection'.

There was to be no great International set for the 1978 World Cup but from time to time if you search them out, you will find Scots in their national kit from over the years in various sets including the likes of eighties heroes Willie Miller, Davie Cooper, Mo Johnston etc.

SCOTLAND GLORY, TEARS AND SOUVENIRS

COMIC CAPERS AND COLLECTABLES

Sadly, this will not be a tribute to some of Scotland's finest comedians, such giants as Chic Murray, Rikki Fulton, Billy Connolly or even Fred MacAulay but a look at one or two Scotland comic collectables from a bygone era i.e. my youth.

Despite Scotland's kids' comic tradition with Dundee-based DC Thomson, there is no *Roy of the Rovers* comic equivalent although as we all know there is *Hot Shot Hamish*. Hamish was a giant of a Scotsman from the Hebrides with the hardest shot in football. The real hot shot was of course, Peter Lorimer known in his Leeds United days as 'Lash'.

I'm sure the makers of the *Dandy* and the *Beano* could re-imagine some of their titles to fit a Scotland format such as Jimmy the Jinks, Willie the Whizz [NB: This relates to Willie Johnston's speed, sorry pace, rather than little yellow pills] and of course, there would be *Denis the Menace. The Bash Street Kids* would of course, be the Celtic young guns from the late 60s and early 70s i.e. Kenny Dalglish, Danny McGrain, David Hay and others dubbed at the time as the Quality Street Gang.

Enough of the fantasy stuff, what about the real collectables. Well, there's nothing that pricey, just the odd bit of nostalgia here and there. I was disappointed in coming across a storyline about Melchester Rovers' Scots duo of Duncan Mackay and Kenny Logan playing for Scotland at Argentina in 1978 to discover it was an on-line story only. Cost me a few pounds to find that out, sadly I now have a collection from the summer of '78 of Roy and the rest of the Rovers playing cricket. However, there was one issue of *Roy of the Rovers* dedicated to Scotland from 1978 called... Roy's Tribute to Scotland!

I don't know if it was a portent of things to come but it is dated April 1st. There is a lot about Scotland in it, including a poster of Gordon McQueen's epic goal at Wembley in 1977, a smattering of black and white photos and a team photo from the '77 South America tour rounds it off.

Other comics worth a look are some of the *Rover* and *Wizard* comics from the 60s portraying Scotland goals on the front cover in their Famous Goals series; one is of Alan Gilzean's winning goal against England in 1964 and rather bizarrely Colin Stein scoring in the 4-1 defeat at Wembley in 1969. There are others but since they're of goals against Scotland let's give them a miss. My other favourite of this type is the *Scorcher and Score* one of May '72 with Scotland on the front as the Top Team with rather odd drawings of Denis Law and Billy Bremner, who stands about six foot tall next to manager Tommy Docherty. However, the real deal is the card giveaways mainly from the likes of the Hornet and Victor. In 1958 just prior to the World Cup in Sweden, DC Thomson released a set of 64 cards via the comics, The Adventure, The Hotspur, Rover and Wizard; among the Scots in the set were Blackpool's Jackie Mudie, a scorer of a hat-trick against Spain in a qualifier at Hampden, a young Dave Mackay and Jimmy Murray who like MacKay played for Hearts. Murray would go on to be the scorer of Scotland's first ever World Cup goal in Sweden against Yugoslavia. The pen-pics style information on the reverse side of these cards averaged around 75 words and included details of their school and works teams!

There's also a great pic of the Scotland team that would play against England at Wembley in 1965 with a ridiculously cheap looking track suit, which was given away in the *Hornet* in the Top Cup Teams set of 1965.

The late 60s and early 70s would see a splash of colour in sets from the *Hotspur*, *Hornet* and *Victor* comics. There's lot of Scottish players among these sets including a grim-faced Eddie McCreadie in his Scotland colours from the 1970 World Cup Star set, which despite its title, only consisted of British footballers. The *Wizard* comic set 'Great Stars of Football' also from 1970 has a rare football card sighting of Scotland striker Colin Stein in a Rangers strip. All those years of A&BC Scottish cards never produced one; I don't know if Stein wanted more than the tenner offered for his image at the time. Stein can also be seen in an Anglo confectionery set from 1969/70 again as a Rangers player.

IPC/Fleetway through their comics *Lion*, *Tiger*, *Scorcher* and others would release sets in the late 60s and early 70s which all had their own small albums. I should also mention the Soccer Super Stars of Britain set from their *Action* comic in 1975/76 which had a host of Scots in the set and included Danny McGrain of Celtic and Ted MacDougall of Norwich City in their national colours.

By the mid-70s most of these comics fell by the way as did the idea of football card giveaways, although from time to time there has been some. The classic years were gone however.

SCOTLAND GLORY, TEARS AND SOUVENIRS

COMMENTATING LEGENDS

As far as Scottish football commentators are concerned there are but two who have achieved legendary status – Arthur 'stramash' Montford and Archie 'a penalty if ever there was one' MacPherson. Quite simply they are the best-loved, most fondly remembered pair of football wafflers in Scotland.

Arthur was the soft-spoken anchorman and/or lead-commentator of Scottish Television's *Scotsport* programme from 1957 to 1989, hosting over 2,000 editions. He was renowned for his trademark checkered-pattern sports jackets [which close-up looked like interference] and some legendary lines of football commentary in which his patriotism often got the better of his professionalism.

In September 1973 when Czechoslovakia took the lead in a vital World Cup qualifier at Hampden a clearly pained Montford bemoaned 'Disaster for Scotland.' Later on in the game he would warn 'Watch your back, Willie' as Morgan looked to be in danger of losing possession, whilst in the closing minutes as Denis Law broke clear an over-excited Arthur implored – 'Come on now Denis, come on, Denis!' Alas, Ivo Viktor in goal thwarted the Lawman. Mercifully however Scotland actually averted disaster against Czechoslovakia in 1973 by storming back to win 2-1. However, the phrase 'Disaster for Scotland' is now an integral part of everyday language in Scotland for a whole variety of reasons, some more obvious than others.

Four years later and we're at Anfield, Liverpool for a World Cup qualifying showdown with Wales and when three minutes from time Kenny Dalglish makes it two-nil for Scotland Arthur's joy is unconfined – 'It's there! Argentina here we come!'

By comparison, the more robust Archie worked for the BBC, Scottish Television, Eurosport, Setanta Sports, Radio Clyde and Talksport but his purple patch was probably whilst working on the *Sportsreel* and *Sportscene* programmes for BBC Scotland between 1969 and 1990 as presenter and/or lead commentator.

His ginger bouffant, when exposed to the extremities of the Scottish weather, meant that on occasion he looked like a giant weetabix in distress. His footballing soundbites included 'Absolute Bedlam!' and 'Woof!'

For the 1996 film adaptation of the Irvine Welsh novel *Trainspotting*, Archie re-voiced his commentary of Archie Gemmill's fabulous goal against the Netherlands at the 1978 World Cup finals for a sex scene which took place at the same time and which ended in a simultaneous climax. Over on the other channel Arthur's take on the genius of Gemmill was equally as joyous.

Arthur, Archie Mac and Archie G – who would have thought that three men in Mendoza would give so much pleasure to around five million Scots?

CZECHOSLOVAKIA

Gone but not forgotten – Czechoslovakia, along with East Germany, the USSR and Yugoslavia were Cold War Europe's 'Communist Fab Four'.

Czechoslovakia, with its capital city of Prague, was a sovereign state in central Europe which existed from October 1918 [when it declared its independence from the Austro-Hungarian Empire] until its peaceful dissolution into the Czech Republic and Slovakia in January 1993. It was a part of the communist Soviet bloc from 1948 until 1990.

In the world of football Czechoslovakia won the 1976 European Football Championship and were World Cup runners-up in 1934 and 1962. At Olympic football they were gold medallists in 1980 having won silver in 1964.

Between 1937 and 1977 Scotland played Czechoslovakia on ten occasions, seven of which were World Cup qualifiers. Scotland won five of the matches, lost four and drew one.

1937, Sparta Stadion, Prague
Friendly, 3-1 - 35,000

1937, Hampden Park, Glasgow
Friendly, 5-0 - 41,000

1961, Tehelne Pole Stadion, Bratislava
World Cup Qualifier, 0-4 - 50,000

1961, Hampden Park, Glasgow
World Cup Qualifier, 3-2 - 51,590

1961, Heysel Stadium, Brussels
World Cup Play-off, 2-4 - 7,000

1972, Estadio Beira Rio, Porto Alegre
Brazil Independence Cup, 0-0 - 15,000

1973, Hampden Park, Glasgow
World Cup Qualifier, 2-1 - 100,000

1973, Tehelne Pole Stadion, Bratislava
World Cup Qualifier, 0-1 - 15,000

1976, Sparta Stadion, Prague
World Cup Qualifier, 0-2 - 38,000

1977, Hampden Park, Glasgow
World Cup Qualifier, 3-1 - 85,000

The Scotland team that defeated Czechoslovakia 5-0 at Hampden Park in 1937 included six players who were making their full international debut. The visitors' line-up included four footballers who played in their losing 1934 World Cup Final against Italy.

Scotland's historic World Cup qualifier against Czechoslovakia at Hampden Park in September 1973 was the last time the official attendance at the national stadium hit the 100,000 mark.

When Scotland defeated Czechoslovakia 3-1 in the World Cup qualifier at Hampden Park in September 1977 the visitors' line-up included six of the players who had helped them win the European Championship Final 15 months previous but not the legendary Antonin 'Penalty chip straight down the middle' Panenka. However Panenka did play against the Scots on the three preceding occasions the two sides met and scored one of the goals in the 2-0 victory in Prague in October 1976.

DALGLISH, KENNY – THE 30 GOALS
Kenny Dalglish and Denis Law are Scotland's joint top goalscorers with 30 goals apiece. Here's a summary of King Kenny's tally which somewhat surprisingly never included a hat-trick.

Goal #1. Unlike Denis it took Kenny a few games to get off the mark having made his debut under Tommy Docherty on 10th November, 1971 coming on just after half-time against Belgium in a Euro qualifier at Pittodrie. It wasn't until his fourth game against Denmark a year later in a World Cup qualifier he netted. Two minutes into the game at Hampden Kenny scored and Peter Lorimer added a second just after half-time to seal a vital World Cup win. It was just six months after the Lawman's last goal for Scotland.

Goal #2. With a minute of the game remaining Kenny scored against Northern Ireland in a British Championship match at Hampden in May 1973 but it was only a consolation as the Scots were two down at this point.

Goal #3. Came in a friendly in Frankfurt in March 1974 against the World Cup hosts West Germany. Kenny took a great through ball from Dundee's Bobby Robinson and despatched the ball past Sepp Maier and into the net. Although Scotland had played well that night, again this was only a consolation goal as they lost 2-1.

SCOTLAND GLORY, TEARS AND SOUVENIRS

Goal #4 was against Wales at Hampden on 14th May, 1974 as Scotland won the British Championship match 2-0 with Sandy Jardine scoring from the penalty spot also.

Goal #5 was in the last four minutes of a friendly against Norway in Oslo on 6th June as part of Scotland's World Cup warm-up plans. Joe Jordan had scored the other as Scotland won 2-1 in their last game before World Cup '74.

Goal #6 Kenny failed to score at the World Cup in 1974 but scored Scotland's third as they beat East Germany in a 3-0 friendly win at Hampden in October '74 with Tommy Hutchison and Kenny Burns netting the others.

Goal #7 came in a 3-0 defeat of Northern Ireland in a British Championship match at Hampden in May '75 with Ted MacDougall and Derek Parlane grabbing the other two.

Goal #8 was in a 3-1 defeat of Denmark on Euro qualifier business but the damage had already been done as the Scots had lost at home to Spain the year before in the group. This was in October 1975 and Bruce Rioch and Ted MacDougall scored the others.

Goal #9 was the final goal against the Northern Irish in a 1976 Home International with Archie Gemmill and Don Masson scoring as the Scots began a couple of years of great football with a 3-0 win.

Goal #10 is among our favourite of Kenny's goals as Joe Jordan raced down the wing and passed inside to Kenny, who evaded the defender and then didn't hit the ball that well but this year [1976] the English had Ray Clemence in goal and not Peter Shilton and so the ball squirmed between his legs and into the back of the net. Kenny raced away with his arms aloft and with a big grin on his face and it was 2-1 to Scotland and the British Championship was ours once more.

Goal #11 came in a friendly rout of Finland in September 1976 as Scotland won 6-0. This is the type of game Law would have scored a bundle but Kenny only netted the once.

Goal #12 was in Willie Ormond's last game in charge as Scotland beat Sweden 3-1 at Hampden in April 1977. An own goal from Hellstrom and Joe Craig's famous Scotland cameo appearance where he scored a goal, before he had even kicked the ball were the other two scorers for Scotland.

Goals #13 & 14 were his first double as Dalglish netted twice against Northern Ireland in the Home Internationals with Gordon McQueen scoring in between them on 1st June 1977 at Hampden as Scotland won 3-0.

Goal #15 Wembley 1977. McQueen and Dalglish score again to do the damage as the Scots win 2-1 under Ally MacLeod. The Tartan Army then did their own wee bit of 'damage' afterwards.

Goal #16 came a far cry from Wembley in the Estadio Nacional, Santiago, Chile on 15 June 1977; a game which many see as Scotland's game of shame. The stadium had been used as a prison camp following a coup d'état by the military in Chile in 1973 under the leadership of Maggie Thatcher's friend, General Pinochet. Scotland won 4-2 in this friendly as part of their World Cup acclimatisation tour of South America. Kenny opened the scoring, Lou Macari hit a double and Asa Hartford netted the other.

Goal #17 was the icing on the cake as Scotland powered to a 3-1 win over Czechoslovakia in a World Cup qualifier at Hampden in September 1977 with Joe Jordan and Asa Hartford bagging the others. This was Kenny's first as a Liverpool player.

Goal #18 is another favourite as Kenny scored that wonderful header against Wales in a World Cup qualifier at Anfield on that unforgettable

111

Kenny Dalglish has made most appearances for Scotland.

night in Liverpool in October, 1977. Argentina here we come!

Goal #19 is one that there are many images of as he managed to strike the ball beautifully from Joe Jordan's knock down to equalise for Scotland against the Netherlands in Mendoza, Argentina on 11 June 1978. The Archie Gemmill show was to follow in the second half as Scotland won 3-2 but alas…

Goals #20 & 21 gave Jock Stein a winning start to his second term as Scotland manager as the Scots toiled to beat Norway in a Euro qualifier at Hampden in October 1978 with an Archie Gemmill penalty in the 87th minute giving them a 3-2 victory.

Goal #22 was once more against Norway in a Euro qualifier in Oslo in June 1979 with Scotland winning 4-0 with goals from Jordan, Dalglish, John Robertson and Gordon McQueen.

Goal #23 was in a drubbing of Portugal 4-1 at Hampden in the final match of the 1980 Euro qualifiers in March, 1980. Goals from Andy Gray, Steve Archibald and Archie Gemmill completed the scoring. Scotland had of course failed to qualify but then again we did have Belgium in our group!

Goal #24 was a vital one as Scotland defeated Israel in February 1981, on their way to qualifying for the Spain '82 World Cup. This match took place in Tel Aviv and would be the only home defeat for Israel in the group and went a long way in helping Scotland qualify.

Goal #25 came in a World Cup warm-up friendly at Hampden in March 1982 as the Scots beat the Netherlands 2-1 with Frank Gray providing the other.

Goal #26 and Kenny opened up our scoring in Spain '82 in the 18th minute which was quickly followed by a double from John Wark against New Zealand in Malaga in June but then Scotland shipped two goals before a late rally to finish 5-2 winners.

Goals #27 & 28 were against Belgium in the Heysel Stadium, Brussels in a Euro qualifier in December 1982. Both goals were exquisite; the first a wonderful one-two with Steve Archibald that finishes with a deft flick past the Belgian goalkeeper. The second sees Kenny weave his way through the Belgian defence before he unleashes a wonderful finish once more but this is the Scotland national team and of course it is Belgium and the Scots lost 3-2 in the end.

Goal #29 was one of six as Scotland routed Yugoslavia in a friendly at Hampden in September, 1984 winning 6-1.

Goal #30 came on his 96th appearance. Scotland had been put 2-0 up against Spain at Hampden in a vital World Cup qualifier in November 1984 with goals from Mo Johnston. However, the Spanish had gotten one back in the 68th minute and some nervy moments followed. However, another magical moment as Kenny cuts inside from the right and seems almost to be moving away from the goals but turns and screws one into the net to give Scotland a memorable win.

Injury kept Kenny out of Scotland's World Cup squad at Mexico 1986 and his 102nd and final appearance came about at Hampden Park on 12 November 1986 in a Euro qualifier against Luxembourg at Hampden. Scotland won 3-0 but alas Kenny was unable to get on the scoresheet and overtake Denis as Scotland's top marksman.

DOCHERTY, TOMMY

Although most of us will think of Tommy Docherty [aka The Doc] and his days in charge of the Scotland team in the early 70s, he also played for the national team 25 times from 1951-59, travelling to two World Cup finals.

Tommy was first capped as a Preston North End player in November, 1951 making his debut against Wales at Hampden. Tommy was what we would think of nowadays as a holding midfielder, making the tackles and threading passes forward at this time. Scotland lined up with one or two legends beside Tommy such as Jimmy Cowan of Morton in goals, George Young, Willie Woodburn, Willie Waddell all of Rangers, Lawrie Reilly of Hibs as well as the two Billys of the time; Steel of Dundee and Liddell of Liverpool. With all that talent on display Scotland still managed to lose 1-0.

Scotland qualified for the 1954 World Cup finals due to a second place finish in the Home internationals. However, it is fair to say that Scotland's first ever World Cup was a bit of a disaster in many ways. Scotland did pick a squad of 22 players but the great minds at the SFA decided to only take a squad of 13 players and also allowed Rangers to take their players on a club tour of Canada instead. Scotland's first game was against Austria in Zurich which they narrowly lost 1-0, however in their next game in the heat of Basel they were run ragged by Uruguay, losing 7-0. Tommy played in both games as did another future Scotland manager Willie Ormond.

Sadly, this was not the last time Tommy was in a Scotland side that shipped seven goals; they would do so again in April, 1955 losing 7-2 to England at Wembley. Aberdeen's Fred Martin was the unfortunate Scotland goalie on both occasions. Tommy would score his only Scotland goal in this game.

Tommy would be part of the side that qualified for the World Cup in Sweden in 1958 but was not fully fit and took on a more coaching, scouting role for the team. Scotland would open with a draw against Yugoslavia followed by two narrow defeats to Paraguay (3-2) and France (2-1).

Tommy moved to Arsenal in 1958 and returned to the Scotland side for the whole of the 1958/59 Home International Series. This first of these games in October '58 was against Wales at Ninian Park where Denis Law would make his entrance to the international stage. Docherty's last game for Scotland was at Wembley in April, 1959 where a solitary goal by Bobby Charlton would prove to be the winner.

Following the departure of Bobby Brown as Scotland manager in late 1971 Tommy Docherty was a surprise choice given his high profile and reputation for speaking his mind but it was to prove a good fit as Tommy revived Scotland's fortunes and paved the way for their qualification to World Cup '74.

Tommy was in charge of Scotland for twelve games winning seven, drawing two and losing three. His first game was against Portugal in a Euro qualifier on 13 October, 1971.

Straight away Tommy was controversial in picking two players of Scottish parentage for the first time and in particular his choice of goalkeeper, Arsenal's Bob Wilson. Bob was very much seen as an Englishman to all and sundry even though Bob himself is very proud of his Scottish heritage. The other player was Hibs' Alex Cropley who was born in the town of Aldershot, as his father was playing for 'The Shots' at the time. Both Alex and Bob would only play twice for Scotland.

Tommy Docherty, Scotland Team Manager

Also making his debut that night would be Sheffield United's centre half Eddie Colquhoun who would win nine caps in total, his last being in Willie Ormond's torrid debut as manager ie the 5-0 whitewash to England in 1973. Colquhoun was replaced in 60 minutes by Martin Buchan who would actually move to Manchester United from Aberdeen prior to the Doc going there. Buchan would go on to play 34 games for Scotland. Scotland won 2-1 against Portugal that night at Hampden with Archie Gemmill and John O'Hare scoring the goals.

Being a wily character, Tommy decided to reinstate Aberdeen's Bobby Clark to first choice goalkeeper in his next game as this was against Belgium in November 1971 in another Euro qualifier at Pittodrie. He also chose the host club's Buchan and debutant Stevie Murray to start. This would be Murray's only Scotland game. In the 48th minute Alex Cropley was replaced by a Scotland legend in the making, Kenny Dalglish. Scotland won 1-0 with O'Hare scoring again.

Docherty established new players into the team but he would also be responsible for bringing back Denis Law to the side for the first time in three years as he would also do for Celtic's Billy McNeill. Law was brought back into the side for a friendly v Peru in April '72 where Willie Donachie and Asa Hartford duly made their debuts. Scotland won 2-0 with goals from O'Hare and the returning Law.

As for the 1972 Home Internationals we would beat both Northern Ireland (2-0) and Wales (1-0) but lose to England (0-1). Only Luigi Macari or Lou to me and you, would make his debut in any of these games, as a sub against Wales and playing the full 90 minutes against England.

Then onto Brazil in June and July 1972 for the Independence tournament or the Mini World Cup as it was dubbed. Scotland would draw 2-2 with Yugoslavia in front of a crowd of 4,000 in Belo Horizonte. Lou Macari scored the Scotland goals. The next game in Porto Alegre would see Scotland draw 0-0 with Czechoslovakia in front of 15,000. The final game saw Scotland lose 1-0 to Brazil with Jairzinho scoring the only goal in 80 minutes at the Maracana in front of a crowd of 130,000. During the tournament the Doc gave debuts to Alex Forsyth of Partick Thistle and Jimmy Bone, then of Norwich City – both had been part of the Thistle side which had sensationally won the Scottish League Cup in October '71 beating Celtic 4-1. Team-mate John Hansen had already been capped at this point by Docherty and Alan Rough and Denis McQuade from that team had also been part of previous Scotland squads.

Tommy would only have two more games in charge, both World Cup qualifiers against Denmark in October/November 1972. The first would see Scotland win 4-1 with goals from Macari, Bone, Willie Morgan and debut player Joe Harper of Aberdeen. His final game in charge would see him give David Harvey of Leeds United his debut against Denmark at Hampden which the Scots won 2-0 with Kenny Dalglish hitting his first Scotland goal and Peter Lorimer netting the other. Tommy would then, in December 1972, take up the management post at Manchester United.

Tommy paved the way for Willie Ormond to take us to the World Cup finals in 1974. His time as Scotland manager was a success, winning all his Euro and World Cup qualifiers. He also gave debuts to important players like Buchan, Dalglish, Donachie, Hartford, Macari and David Harvey, all of whom served their country well and unlike a lot of teams Docherty took charge of, he never got us relegated!

EAST GERMANY

In 1945, at the end of the Second World War, Germany was divided into four sectors by the Allied powers. The British, French and American sectors later became the Federal Republic of Germany [West Germany] whilst the Communist Soviet Union sector became the German Democratic [misnomer surely?] Republic [East Germany]. Just to confuse matters, the western half of the city of Berlin remained outwith the jurisdiction of East Germany.

East Germany [like Scotland] qualified for the 1974 World Cup finals in West Germany. However, unlike Scotland they reached the second round thanks in no small way to a 1-0 win over their hosts and neighbours at the initial group stage. The GDR then won the Olympic Games football gold medal in 1976 and the silver four years later. In October 1990 as a result of the collapse of communism in Europe, East Germany was dissolved and Germany re-unified.

Between 1974 and 1990 Scotland played East Germany on six occasions [more than any other 'Home' nation], winning two, drawing one and losing three – where was Harry Palmer when we needed him?

1974, Hampden Park, Glasgow,
Friendly, 3-0 - 39,445

1977, Weltjugend Stadion, East Berlin,
Friendly, 0-1 - 50,000

1982, Hampden Park, Glasgow,
Euro Championship qualifier, 2-0 - 40,355

1983, Kurt Wabbel Stadion, Halle,
Euro Championship qualifier, 1-2 - 18,000

1985, Hampden Park, Glasgow,
Friendly, 0-0 - 41,114

1990, Hampden Park, Glasgow,
Friendly, 0-1 - 21,868

Under manager Willie Ormond, Scotland's first game against East Germany [at Hampden Park in 1974] saw Graeme Souness of Middlesbrough and Celtic's John 'Dixie' Deans make their full international debuts.

Gary McAllister of Leicester City made his debut in the game against East Germany in 1990, which was in preparation for

Scotland going to the Italia 90 World Cup finals. It was also the third-last match to be played by the Communist state – Brazil then Belgium were their final two opponents. Thomas Doll who scored the winner against Scotland in 1990 made his last-ever international appearance in 1993 when he faced Scotland in a re-unified German side which also triumphed 1-0 in a friendly in Glasgow.

ENGLAND

England are Scotland's next door neighbour and are the 'senior partner' in a political union which also involves Wales and Northern Ireland. England is a larger country than Scotland – they are also more populous, powerful and wealthier than Scotland. By and large England even has a better climate than Scotland and on occasion some of their inhabitants [eg their media and their politicians] can be patronising and arrogant towards the Scots [if not the world]. So sometimes, just sometimes, England gets on Scotland's 'Thrupenny bits'. Big Style!

England also has the oldest Football Association on the planet [founded 1863] with the Scottish Football Association [the second-oldest] being founded in 1873. The Scotland – England international [first played in Glasgow in 1872] is also the oldest international football fixture in the world. Our football rivalry therefore goes back almost 150 years – our 'history' much longer. England are still often referred to as Scotland's 'Auld Enemy' even when it's just a game of footie.

Scotland have played England on over 100 occasions [with England now narrowly ahead in the series] and for decades many Scots regarded the fixture [ie the climax to the annual British Championship] as THE game on the calendar until we eventually realised that there were bigger pictures called the World Cup and European Championships.

Getting beaten by England at football remains a painful experience [especially scorelines like 2-7 in 1955 and 3-9 in 1961] but not as painful as being hung, drawn and quartered. Conversely defeating England at football will always be a coveted, pleasurable experience – especially at Wembley [eg 5-1 in 1928, 3-1 in 1949, 3-2 in 1967 when England were world champions and 2-1 in 1977 when the Caledonian horticulturists were a wee bit exuberant]. However, these landmark victories don't tackle issues such as poverty and inequality.

Bobby Moore, Alan Ball, Emlyn Hughes and Mick Channon were notable England players which Scotland fans loved to hate – possibly because we secretly admired them. As an aside, I still maintain that having the works of Charles Dickens and William Shakespeare inflicted upon us at secondary school was a much more unpleasant experience than anything Bobby Charlton, Jimmy Greaves or Ted 'Wembley ban' Croker ever did to us.

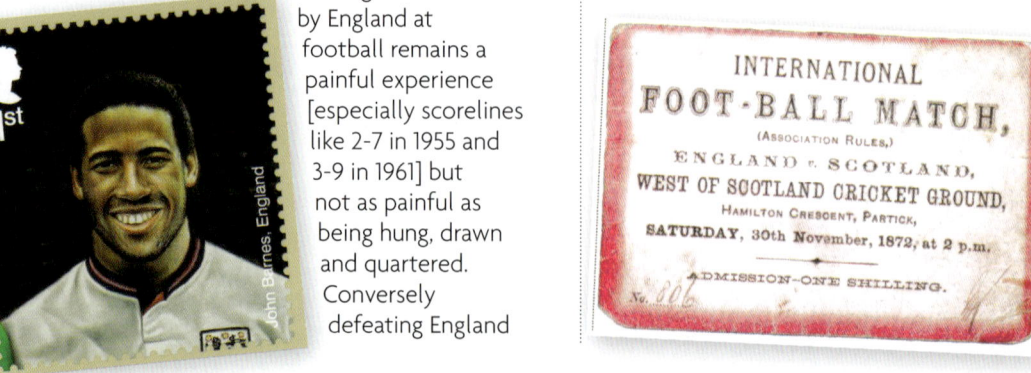

SCOTLAND GLORY, TEARS AND SOUVENIRS

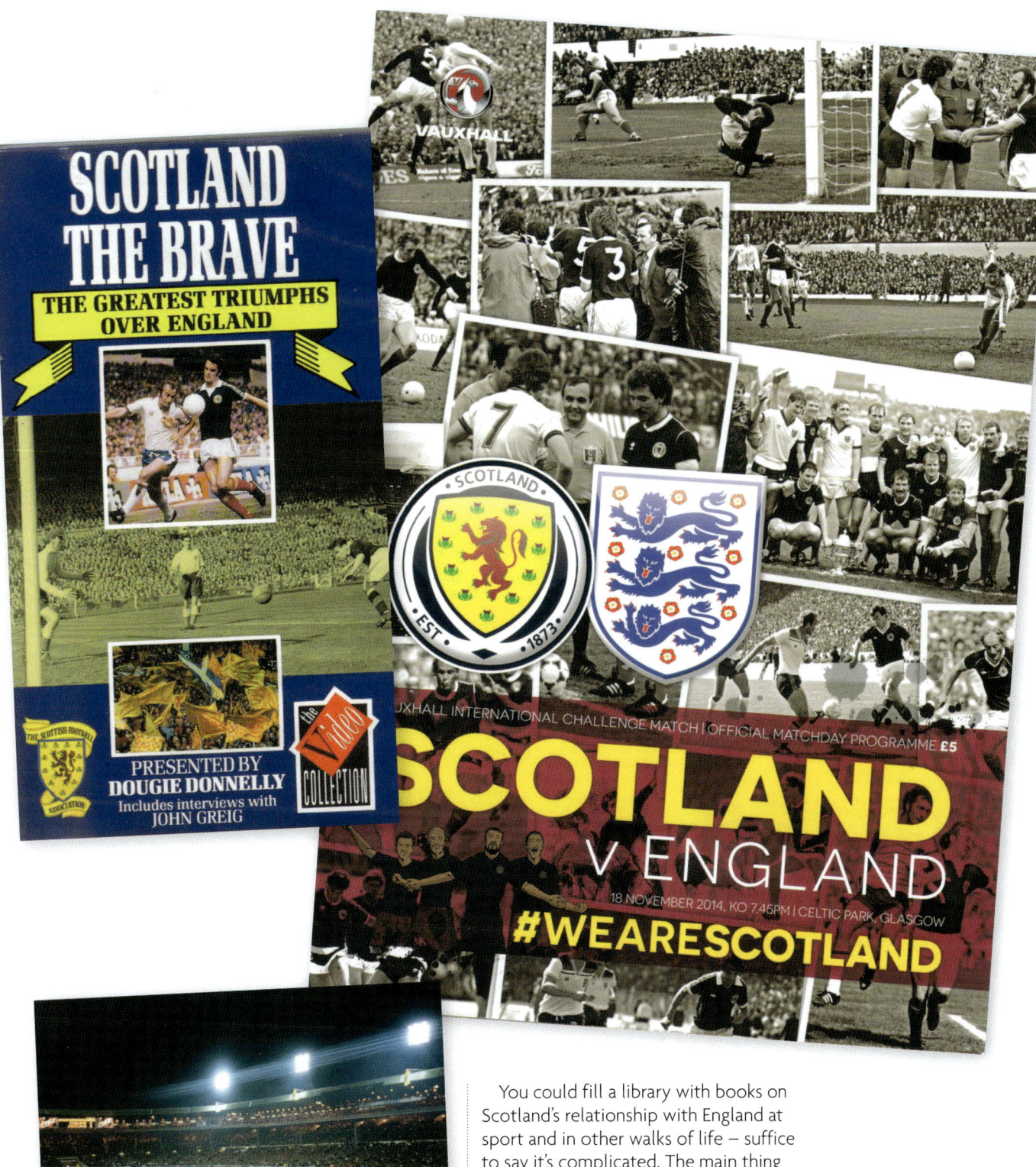

You could fill a library with books on Scotland's relationship with England at sport and in other walks of life – suffice to say it's complicated. The main thing is to keep a sense of perspective and for both of us to recognise just how important it is that neighbours should also be friends. There, I said it....

FANZINES

From a popular culture perspective several good things came out of the 1980s – Kajagoogoo and Beadle's About are two examples that weren't but football fanzines most certainly were. Thanks to fanzines, supporters now had an outlet [which was largely uncensored] for anger, disappointment, joy, ideas, and self-effacing humour.

Right at the forefront of the fanzine revolution in Scotland was the Edinburgh-produced *The Absolute Game* [*TAG*] which first appeared in late 1986. *TAG* [a black and white typewritten masterpiece] was about Scottish football in general but the national team usually rated a big mention. Serious issues such as supporter ID cards and stadium overcrowding were covered and around 60 issues were produced until its demise in 2002.

Alotta Balls [1987 to 1992] was a West of Scotland equivalent of *TAG* only not as 'highbrow'. Indeed, *Alotta Balls* prided itself on its puerile humour, including a spoof advert in 1990 for 'Ally-Mo' condoms as protection against World Cup Willie. Ally-Mo being an abbreviation for Scotland strikers Ally McCoist and Mo Johnston.

Two fanzines which were solely dedicated to the exploits of the national side were *Que Sera Sera* [late 1990s] and *Haggis Supper* [1999 to 2002]. *Haggis Supper* was produced by Scotland supporters 'operating behind enemy lines' [ie they lived and worked in London] and one of their campaigns was in support of Scotland and Ireland's joint bid to host the finals of Euro 2008 which unfortunately proved unsuccessful.

Fast forward to 2014 and attempting to buck the online trend there is *Scotland Epistles, Bullshit & Thistles*. The plan was that *Scotland Epistles* [a glossy, full colour, historian come optimist publication] would be produced in tandem with a successful Euro 2016 qualifying campaign. The best laid plans etc etc. Occasionally the editor dares to dream of selling a Scotland World Cup special issue outside the Kremlin in 2018 and the Doha Tower, Qatar in 2022. However, he knows it is wrong to think such things and so he tightens his barbed-wire cilice and goes back to sending 'begging emails' to potential advertisers.

SCOTLAND GLORY, TEARS AND SOUVENIRS

FATHERS & SONS, WEE BROTHERS AND THE OCCASIONAL NEPHEW TOO

One of the hardest things to do in life is follow in your father's footsteps particularly in the world of football. You would think it would be easy, after all there's your Dad out kicking a ball with you in the back garden before you're even knee high to a grasshopper and he knows all the moves but do you make it as a world superstar and become a Scottish internationalist? Scotland legends Dave Mackay, Kenny Dalglish and Gordon Strachan all had footballing sons who never came close to reaching the peaks of their famous fathers.

Some, however, do manage to make an impact and among them was Ronnie Simpson. His father Jimmy played centre-half for Rangers from 1927 to 1940 winning five League and four Scottish Cup medals. He would play for Scotland on 15 occasions and captained them 13 times including two wins against England in 1935 and 1937. It took a very long and winding road for Ronnie to don the yellow goalkeeper jersey of Scotland. Starting off just after the Second World War at Queen's Park, Ronnie actually represented Great Britain at football in the 1948 London Olympics but he would then move to Newcastle United in the 50s winning the FA Cup twice, before heading back north to play for Hibs and finally Celtic.

Ronnie was first capped in April '67 at the not so tender age of 36 years and 196 days making him the oldest player to make his debut for Scotland. The game was of course, the famous 3-2 victory at Wembley against England and a few weeks later Ronnie was to write himself further into the history books as part of the famous Lisbon Lions Celtic team that won the European Cup. Ronnie would win five caps in total.

Scot Gemmill or to give him his full name; Scotland Gemmill was always going to struggle to step out of his father's shadow. His father Archie, after all, scored one of the most iconic of Scotland goals at the World Cup finals in Argentina '78, gained 43 caps [between 1971 and 1981], netted eight goals in total and captained Scotland on 23 occasions. Scot would gain only 26 caps and perhaps had a frustrating Scotland career as he was in and out of the team over an eight-year period from 1995 to 2003. He would also make the squads for both Euro '96 and World Cup '98 finals but would not get any playing time.

There have been a few brothers to play with Scotland too with perhaps Eddie and Frank Gray among the most successful. Eddie was a big part of the great Leeds United team of the 60s and 70s along with several other Scots including Billy Bremner, Peter Lorimer and latterly his wee brother Frank. Eddie was voted as the third greatest Leeds United player of all time but he would only gain 12 caps in total [1969-1977], due to Scotland's plethora of wing talent around the time including Jimmy Johnstone, Charlie Cooke and others. His young brother Frank played in the less sexy position of left back but was able to perform as a solid player for Scotland on 32 occasions including three games at the 1982 World Cup finals.

Other capped brothers include John and Alan Hansen [Partick Thistle and Liverpool respectively] plus Derek and Barry Ferguson [Rangers and Rangers/Blackburn Rovers]. However, they would never play together at international level unlike the Shaw and Caldwell brothers.

Davie Shaw of Hibernian and Jock 'Tiger' Shaw of Rangers were both capped against Switzerland in a

post-war 3-1 friendly win at Hampden in May, 1946 in front of a crowd of 111,899. This would be their only game together and this feat was not repeated until Gary and Steven Caldwell [aka The Chuckle Brothers] played together against Moldova in October, 2004 in a World Cup qualifier in Chisinau. The game would end 1-1 but in their only other starting appearance together they shipped four goals without reply to Norway in August 2009, in another dismal World Cup campaign.

Midfield man Craig Burley and former Scotland defender and manager George Burley are related too with Craig being George's nephew. Craig would gain 46 caps between 1995 and 2003 scoring three times including a memorable one against Norway in the 1998 World Cup finals; as for George he would gain only 11 caps [1979-1982] and a whole lot of notoriety for his time as manager [2008-2009].

FKS STICKERS

Ah, the summer of 1974 and as Scotland prepared to take its rightful place among the football elite at the West Germany World Cup finals I was enthralled by my first sticker set. Prior to this there may have been sets from Panini via Top Sellers or FKS sets available in the UK but none had reached the north of Glasgow until the FKS World Cup set landed at my local newsagents in 1974.

Year after year I had collected each new footballer set but this time it was different; no more duff players from Clyde, East Fife or Arbroath, here was the Johan Cruyffs, the Gerd Mullers and the Rivelinos as well as players from exotic countries like Haiti and our future opponents Zaire.

I collected like I always collected the footballer cards each winter, scraping pennies together as voraciously as I could including scouring the wastelands of the Milton district of Glasgow for empty ginger bottles [ie soft drink bottles with a returnable deposit]; all to get my hands on that vital packet of stickers and hope to God I didn't get another of that clown Jan Tomaszewski.

As for the Scotland players – the tough-looking, straight out of *The Sweeney* images included most of the World Cup big hitters including Bremner, Dalglish, Law, Jordan and Lorimer but there was also added a few who

SCOTLAND GLORY, TEARS AND SOUVENIRS

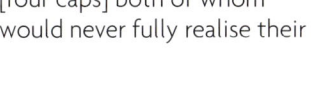

never got to Germany. Ally Hunter of Celtic [four caps] had been the goalkeeper the night Scotland qualified but had conceded a goal that he should have done better with, so was discarded for David Harvey. There were stickers too of Celtic's George Connelly [two caps] and Jimmy Smith of Newcastle United [four caps] both of whom would never fully realise their potential. Connelly was lost to football following mental health issues and Smith to injury at the age of 29.

There were also included within the associated album some players that had once played with such glamorous clubs as Montrose, Airdrie and even Junior Scottish side Bonnyrigg Rose. These were of course members of the Australian squad.

FKS would release sets for both the 1978 and '82 World Cups but sadly I had moved on from sticker collecting to vinyl record buying and it is only now that occasionally I sit with my 1978 FKS sticker album with a glue stick attempting to complete the set. As for the 1982 set which is probably the best looking set, I am as yet albumless but have some glue set aside for the grand day the album is acquired – probably from the great God ebay. Sad but true.

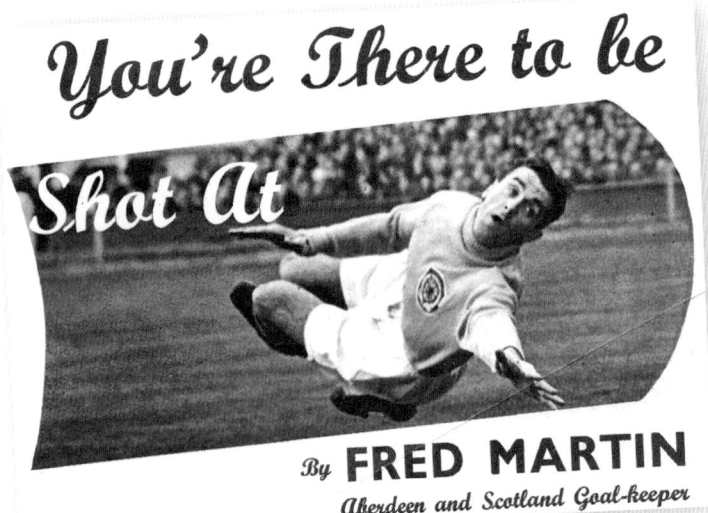

You're There to be Shot At
By FRED MARTIN
Aberdeen and Scotland Goal-keeper

GOALKEEPERS' GRAVEYARD

A trip to Wembley to see Scotland take on the old enemy was for many years the ultimate dream for countless young Scots boys growing up but it was also known as a place of nightmares for some Scottish goalkeepers; leaving their international career in tatters and being forever cursed by their fellow countrymen.

Although for the first Scotland goalie to let in a barrowload this was not the case. Jack Harkness of Hearts shipped five goals in a 5-2 defeat at Wembley in 1930 but would go on to make a few more appearances in a Scotland jersey. Perhaps in Jack's favour was the fact that two years earlier he had stood between the sticks as part of the Wembley Wizards team that had delivered a 5-1 thrashing to England and indeed had been part of the side that had beaten England at Hampden in 1929 too.

However, there is one mitigating factor in his return to a Scotland team after the Wembley fiasco and that was the tragic death of Celtic goalkeeper John Thomson who had been his immediate replacement the month following that game. Thomson would play four times for Scotland with only one goal conceded and he too would taste victory over England at Hampden in March, 1931. Although neither Thomson, nor any Celtic or Rangers players took part in Scotland's European tour in the summer of 1931 [with John Jackson of Partick Thistle deputising], there is no doubt had he not lost his life following an accidental collision with Sam English of Rangers on 5th September 1931, that Thomson would have won many more caps.

If there was a good time to lose heavily to England at Wembley and not suffer the ignominy and cutting humour that would follow these goalkeepers around, it would be during the Second World War. Joe Crozier of Brentford would be the fortunate 'unfortunate' goalkeeper in this era. Joe would be in goals for the 6-2 defeat at Wembley in February 1994 and even worse three months before was part of the Scotland side that lost 8-0 at Maine Road, Manchester although contemporary reports at the time suggested only Crozier's courage kept the English goal-tally down to single figures.

Walking off the pitch in the sweltering heat of the Sankt Jakob Stadion in Switzerland on 19th June 1954 after suffering a humiliating 7-0 defeat to Uruguay in the World Cup finals, Aberdeen goalkeeper Fred Martin must have thought it couldn't get much worse than this. The 1954 finals did have other high scores with Hungary posting wins of 9-0 v South Korea, and 8-3 against the team that would beat them in the final; West Germany. Turkey also won 7-0 v South Korea and even in the knockout stages there were scores such as Austria 7 Switzerland 5 followed by West Germany 6 Austria 1 in the semi-finals.

Joe Crozier

As for Martin and co. it was to get worse ten months later, in April 1955, as they lost 7-2 to England at Wembley. Fred was blamed for fumbling two of England's early goals with the Scots 3-1 down after 25 minutes. Dennis Wilshaw of Wolves would hit four that day but it was 40 year old Stanley Matthews who won all the plaudits for his wing play. As for Martin he would never play again for Scotland,

SCOTLAND GLORY, TEARS AND SOUVENIRS

however he was not the only player who had suffered these two seven-goal defeats; Preston North End's Willie Cunningham and Tommy Docherty as well as Partick Thistle's Jimmy Davidson and Johnny McKenzie also suffered the same fate with only Docherty ever pulling on a Scotland jersey again.

And so to Hapless Haffey. Celtic goalkeeper Frank Haffey would only play twice for Scotland and both times against England. In the first game at Hampden in 1960 it ended in a 1-1 draw with Bobby Charlton scoring one penalty for England and missing another – twice! Haffey was lucky at Charlton's second penalty as the ref blew his whistle for encroachment which was just as well as Frank literally fumbled the ball into the net. One year later and he was not so lucky.

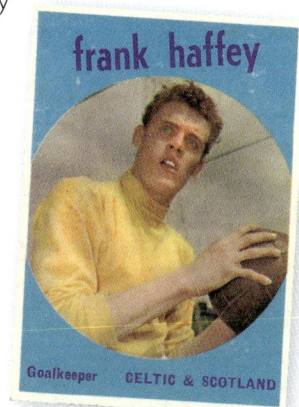

Wembley '61 and Scotland were to lose 9-3 with Haffey looking poor at quite a few of the goals. Frank was actually third choice that day but injuries to Bill Brown of Tottenham and Lawrie Leslie of Airdrie saw him take his place between the sticks. Haffey would emigrate to Australia a few years later, in a move which many saw as truly fitting for his criminal goalkeeping that day in April 1961.

Stewart Kennedy would be the final entry into our Hall of Shame and yet it had all been going well for the Rangers goalie in the yellow jersey of Scotland up until May 1975. Stewart had played in four internationals, had kept clean sheets in two games and had yet to be on a losing side. However, his trip to Wembley was to see him be vilified in his homeland for years to come as Scotland lost 5-1. In fairness to Kennedy the defence in front of him were not much better. A week later and Jim Brown of Sheffield United was brought in to the side for his only international appearance – a Euro qualifier against Romania. Stewart, alas, never played again for Scotland but after leaving Rangers in 1980 he would play on past his 40th birthday amassing over 300 games with Forfar Athletic, so I think he still enjoyed the game.

Wembley hasn't always been a Scotland goalie's nightmare but there are only three who have kept a clean sheet there. The first was Dave Cumming of Middlesbrough in his only international which took place in April, 1938 as Scotland won 1-0 thanks to a goal from Tommy Walker of Hearts. The much and unfairly maligned Alan Rough of Partick Thistle also achieved this feat in the 1981 victory where John Robertson of Nottingham Forest netted the winner from the penalty spot. Rough would also play in the 2-1 win in 1977 as well as a 2-1 defeat in 1986 but as most Thistle fans will point out by then he was a Hibernian player.

The final goalie not to concede was Neil Sullivan of Wimbledon as Scotland triumphed 1-0 in the second leg of the Euro play-off against England in November, 1999. Jerry Dawson of Rangers would also take part in a 0-0 draw during the war period in an unofficial match in 1942 which also deserves a mention given how dominant England were in that era.

Finally, often seen as the greatest performance by a Scotland goalkeeper was Jimmy Cowan's in the 1949 match at Wembley which saw Scotland win 3-1. Most of the praise that day was heaped upon Cowan of Greenock Morton who had only agreed to travel to London on the insistence of his seriously ailing mother. He did his Mum, and indeed the whole country, proud that day.

123

HAMPDEN PARK

Hampden Park [aka Xanadu] is the national football stadium for Scotland and is situated in the Mount Florida area of south-east Glasgow. Technically Hampden is also home to Scotland's oldest football club Queen's Park – a cuckoo in their own nest who celebrated their 150th birthday in July 2017.

The Mount Florida location is the third site in the vicinity to contain a stadium named Hampden – which incidentally takes its name from John Hampden, a Parliamentarian from the 17th century English civil war. The stadium on the current site was completely rebuilt in the 1990s [albeit in much the same style as the old stadium] and was officially inaugurated in March 2000 with a visit from world champions France [who won 2-0]. As such, our national stadium, which has a capacity of around 52,000 is actually new, third Hampden – are you still with me? It also contains a marvellous Museum of Football that is well worth a visit.

For the baby-boomers generation, old third Hampden is the stadium that we still dream about. It opened in 1903 and with the addition of a new stand atop the north enclosure [ie terracing] in 1937, it was for a time the largest football stadium in the world with an official capacity of 150,000 until usurped by Rio's Maracana stadium in 1950. Somewhat surprisingly, floodlights [four large pylons] weren't installed until 1961.

On 17th April 1937 the Scotland v England match attracted a crowd of 149,547, the highest official attendance ever recorded in the UK although it's reckoned that at least another 10,000 entered the stadium after smashing down gates. Scotland came back from 1-0 down to win that match 3-1. Yessss!

For many youngsters it was something of a rite of passage to attend a big match at Hampden outwith the company of an adult and to experience with your teenage peers, the magical assault on all your senses. Games played in glorious technicolour, the deafening roar of the crowd, the hugging of total strangers in a macho-bonding sort of a way together with the tasting of dust from the terracings when Scotland scored and the crowd morphed into dancing dervishes. And then there was the special aroma – a magical fusion of fast food, stale alcohol, cigarette smoke and urine. Not even Chanel's finest perfumers could bottle anything that comes remotely close to this veritable elixir.

Anyway, Hampden Park went on to set all sorts of attendance records at club and country level. However, as safety standards improved, the capacity shrunk [135,000 in 1949, 81,000 in 1977] and the truth was that by the late 1960s the grand old lady of Mount Florida was in serious need of a facelift. Ultimately she got a new body altogether but it's a body with many seats too distant from the action. In short, the sightlines are poor and the rain [it does occasionally rain in Glasgow] can still reach a number of the spectators.

In its current guise, Hampden's last big UEFA hurrah could be as a co-host of the 2020 European Championships. As a traditionalist [aka a Glaswegian who likes having the national stadium on his doorstep] I would hope for a re-modelling exercise in the future as opposed to a re-build somewhere else in Scotland or worse still a permanent re-location to Murrayfield rugby stadium in Edinburgh!

It goes without saying however that over the years Hampden has played host

SCOTLAND GLORY, TEARS AND SOUVENIRS

to some memorable games of football [as well as some no bad rock concerts]. Joy and despair, satisfaction and frustration, laughter and tears – they've all been experienced to varying degrees. One last thing to remember then about the national stadium is that in Hampden Park, no-one can hear you scream... unless you're attending a Queen's Park home game.

HOME VENUES [OTHER THAN HAMPDEN]

Since 1990 for a variety of reasons, but mostly due to renovation/reconstruction work at Hampden, Scotland have played over 30 full internationals at half a dozen other stadia located throughout the country. The super six are Rugby Park, Kilmarnock; Celtic Park and Ibrox Park, Glasgow; Easter Road Stadium and Tynecastle Stadium, Edinburgh; plus Pittodrie Stadium, Aberdeen. The associated opposition have included the defunct [USSR], the re-born [Estonia], the exotic [Trinidad and Tobago], the Teutonic [Austria], the ancient [Egypt and the Faroes – sorry] and that rugby-mad country where they filmed *Lord of the Rings* [New Zealand].

Incidentally, between May 1997 and October 1998 half a dozen of Simon Donnelly's ten Scottish caps were won at the aforementioned six stadia. Curiously enough though, the Celtic striker never appeared for Scotland at Hampden.

Anyway, the obvious omissions in the said list of venues are Murrayfield rugby stadium in Edinburgh and the city of Dundee! It's a shame that Scotland's fourth city doesn't have a stadium which merits the hosting of a full Scotland international match. From a perverse perspective, why should Taysiders escape the pain?

The record books reveal however that Dens Park, Dundee did stage three Scotland games in 1904, 1908 and 1936 [all versus Wales] whilst Carolina Port, Dundee got the 1896 Scotland-Wales gig which we won 4-0 with no less than nine Scottish players making their debuts! Some other one-game wonders from way back include Fir Park, Motherwell [Wales 1898]; Cappielow Park, Greenock [Wales 1902]; Love Street, Paisley [Wales 1923]; plus the Maryhill Pleasuredrome [aka Firhill Stadium, Glasgow] [Ireland 1928].

IRELAND/NORTHERN IRELAND

Over the centuries there has been much to-ing and fro-ing of the Scots and Irish peoples across the water to one another's countries, mostly in a peaceful manner – it is only 110 miles, as the crow flies, from Glasgow to Belfast. Indeed the history of Irish soccer arguably began in 1878 when John McAlery, a Belfast merchant, saw his first organised football match when he was on his honeymoon in Edinburgh. So impressed was he that he formed Cliftonville FC, the first known football club in Ireland. It is not known if Mrs McAlery was equally impressed.

The Belfast-based Irish Football Association [IFA] were the fourth such association to be created – in 1880. As such, Ireland [as they were then known] provided Scotland with their third, different, opponents [our game no. 21] when both sides met at Ballynafeigh Park in Belfast in the inaugural match of the British Championships in 1884. Other regular early venues included Solitude Park, Belfast and Dalymount Park, Dublin before Belfast's Windsor Park took over as the norm.

Ireland was partitioned in 1921 with the IFA becoming the governing body for the successor team – Northern Ireland. However for a time and just to confuse matters there were two international teams calling themselves Ireland and some footballers played for both sides. In 1953 though FIFA ruled neither team could be referred to simply as Ireland, decreeing that the Dublin-based Football Association of Ireland team be officially designated as the Republic of Ireland, while the IFA team was to become Northern Ireland. [See also Republic of Ireland.]

Scotland have played Ireland/Northern Ireland on almost 100 occasions [mostly British Championship matches] with Scotland well ahead in the series which includes some big victories in the 'early days' such as 11-0, 10-2, 9-1, 8-2 and 7-2. It goes without saying however that the Irish have produced some great individual footballers who at some time have either frustrated or tormented the hell out of Scotland, such as Danny Blanchflower, Billy Bingham, George Best, Derek Dougan, Pat Jennings and Norman Whiteside.

It's also a wee bit annoying [yes I'm green with envy] that on three occasions Northern Ireland have progressed beyond the group stages at the finals of major competitions [1958 and 1982 World Cups and 2016 European Championships] – a trick Scotland haven't managed once!

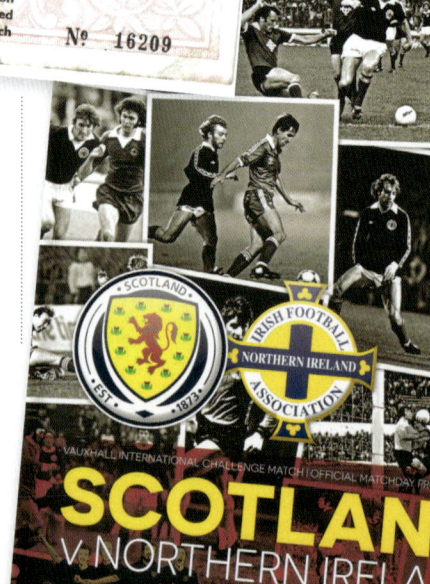

SCOTLAND GLORY, TEARS AND SOUVENIRS

revered by the Tartan Army although not so much loved down in Wales.

His first Scotland cap would come just four days after he played for Leeds United against AC Milan in the European Cup-Winners' Cup Final in May 1973. Joe would come on for Lou Macari as part of a double substitution in the 70th minute of the game against England at Wembley. Scotland

JOE JORDAN

On 26th September, 1973 three heroes emerged from Scotland's decisive victory over Czechoslovakia none of whose lustre will dull with time in the eyes of many a Scotland fan.

First there was manager Willie Ormond, who after a difficult year or so in charge had finally got it right. After a run of five defeats in six games, he took Scotland to the World Cup for the first time in sixteen years.

Then there were the two goalscorers that night – Jim Holton and Joe Jordan. Holton had a brief Scotland career of only fifteen games but his physicality and presence in the heart of defence that would terrify many a centre forward endeared him to Scotland and Manchester United fans.

As for Jordan, he was built of the same stuff as Holton [girders perhaps] and would eventually score for Scotland in three World Cups and is

Flashback MAGIC

Match-winning sub

Date: September 26, 1973
Match: World Cup qualifier
Result: Scotland 2 Czechoslovakia 1
Venue: Hampden Park

Joe Jordan heads powerfully home for the winning goal as Willie Ormond's team book their place in the 1974 World Cup Finals in West Germany. Big Jim Holton had scored Scotland's first, but it wasn't until Jordan appeared as a substitute for Kenny Dalglish that they settled the match.

were to lose 1-0 thanks to a Martin Peters goal. The other sub was Colin Stein then of Coventry who was making his 21st and final international appearance.

Joe was initially left out of the squad for summer friendlies that year in favour of Stein but injury to the Coventry man would see Jordan make a sub's appearance against Switzerland in Berne and then play from the start of the SFA Centenary Celebration match against Brazil at Hampden in June 1973.

Joe was seen as the solution to Scotland's problems, they needed a target man to head knockdowns, to hold the ball up and do all the selfless running for the striker. Kenny Dalglish fitted into the Scotland side as a midfield player at the time; the striker role was to be centred on Derek Parlane of Rangers.

Parlane was to fall out of favour however and by that wondrous September night, the front pair would be Dalglish and Denis Law. Joe would, of course, come on as a sub for Dalglish in the 63rd minute and by the 75th would begin his legendary status with the goal that put Scotland on the plane for West Germany in the summer of 74.

Joe's next Scotland goal would come in the game against England at Hampden in May 1974. This game would be seen by many as Jimmy Johnstone's finest in a Scotland shirt but it was Joe who scored the opener, although if truth be told it was really Mike Pejic of Stoke City who got the last touch. As far as I know Pejic has never tried to claim it as his own and I don't think he is ever likely to. No such luck beheld Colin Todd as he was very much credited for an own goal in the game to give Scotland the 2-0 win.

Next stop in legendary status was in the German city of Dortmund where his knockdown from a free kick would be placed perfectly for Peter Lorimer to score Scotland's first goal against Zaire. It was Jordan who would score the second as the African defence

SCOTLAND GLORY, TEARS AND SOUVENIRS

stood stalk still to allow him a free header which the keeper stumbled into the net.

There would be no goals for Joe against Brazil but he would score a very late equaliser against Yugoslavia that ultimately would not be enough for Scotland to progress but it would be enough to see them leave the tournament as the only undefeated team in the competition.

It's hard to believe but Joe wasn't an automatic selection for Scotland after the World Cup finals but he would always seem to get back in there for the big matches. May, 1976 would see him bustling down the wing at Hampden against England with one touch, moving away from Roy McFarland before looking up and finding Kenny Dalglish with the perfect pass. 2-1 Scotland.

Fast forward to 21st September, 1977 and almost four years to the day Scotland face Czechoslovakia in a vital World Cup qualifier once more. Big Joe rattles in the first one from a corner and then for the second goal it is the Czechs that are truly rattled as they struggle to get a cross from Willie Johnston under control. Two defenders and the goalie all try to get the ball but as Jordan gets in among the mix chaos abounds and the Czech keeper loses the ball for an easy tap-in for Asa Hartford. Scotland would win 3-1. Next up Wales at Anfield.

Lots of Scots love Joe Jordan but I don't think our idolisation of him is shared in Wales where he is seen as the man that cheated them out of a place in the World Cup finals in Argentina. As for Joe, he still won't admit he [and not the Welsh defender] handled it but as far as I'm concerned . . . he might have. Anyway Scotland were awarded a penalty and you know the rest.

And so to Argentina. I remember in the months leading up to the World Cup there was an interview with the Peru team and when asked who they feared most their reply was 'Hoe Hordan.' Oh how we laughed until we cried in June 1978.

Joe would of course, score for Scotland against Peru and we all thought Ally MacLeod's bandwagon was on course until the wheels fell aff into the second half with Masson missing a penalty and then Cubillas showing his class.

Joe would of course be on hand to knock down the ball to Dalglish to score against the Dutch in the legendary game that saw Scotland go out of 1978 with their heads held a wee bit higher.

Joe would gain 52 caps in total [scoring 11 goals] and 47 of them would be won playing alongside Dalglish. No wonder they had such a good understanding.

Jock Stein used Joe more sparingly after taking over the side in 1979 but when he needed his power, his running and his goals, Joe would show up. Joe played in the side that won at Wembley in 1981 and in yet another vital September World Cup qualifier, in 1981, it was Joe who drew first blood. Scotland would win 2-0 against Sweden with a John Robertson penalty adding to Joe's piledriver of a header.

Spain 1982. Joe was by this time 30 years old and was plying his trade with old foes AC Milan. He was named in Stein's squad but was not expected to play a big part in the World Cup with younger players such as Steve Archibald and Alan Brazil available for selection and indeed he would be left out of the first two group games. However, with a win needed against the USSR, Joe was once more called upon to make his mark and Joe didn't let big Jock or Scotland down.

Fifteen minutes into the match and Archibald gets hold of a loose ball hitting it past the last defender and Jordan runs onto it to unleash a left foot shot past the advancing Dasaev in the Soviet goal.

Scotland would blunder in the second half and with us 2-1 down, Joe was replaced by Alan Brazil. A last-gasp goal by Graeme Souness was not enough and so Joe's Scotland career ended with our exit from the World Cup.

Joe rates as my all-time Scotland hero in many ways and as we struggle to qualify for a tournament nowadays it's hard to believe there's a Scotsman who has scored at three different World Cups. Over a thousand words on Joe and I never mentioned his missing teeth or nickname, 'Jaws'. Damn, I was so close there.

KICK-OFF TIMES AND MATCH DAYS

7.45pm on a Saturday; 7.45pm on a Sunday; 5.00pm on a Saturday; 7.45pm on a Monday; and 7.45pm on a Thursday – these were the days and kick-off times of Scotland's five home matches in the 2018 World Cup qualifying campaign. It's all part of FIFA [and UEFA's] 'week of football' and their homage to the great God *TelevisionCoverageIsAllThatReallyMatters*.

It's a week of football that therefore doesn't give a damn about work/childcare/ travel arrangements of supporters.

Now both of us authors live within three miles of Hampden Park – indeed David Stuart can see the East Stand from his front garden – so it's no real problem for us or for many fellow Weegies and our near neighbours. However, what about those supporters who don't reside within the Greater Glasgow area [eg loyal footsoldiers from the likes of Fife, Tayside and Grampian as well as the Highlands and Islands] for whom some of these dates and times are just totally unsuitable. Indeed there are also those supporters who live outwith Scotland for whom being mucked about with dates and times presents even more of a logistical nightmare.

From the late 1960s right through to the early years of the 21st century things were much more regimented and consistent with the vast majority of internationals being played either on a Saturday at 3.00pm or a Wednesday at 8.00pm and that is the pattern that I suspect most of us would like to return to.

Looking back at the 1950s however there were many weird and wonderful Wednesday internationals with kick-off times such as 2.15pm, 2.30pm, 2.45pm, 6.30pm and 6.45pm. An absence of floodlights might have had something to do with it but despite work commitments, inclement weather, etc., some of the attendances were pretty damn impressive.

On Wednesday 1st November 1950, a 2.45pm kick-off did not deter 83,142 spectators from turning up to see Scotland beat Ireland 6-1 in the British Championship. Incidentally, Dundee's Billy Steel got four of the goals whilst Celtic's John McPhail netted the opening brace. Six weeks later on Wednesday 13th December and despite a 2.15pm kick-off just twelve days before Christmas, our true love [Scotland] were sent a crowd of 68,000 for a friendly match against Austria. One can only speculate as to just how many sick-lines and phoney Granny's funeral excuses these two matches generated.

It's just possible however that if the SFA arranged a game with a kick-off time to coincide with sunrise a fair number of us would still trundle along to the national stadium just for the sheer novelty of it all. A coffee, a roll and square sausage and an 8.00am charity match against Tahiti [former Oceania champions by the way] – it sounds good to me!

KIRIN CUP, ETC.

Since 1992 the Kirin Brewing Company have regularly organised an annual international football competition involving the hosts Japan and usually two other invited teams. Scotland have been invited to participate in the Kirin Cup on two occasions and groundhoppers should note that although Scotland never made it to the 2002 World Cup finals in Japan and South Korea, thanks to Kirin and the Japan Football Association we got to play in three of the host stadia for that tournament as well as other interesting arenas.

On 21st May 1995 Scotland drew 0-0 with Japan in the Big Arch Stadium, Hiroshima in the opening game with manager Craig Brown giving debut caps to five players – Brian Martin and Paul Lambert [both Motherwell], Scot Gemmill [Nottingham Forest], Craig Burley [Chelsea] and Paul Bernard [Oldham Athletic].

Three days later Scotland travelled to the Prefectural Sports Park in Toyama where they defeated Ecuador 2-1 with the goals coming from John Robertson of Hearts and debutant Steven Crawford of Raith Rovers. Japan then beat Ecuador 3-0 in the Olympic Stadium, Tokyo to win the competition on goal difference.

In May 2006 Walter Smith's Scotland did the unthinkable however and won an international competition outwith our own continent. It would have been preferable if this achievement had taken place at Argentina 78 but beggars can't be choosers.

The opening match saw Japan surprisingly lose 1-2 to Bulgaria in the Nagai Stadium, Osaka. Scotland then demolished Bulgaria 5-1 in the Kobe Wing Stadium, Kobe – a 2002 World Cup finals venue. Kris Boyd then Chris Burke [both Rangers and both making their full international debuts] netted doubles either side of a goal from Everton's James McFadden. In the final match goalkeeper Neil Alexander [then of Cardiff City] kept a clean sheet as Scotland and Japan drew 0-0 in the Saitama Stadium, Saitama – another 2002 World Cup finals venue. Scotland had won the Kirin Cup and commemorative limited edition replica jerseys were duly produced. Yes really.

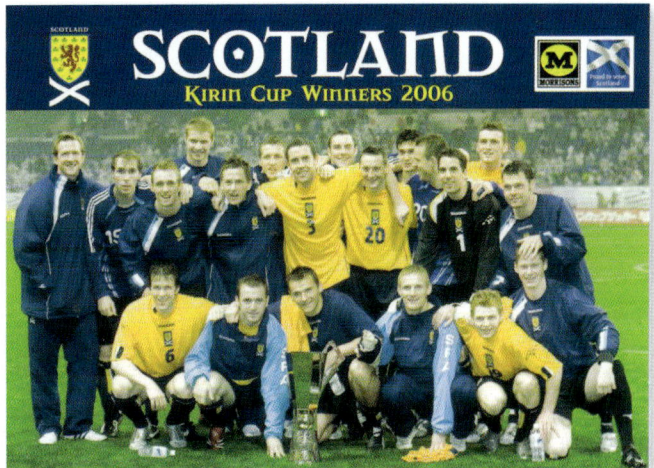

Scotland, under the management of George Burley, also played Japan in a friendly match in 2009 losing 0-2 in the Nissan Stadium, Yokohama – the venue for the 2002 World Cup Final between Brazil and Germany.

Now surely it's about time the SFA did the decent thing and invited Japan over to Scotland either for a friendly match or to take part in some contrived triangular tournament.

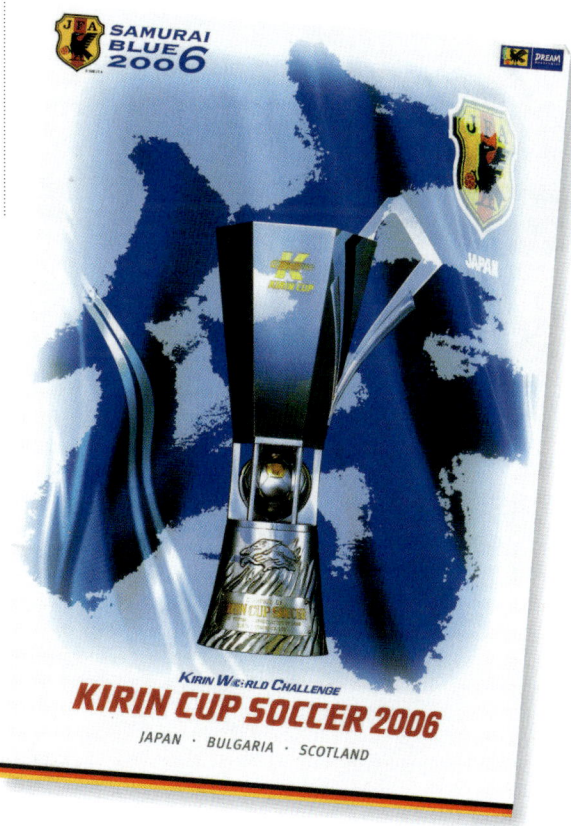

LAW, DENIS – THE 30 GOALS

Only two Scotland players have ever reached the 30-goal mark for Scotland; Denis Law and Kenny Dalglish. Denis was of course first to achieve it hitting the mark in 55 games. Here's how he did it.

Goal #1 came on his debut at the age of 18 at Ninian Park, Cardiff in a Home International match against Wales on 18th October, 1958. Scotland won 3-0 with Denis scoring the second in the 70th minute. Denis was a Huddersfield Town player at the time.

Goal #2 came on 4th May, 1960 in his eighth Scotland game in a friendly v Poland at Hampden. Scotland lost 3-2. Law scored in the 23rd minute. Denis had moved to Manchester City by this time.

Goal #3 was in 5-2 defeat of Northern Ireland in a British Championship match at Hampden on 9th November, 1960. Denis had opened the scoring in eight minutes.

Goals #4 and #5 came in a memorable World Cup qualifier 3-2 win against Czechoslovakia in 1961 with the Scots going behind twice but Denis's double in the 62nd and 83rd minutes [plus Ian St. John's 21st minute goal] did the trick. These would be Denis' only goals scored for Scotland as a Turin player.

Goal #6 was once more in the Home Internationals as Scotland won 3-2 down at Ninian Park, Cardiff in October 1962. Denis had scored the second goal for Scotland and of course was now a Manchester United player.

Goals #7, 8, 9 and 10 came in the one Home International at Hampden on 7th November, 1962 against a luckless Northern Ireland as Denis unleashed a four-goal blitz in a 5-1 win.

Goals #11 and 12 are a bit controversial as Scotland beat Austria 4-1 in a stormy match at Hampden in a so called friendly on 8th May, 1963. The controversy is that the match was abandoned as referee Finney of England felt a full scale riot among players would have happened had the game continued but the goal and result (4-1) stands as such. However, in fairness to Denis in January, 1961 he once scored a double hat-trick against Luton Town only for the game to be abandoned in the 62nd minute. The goals were expunged from the records and worse was to follow as Manchester City lost the replay.

SCOTLAND GLORY, TEARS AND SOUVENIRS

Goals #13, 14, and 15 all came as Denis scored a hat-trick against minnows Norway in a friendly in Bergen on 4th June 1963. Sadly, the 'minnows' scored four that day! Yep, 'William Wallace, Robert the Bruce, Mary Queen of Scots, Bonnie Prince Charlie and Harry Lauder we gave your boys one hell of a beating!'

Goal #16 came a week later as Scotland humbled Spain 6-2 in the Bernabeu in a friendly game. This would be one of five games in which Denis would be the captain of the side.

Goals #17, 18, 19 and 20 as Denis and Scotland got their revenge on Norway for that defeat five months earlier as they crushed the Norwegians 6-1 in a friendly at Hampden in November '63.

Goal #21 came as Denis completed a stunning year with 11 goals for Scotland. The last came against Wales at Hampden on 20th November as Scotland ran out 2-1 winners.

Goal #22 was the first goal of Scotland's 1966 World Cup qualifying campaign and came in two minutes against Finland at Hampden in a 3-1 win on 21st October, 1964.

Goal #23 came against the Auld Enemy at Wembley in April 1965 as Scotland came from 2-0 down to draw 2-2 with Denis netting the first of the comeback goals.

Goal #24 came on the campaign trail once more as the Scots fought out a tough 1-1 draw in Chorzow, Poland in May, 1965.

Goal#25 came once more against England in a seesaw British Championship match in April 1966 which Scotland lost 4-3. Denis describes his goal as his best for Scotland. It really is a classic header as he rises to power the ball into the net from a corner and is well worth seeing, as is the last-minute penalty that Scotland were denied as Law is pole-axed to the ground by Keith Newton.

Goal #26 was back where it all began at Ninian Park, Cardiff against Wales in October 1966 in a game that doubled up as a Euro qualifier and Home International with Denis equalising with four minutes to go.

Goal #27 came at Wembley as Denis finally scored a goal in a winning game against the Auld Enemy. This was of course the famous 1967 win as the Scots hammered the English 3-2 and like the Welsh game doubled as a Euro qualifier and Home International. Denis opened the scoring in the 27th minute.

Goal #28 came in a World qualifier against Austria at Hampden on 6th November, 1968 with Denis scoring an equaliser seven minutes

A great goal — by a great player. Denis Law scores Scotland's first goal in last season's game against Northern Ireland.

SCOTLAND GLORY, TEARS AND SOUVENIRS

into the match which Scotland would edge 2-1 with Billy Bremner scoring the other. Denis would play in the first game against West Germany in the World Cup qualifying group but was not played in either of the games against Cyprus. He was thus denied ample opportunity to rack up some more goals and didn't feature further in that campaign.

Goal #29 would come after a couple of years on hiatus, and as Man United's stock deteriorated with the departure of Sir Matt Busby, so did Denis's. However, on 26th April, 1972 Tommy Docherty brought Denis back from the wilderness and made him captain for a friendly against Peru. Denis repaid the Doc's faith by scoring the second in a 2-0 win. Incidentally, playing at Hampden that night would be architects of Scotland's 1978 doom Hector Chumpitaz and the talented Teofilo Cubillas. Remarkably Chumpitaz would return to Hampden in 1979 also, which ended in a 1-1 draw.

Goal #30 and his final would be a typically acrobatic effort as he scored against Northern Ireland in a Home International at Hampden on 20th May, 1972. Scotland would win 2-0 and although he would play another 11 times for Scotland ending with an appearance against Zaire at the 1974 World Cup finals; The Lawman never scored again.

LEVEIN, CRAIG

Dunfermline-born Craig Levein was appointed Scotland manager a month after the departure of George Burley in November 2009. Craig gained 16 caps for Scotland and probably should have won more but persistent injuries prevented the Hearts man from establishing himself as first choice centre-half for any great length of time, although he would play against Sweden in the 1990 World Cup finals.

His time as Scotland manager saw him make some choices and decisions that were deeply unpopular and in many ways failures, and which would eventually unseat him from the job as national coach.

It started well with a victory over the Czech Republic in a friendly at Hampden but a blank-score draw in the first of the Euro 2012 qualifiers in Lithuania where we seldom do well, was followed by an embarrassing victory over Liechtenstein where Stephen McManus's winner in the 97th didn't quite save our blushes. Levein also took James McFadden off at half-time which was not popular with the Tartan Army given the amount of times that his individual brilliance had dug us out of a hole. Sadly, this would be McFadden's last Scotland appearance as injury would blight his career thereafter.

Next up was one of the most controversial tactical decisions ever made by a Scotland manager, when Levein decided to utilise a formation of 4-6-0 having seen Russian side Rubin Kazan gain a draw at home to Barcelona with this strategy. To me the most embarrassing aspect of it, was that Levein didn't think Scotland were good enough to play with a lone striker up front, a role in which Kenny Miller was ably suited to particularly against an ordinary Czech side. Poor James Mackie of QPR was selected for his first game for the national side and asked to play in a non-striking striker's role! Alas, there was no Plan B when the Czechs scored, chasing the game was not part of Craig's strategy but then again they were no Barcelona!

The match against world champions Spain at home was next and Levein sent out a side to attack which you only wished he had done four days before. The Scots went two goals down before coming back

CRAIG LEVEIN
Heart of Midlothian

to equalise through Steven Naismith and a Pique own goal, only to have our hearts broken again as Fernando Llorente scored the winner with ten minutes remaining. The manner of defeat encouraged some that maybe Levein was getting a handle on international management, however there were some dissenting voices still in regards to the Czech fiasco and among them would be Steven Fletcher of Wolves. This would lead to Fletcher and Levein carrying out a media-based mudslinging contest where neither came out with much credit.

Levein took Scotland to Dublin for the Carling Nations Cup in 2011 where they beat both Northern Ireland and Wales before a defeat to the Republic saw them fail to win the tournament but come September it was back to Euro duty.

The name Kevin Blom will go down in infamy among Scotland fans for giving the Czech Republic a penalty in the final minutes of the game at Hampden, when it was clearly a dive and then denying Christophe Berra one a few moments later. There are those who would say the ref had denied the Czechs a penalty earlier in the game too but nobody likes level-headed football supporters.

Ultimately this result more than any other would put paid to Scotland progressing to the play-offs but Levein was expected to continue for the 2014 World Cup qualifying campaign. However, before that there was more controversy on its way. 6th August 2012 and Levein announces his team for the upcoming friendly v Australia, giving his reason for omitting Rangers full back Lee Wallace as because he was playing in the fourth tier of Scottish football following Rangers' fall from grace. 13th August and Ian Black of the same club was called into the squad – apparently Levein's previous statement had been 'misconstrued'. Black made a cameo appearance for the last three minutes of the match and was roundly booed by some Scotland fans in the crowd. Given he had been part of the Hearts side that had beaten Hibernian 5-1 in the Scottish Cup Final the previous May, that the game against the Socceroos was at Hibs' Easter Road Stadium and that he also joined Rangers weeks before perhaps the reaction was not surprising.

And then the World Cup campaign got off to a dire start with two toothless displays at home to Serbia and Macedonia which ended in scores of 0-0 and 1-1 respectively. Levein patched things up with Steven Fletcher and also Kris Commons of whom he had been previously quite dismissive, saying that he had seven better players ahead of him in his squad when he had not selected him. However, it was too little too late for despite their inclusion, Scotland lost away to both Wales and Belgium and time was called on the Levein era. Although you could probably point to games where Levein's side had been unlucky, in my humble, ticket-buying opinion ultimately he was clueless and I haven't even mentioned the embarrassing 5-1 away defeat to the USA in May 2012. Nuff said.

SCOTLAND GLORY, TEARS AND SOUVENIRS

LYONS MAID: MORE FOR YOUR LOLLY

You know, for someone who collected all sorts of cards in the early seventies whether from footballer packs, comics, tea bags or sweet cigarettes I don't recall ever really having any of the sets that *Lyons Maid* released in the sixties and seventies.

There were sets of pop stars, famous people and modes of transport all of which I would have collected but even worse I never had any of the two football or soccer, whatever that is, sets they released.

The first was the *Soccer Stars* set of 1970/71 which was free with the Score ice-lolly and which comprised of 40 cards of notable British players of the day that included the likes of Denis Law, Dave Mackay, Charlie Cooke, John Greig and Tommy Gemmell. There was also Colin Stein of Rangers playing for Scotland against Cyprus at Hampden in May, 1969 during which he scored four goals in the 8-0 World Cup qualifier rout. In addition, there were tokens attached that you collected to send away for a Soccer Chart of League Tables / Ladders – in case you had lost your *Shoot!* version that season no doubt. Furthermore, in return for a one shilling [five pence] postal order you could receive a full colour soccer star chart for your cards. We were spoiled back then!

Lyons Maid then followed up with an International Footballers set the following season. Once more it had many stars of the day and it is a rather tasty collection including 1970 World Cup winners such as Pele, Jairzinho and Rivelino, among others. There was also the likes of Cruyff, Beckenbauer, Muller, Yashin and the relative unknowns of Peru: Hector Chumpitaz and Teofilo Cubillas. As for Scotland we were represented by the inclusion of Billy Bremner with Tommy Lawrence of Liverpool tucked in behind him for good measure and Tommy Gemmell once more.

Perhaps the reason I never really got a hold of these cards is down to the vagaries of the Scottish summer which only ever seems to last for a few good days and is then gone. I may have grown up in a couple of the roughest housing schemes in Glasgow where it was quite natural upon the first sight of the summer sun to get yer taps aff and play football bare-chested but to do that and eat an ice lolly – I was never that hard.

Kenny Miller celebrates scoring the equalising goal against Macedonia in Scotland's 2014 FIFA World Cup qualifer at Hampden Park.

MACLEOD, ALLY

With the departure of the quiet and restrained character of Willie Ormond, the SFA went in a completely different direction with the appointment of the exuberant, Ayrshire-loving Glaswegian, Ally MacLeod. Jock Stein was first choice for the job but he declined and so the SFA turned to MacLeod.

MacLeod as a footballer had never been capped but he had a decent playing career as a left winger with Third Lanark, St Mirren, Blackburn Rovers and Hibernian before finishing up at Ayr United. MacLeod took over the reins at Ayr United in 1965 and began to build a team that had a reputation as playing good football and would steer them to a Second Division championship in 1965/66 and then to a second promotion in 1968/69. It was after this advancement that his team began to flourish and were a hard team to beat especially down at Somerset Park. He also became a spokesperson for the town of Ayr promoting it whenever and however he could and in 1973 was named 'Citizen of the Year'.

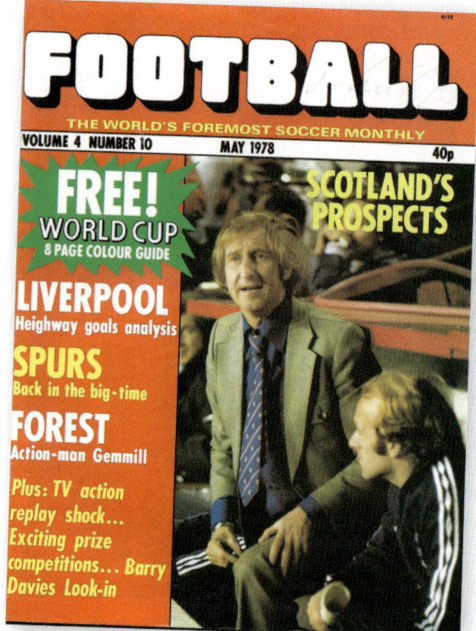

Ally then moved on to Pittodrie and Aberdeen in 1975 where once more he would be a one man publicity show for the club and the city of Aberdeen. In season 1976/77 his side won the Scottish League Cup defeating Celtic 2-1 in the final having swept aside Rangers 5-1 in the semi-final. These were pivotal moments in the growth of the Aberdeen club that would develop into Scottish champions under Alex Ferguson.

In May 1977 Ally introduced himself as Scotland manager with the statement 'My name is Ally MacLeod and I'm a winner' and for a time he was. His Scotland career started with a sedate blank draw with Wales with not many changes from the nucleus of Ormond's side although there was the inclusion of Rangers player Derek Parlane who had been out of the side for two years. His squad for the Home Internationals and tour of South America also included Davie Cooper of Clydebank and Joe Smith of Aberdeen. Cooper of course would go on to play for Scotland under Jock Stein.

Four days after the Welsh game, Scotland turned over Northern Ireland 3-0 at Hampden and so the stage was set for Wembley '77. Scotland would win 2-1 with goals from Gordon McQueen and Kenny Dalglish and so began a mass invasion of the hallowed turf and unheralded devotion to Ally.

The South American tour was a success in many ways starting with a victory over Chile that for many was a bit controversial as the game took place in the Estadio Nacional, Santiago. Following a coup d'état in 1973 the stadium had been used as a detention centre, where torture and deaths took place with the country under the rule of General Pinochet.

This was followed by a draw with future World Cup hosts Argentina in Buenos Aires. A defeat to Brazil in the Maracana rounded off the trip but despite that reverse Scotland's stock was seen to rise. During their time in Argentina, MacLeod and SFA secretary Ernie Walker were also scouting out possible training camps for the squad were they to qualify for the World Cup. Despite this advantage over many of their competitors they would choose poorly.

There was a slight stutter at this stage in September as Scotland lost a friendly to East Germany but this was quickly followed by two World Cup qualifiers that would cement Ally's reputation as a hero to the Tartan Army. Group 7 was a three-team grouping and so far the home sides had won each game, with Scotland losing to Czechoslovakia in Prague but winning against Wales at Hampden under Willie Ormond.

Scotland would, of course, go one better and not only beat Czechoslovakia at Hampden but also the Welsh (supposedly) away at Anfield, Liverpool and so Argentina here we come!

Everybody wanted a piece of Ally MacLeod and he ensured there was plenty of him to go around as he and his Scotland side became Britain's only World Cup finalists. 1977 had been a great year for Ally and Scotland; 1978 not so much. As if the bandwagon didn't need much to get it going Andy Cameron's 'Ally's Tartan Army' rode high in the music charts from April and never seemed to be off the radio in Scotland for months as we all awaited Argentina.

1978 got off to a slow start with a 2-1 victory over Bulgaria in which Ally fielded three new starts in Coventry goalkeeper Jim Blyth, Aberdeen defender Stuart Kennedy and striker Ian Wallace also of Coventry. Only Kennedy would feature in the World Cup.

The Home Internationals became an anti-climax after the anticipation and expectation that was building up to the World Cup. Scotland performed poorly throughout, drawing with Northern Ireland and Wales and then losing to England – all at Hampden. Scotland and MacLeod were further hampered with the loss of Gordon McQueen to injury in the Irish game; they had already lost Danny McGrain prior to the Welsh qualifier for the tournament. The only bright spot was the scoring form of Scotland's Player of the Year, Derek Johnstone.

Don't cry for me Argentina! We in Scotland did an awful lot of that for ourselves following the debacle that was the World Cup '78. We were going to win it, weren't we? I mean all that big send-off, Ally's exuberant claim that we were going to at least win a medal and we had a great team. What could go wrong?

Everything it seems, from the choice of training camp to the assumption that Peru were pushovers, the loss of form and confidence some of the players were showing and Willie Johnston's little yellow pills.

Some of the blame surely lies at MacLeod's door. Scotland were seeded third in the group but MacLeod had decided against checking out Peru at any point prior to the World Cup. He had not taken the English Player of the Year and Young Player of the Year Andy Gray to South America with him and would not play his Scottish counterpart either, instead opting to bring on Joe Harper against Iran for his first international in three years.

The training complex fiasco apparently led to a lot of discontent among the players and furthermore, to a lot of observers the holding back on using Graeme Souness was also seen as a failure. To be fair to MacLeod he was brave enough to go with the generally untried John Robertson in the Iran game but with the loss of Willie Johnston perhaps there was no other option. The sight of MacLeod as a broken man in the dugout for the Peru and Iran games are images that I still find haunting.

He would get it right for the Holland game and of course, it allowed Scotland once more to be recorded as glorious failures and perhaps that is how we should view MacLeod. Ally took charge of one post-World Cup match and then resigned his office to have further management spells with Ayr United, Motherwell, Airdrie and Queen of the South.

For all his failings Ally gave us some marvellous highs such as Wembley and Anfield in 1977 and even now I long for a Scotland manager who could talk about his players and team with such enthusiasm and muster the Tartan Army in the way Ally did in his 500 days or so in charge.

MAKE MINE MONTY

I'm not sure why but I love Monty Gum football cards. I think it's their basic naffness that appeals to me. The way they would regurgitate cards for different sets even if it didn't make any sense always made me chuckle.

Monty Gum was a Dutch company that started just after World War Two but in Britain it was a set from 1975 that I would first come across them. It was quite a random set in that some English clubs featured in it, like Coventry

City, Ipswich Town and Everton but there was no Liverpool, Arsenal or Spurs to be found. In Scotland, one has to feel sorry for the Celtic supporter who continually bought the cards hoping for a glimpse of his side only to find 20 Rangers players in the set as the sole Scottish side featured.

Of course, this being Monty Gum cards they obviously sent a guy to Ibrox during a training session for the Rangers players in old strips but not only do you get the stars such as John Greig, Sandy Jardine and Derek Johnstone but you also get such unknowns as George Donaldson, Alex Morrison and Donald Hunter.

Monty Gum cards were quite cheaply made, printed on thin cardboard with no details on the back and were supposed to be pasted into an album. I have yet to acquire an album but apparently they are just as cheaply made as the cards.

In the 1970s I did collect all sorts of cards and so Monty Gum sets such as Kojak, Starsky and Hutch and Charlie's Angels were sought out but the one I really loved was the World Cup 1978 set.

Monty Gum had released a 1974 sticker set which as far as I know never surfaced in the UK but I have bought some since and they are more a sticker than a card and once again there was an album. Scotland featured in the set with a total of 13 cards out of 200. There was a team photo taken just before the friendly with Brazil at Hampden in June 1973. Among the individual players are legends such as Denis Law, Jim Holton and Kenny Dalglish. However, two players who didn't make the World Cup squad were also included: Derek 'own goal against Brazil' Johnstone and Ally 'soft goal conceded v Czechoslovakia' Hunter.

The 1978 was a full size card set and is a very attractive and colourful one, full of classic players in classic strips such as Ardiles of Argentina, Zico of Brazil and Cubillas of Peru as well as the unknowns of Tunisia and Iran. Each nation had a team photo; Scotland's was from the friendly in Argentina in the summer of 1977. I suspect the Argentina one also came from that day too as in some of the shots of the Argentine players in action there are Scots players to glimpse.

SCOTLAND GLORY, TEARS AND SOUVENIRS

As to the Scotland cards it features the likes of Alan Rough, Bruce Rioch, Willie Johnston and Kenny Dalglish. Gordon McQueen and Danny McGrain are in there too, sadly reminding us that they didn't board that plane down South America way due to injury. Derek Parlane of Rangers is a bit of a strange choice for inclusion but manager Ally MacLeod did name him in his first Scotland side against Wales in May 1977.

It's when we get to the 1982 World Cup the wheels fall off the barra. Monty Gum in their infinite wisdom decided to halve the size of the cards, perhaps in a ruse to fool us they were new as they took the 1978 cards, made it more a headshot and just re-produced the same Scotland players. You do get the likes of Rough, McGrain and Dalglish who all played in Spain but then you still get Derek Parlane, Don Masson and the player with the lifetime ban Willie Johnston. However, Monty also released a postcard sized team set for that competition and apparently there are two Scotland ones and only one of every other team.

As if it wasn't getting ropey enough by the 1986 World Cup they had just stopped trying and produced a set of 100 with only four Scots included. Step forward Gordon Strachan, Arthur Albiston, Alan Brazil and Graeme Hogg! This selection used to confound me for years; I mean Strachan and Albiston played at Mexico '86 but Alan Brazil last played for Scotland in 1983 way before the strip he was wearing was released. As for Graeme Hogg he only played for the Under 21 team a few times and never came close to selection for the full international team. In fact, Hogg is more famous for being floored by a punch by future Scotland manager Craig Levein in a pre-season friendly against Raith Rovers when both were playing for Hearts. Both players were sent off for fighting, Levein walked off whilst Hogg with blood gushing from his face was stretchered off.

It wasn't until recently I came across one of those corny photos from the 80s where a club dresses up all their players in their national strip and has a photo taken. The club in question was Manchester United and there's Brazil, Strachan, Albiston and Hogg in amongst Mark Hughes of Wales, Norman Whiteside of Northern Ireland and Bryan Robson of England. All Monty have done is crop the pictures and use them as cards; perhaps the arm of a black player in a green top i.e. Paul McGrath in the background might have been a clue to the origin of the photos.

There would be another couple of Monty sets, Euro 88 with Hogg et al, of course and World Cup 90 before Monty Gum would go out of business but if you only go for one Monty set it has to be the 1978 one.

MASCOTS

When Scotland next qualify for the finals of a major competition they'll have some tough decisions to make – like who to include in the squad and will we require a new mascot for the tournament. By mascot I don't mean the wide-eyed [and sometimes frightened-looking] children who get

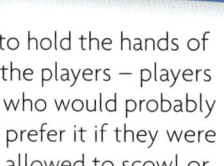

to hold the hands of the players – players who would probably prefer it if they were allowed to scowl or swear their way on to the pitch rather than be nice to someone else's kids.

Nor am I referring to football's furry friends – adults cunningly disguised as birds or animals – and in Scotland's case a lion by the name of *Hampden Roary* who was introduced by the SFA in 2012 and whose antics include circling the perimeter track on a Harley Davidson motorcycle.

No, I mean the images, the artistic gems which are dreamt up by the Football Associations' commercial department/advertising agency in celebration of appearing at the World Cup or Euro finals as well as to generate some income at the same time.

Looking ahead to better times how about something completely different, like a caricature transposing the head of Alex Salmond on to the body of Nicola Sturgeon and calling it *Homerule Hermie*? Then again maybe not.

Probably better to draw inspiration from our old World Cup mascots. *Roary Superscot* was the Billy Bremneresque lion mascot from 1974 complete with the letter S on the front of his shirt. [I foolishly thought it was a number 5 and that he had put his shirt on back to front – duh!]. In 1978 we went with a Thistle-like emblem instead of a mascot and in 1982 we had the rather glaikit-looking *Sandy*. This young lad sported a Scotland strip and a tartan bunnet but he looked like he had just collided with either Willie Miller or Alan Hansen or both.

For the Mexico 86 World Cup we roared back [sort of] in the shape of *McMex* - a pissed-looking lion in a sombrero – or maybe it was the altitude that had got to him. Whilst the lion is a recurring theme, Scotland's national animal is actually the unicorn although a pantomime horse might be more appropriate.

Anyway, I think we lost the plot altogether though with *Scoticus* our mascot for Italia 90. *Scoticus* was a tartan-clad Roman centurion who looked disturbingly like Kenneth Williams in the film *Carry on Cleo*. As manager Andy Roxburgh might have repeated after the defeat by Costa Rica – 'Infamy! Infamy! They've all got it in for me!'

Back to the future then and I suppose *Hampden Roary* could be given a tournament makeover when the time comes. Ditch the kilt and replace with tartan trews, waistcoat and bunnet to create something that is part-lion, part Tartan Army and part comedy great Chic Murray. I think we're on a winner here if only we could bloody well qualify.

McCOLL, IAN

Like Andy Beattie before him, Scotland manager Ian McColl also played for his country on a number of occasions, gaining 14 caps between 1950 and 1958. Dunbartonshire-born Ian was part of the Rangers defence that was known as the Iron Curtain and won a number of championship and cup medals throughout his time with the Ibrox club.

His first Scotland game saw him play with the rest of the Iron Curtain outfield players who were George Young, Sammy Cox and Willie Thornton but would see Morton's Jimmy Cowan play in goals instead of Bobby Brown. Scotland were to lose 1-0 to England at Hampden that day in April 1950 but McColl would take part in a 6-1 victory over Ireland later in the year and also a 5-0 rout of Belgium in the Heysel Stadium in 1951.

He would then disappear from the international scene for a few years before returning in season 56/57. Ian would play in the opening two of Scotland's World Cup qualifiers; victories against Spain and Switzerland and also face England for a third time in April 1958 where once more he was on the losing side. This 4-0 defeat to the Auld Enemy [with Bobby Charlton making his international debut] would be his last game as a player and although Ian would travel to Sweden for the 1958 World Cup finals he was never involved in any of the matches.

His last Rangers game was in the Scottish Cup Final of 1960 against Kilmarnock with Rangers running out 2-0 winners. A few months later and he was installed as the new Scotland manger following the departure of Andy Beattie.

Like his predecessors, Ian's role was mainly in the build up to games and on match days, he had no control over squad and team selection. However, Scotland were blessed with many fine players at the time and Ian led them to the brink of World Cup qualification plus three successive victories over England but before that there was humiliation as Scotland were walloped 9-3 at Wembley in April 1961 in only his second game in charge.

Three weeks after the Wembley defeat McColl's team faced the Republic of Ireland in their World Cup qualifying group in a four-day double-header. Scotland won both games comfortably; 4-1 at Hampden

and 3-0 at Dalymount Park. However, Scotland were brought back down to earth with a bump as they were thrashed 4-0 by Czechoslovakia in Bratislava a week later.

Scotland returned to more a full strength team for the final qualifier against the Czechs at Hampden and despite going behind twice, Scotland would see out the game 3-2 winners due to a late Denis Law goal to set up a play-off. Injury plagued Scotland for the play-off and they were missing some vital players and so the likes of goalkeeper Eddie Connachan and winger Hugh Robertson were drafted in for their debut caps. This time it would be Scotland who would be pegged back twice and so the game headed to extra-time. Over 50 years on and this is still the only occasion in which a Scotland game has gone into extra-time. Sadly it was a bridge too far as the Scots lost two further goals to lose out on a place at Chile '62.

For McColl and the Scots the next few years would prove quite successful as they would produce three wins over England in succession as well as two outright British Home International Championships and a share of a third.

In April 1962 Scotland recorded a Hampden victory against England in an official game for the first time since before the war with goals from Davie Wilson and Eric Caldow giving Scotland a 2-0 win. The following year a Jim Baxter double at Wembley would see Scotland record a second successive whitewash of the Home Internationals. Season 1963/64 would also see them defeat England once more at Hampden through an Alan Gilzean headed goal, however, a defeat to Northern Ireland earlier in the series would see them share the Championship honours with both the Irish and English.

So what went wrong for McColl? How did he go from these highs to being coerced from his job in May 1965?

The reality is despite his glorious wins over England in the past, the failure to defeat them at Wembley in April, 1965 was laid firmly at his door. Scotland drew 2-2 with England and in doing so incurred the wrath of the press and supporters alike. It was not so much for the first half performance which saw Scotland go in 2-1 down but for the second half in which they competed against an England side that went down to nine men early in the period. Ray Wilson had failed to appear after the break following an injury in a tackle with Willie Henderson but within three minutes of the restart John Byrne also limped off.

This game was followed by a poor team performance against Spain in May at home, where a less than enthralling 0-0 draw took place and with the Scotland team devoid of ideas and also deploying one or two dirty tackles. Within days of the Spanish draw, McColl was advised to resign as the SFA committee were about to sack him. Jock Stein of Celtic was asked to take over for the World Cup double header that was to follow away to Poland and Finland later that month.

McColl would claim he was sacked but it was a story that disappeared fairly quickly from the newspapers as Stein's appointment seemed to drive the narrative towards a more optimistic outlook as Scotland chased a place in the 1966 World Cup but hey, that's another story.

So how do you judge McColl's time in charge; given it was a part-time role where he never chose the squad or even the final XI it can be difficult to do so. It was a time of quality players for Scotland such as Law, Mackay, White, Baxter and so many others and McColl had some great victories achieving almost a 60% success rate of wins. But ultimately it was an era of little tactics by British sides and so it came down to the players more than it would in subsequent decades and so it is hard to credit him as highly as we can with some of his successors.

McColl would go on to manage Sunderland a short while after his departure from the Scotland job and would actually sign Jim Baxter in his time at Roker Park but he would ultimately fail and be sacked in 1968. He never returned to management after this and spent the rest of his working life in civil engineering.

ALEX McLEISH

The SFA quickly appointed Glasgow-born Alex McLeish as the next Scotland manager following the departure of Walter Smith. Although, like Smith, McLeish had once managed Rangers he was seen as a Scotland man through and through. As an Aberdeen player McLeish had been capped 77 times, appearing at three World Cup finals and captaining the side on eight occasions and as such seemed to be the perfect choice.

Although his tenure was quite short, it was something of a roller-coaster ride and provided one of the great Scotland victories of this and any other millennium. Even in his first game in March 2007 Scotland left it late with a last-gasp winner from substitute Craig Beattie to give us victory at Hampden against Georgia. This was followed by a 2-0 defeat to Italy in Bari with the Scots second best throughout the contest but a comfortable win in the Faroes in June, saw Scotland well in contention to qualify for the Euro finals in Austria and Switzerland.

Come September '07 and once more it is late substitutions that make a difference

SCOTLAND GLORY, TEARS AND SOUVENIRS

– with Scotland struggling to overcome Lithuania at home, McLeish brings on Shaun Maloney for Lee McCulloch in the 76th minute and within moments Scotland are in front. Maloney has been passed the ball as he is still on his run on from the sidelines, takes a touch and then hits a mean cross into the area and Stephen McManus pounces to put Scotland ahead. Hampden goes berserk and goes more so a few minutes later when another of McLeish's subs James McFadden hits a third. Could it get any better?

Yes, oh yes, it really did – just four days later in Paris. James McFadden hit the back of the French net from distance and gave us all a giant knot in our stomachs as we awaited the final whistle a mere 26 minutes away. How the defence once more held out against the French I don't know but hold out they did and like many a Scotsman I have thought myself accurs'd for having not been there on St Faddy's day. [That bugger Marshall was there of course.]

A month later and Ukraine came to Hampden and unusually Scotland decided to get themselves in front early, add to it and generally keep the opposition at bay. Kenny Miller had opened the scoring in four minutes with McCulloch adding to it eight minutes later and although Ukraine would get one back, Scotland never looked in trouble and once more McFadden produced a moment of magic to give Scotland an unassailable lead late in the second half.

Tbilisi, feckin' Tbilisi – when will a Scotland side go there and get a result against a team that is always ranked so far below them? Just like Gordon Strachan and his failed attempt to get to Euro 2016, Alex McLeish's side came unstuck and lost 2-0 to Georgia. Scots don't have a lot of luck in the Boris Paichadze Stadium, indeed under its previous name, the Lenin Dinamo Stadium; Liverpool [with Alan Hansen, Graeme Souness and Kenny Dalglish all playing] came undone there and lost 3-0 to Dinamo Tbilisi, to crash out of the European Cup at the first round stage in 1979.

Scotland had one throw of the dice left; a win against Italy at Hampden would see them progress as group winners. The weight of anticipation and expectation was heavy in the air that night. It seemed to take an

age for the game to start with a 5pm kick-off chosen. Within two minutes disaster struck with Luca Toni giving the Italians the lead but then a scrambled Barry Ferguson effort saw a glimmer of hope only for it to be doused late in the game as the referee gave a foul against Alan Hutton when clearly it was him who had been impeded. Italy would score from the resultant free kick and any hopes of qualifying were crushed.

A disappointing end to what had been a great campaign in many ways with some memorable moments that Scotland fans will hold on to for years. McLeish had been a big part of it after taking over from Walter Smith. However, in many ways it became tarnished with his departure to Birmingham City, a few weeks later. Recent years have seen McLeish go through a series of unfortunate appointments and perhaps in some ways it could be seen as karma for his hasty departure from the Scotland and Birmingham jobs but no matter how we feel about him, we will always have Paris.

NATIONAL ANTHEMS

Until 1982 Scotland supporters had to endure the UK national anthem – 'God save the Queen' – prior to kick-off. Throughout the 1970s and against a backdrop of increased Scottish nationalism, 'God save the Queen' became viewed more and more as an 'English imposition' and the knowledge that at one time that anthem included reference to 'crushing rebellious Scots' did not help matters. As such it was roundly booed by many of us on the Hampden terraces much to the embarrassment of the Scottish Football Association. It was our 'voice of protest' [or so we told ourselves] whilst for some sitting in the old south stand it was just plain bad manners.

When Scottish athletes were presented with gold medals at the 1970 Commonwealth Games in Edinburgh 'Scotland the Brave' was the victory anthem until being replaced with 'Flower of Scotland' at the 2010 Games. The dour and somewhat anti-English 'Flower of Scotland' was first introduced to Scotland football matches in 1993 [some six years before a Scottish Parliament was established in Edinburgh] but I've always preferred the more upbeat 'Scotland the Brave' which the SFA nominated as Scotland's 'football tune' at the 1982 World Cup finals in Spain in an attempt to differentiate ourselves from fellow UK finalists England and Northern Ireland. 'Flower of Scotland' is no Marseillaise but I'll still belt it out of course, when required.

In recent years the SFA have seen fit, on occasion, to invite a 'star name' to lead the singing of the national anthem and which have included the likes of Amy MacDonald [the singer-songwriter not the squeaky-voiced actress], Caledon [Scotland's Three Tenors] and Ronnie Browne [surviving member of The Corries who released the song on vinyl in 1974].

There is always however the question of timing – the crowd's version of the anthem is usually completed quicker than that of the lead singer. Furthermore the supporters in the four stands also tend not to start and finish simultaneously. A bevvied barbershop quartet comprising of around 30,000 plus 'half-cut harmonisers' – and I guess that's just the way we like it.

NEARLY MEN

This is perhaps one of the most subjective pieces in this book as it's about players that never received international recognition for Scotland. People's views tend to be clouded by which team they support and often players down south are never thought of in such lists.

If I miss out one of your favourites I'm sorry but it's only a taster. One of the names that always come up in these is Bobby Russell of Rangers. Bobby played on the right side of midfield for Rangers in the late 70s through to 1987 and had a great footballing mind and passing ability. He would go on to play for Motherwell and lift the Scottish Cup with them in 1991. One of his Rangers team-mates, Gordon Smith, was also touted as a player who deserved international recognition but if you're a Brighton fan you maybe think not so much.

Andy Ritchie of Morton was Scotland's Football Writers' Player of the Year in 1979 and rightly so as he had great ability and was able to change games with one sublime touch after another. If Morton

SCOTLAND GLORY, TEARS AND SOUVENIRS

got a free kick you knew Ritchie would bend it in. The problem for Ritchie was that he didn't look like a football player as he carried a bit of weight but then again that never did John Robertson of Nottingham Forest much harm.

Of course at Forest you also had John McGovern who captained his side to two European Cup triumphs but never sniffed a place in a Scotland side. Forest fans from an older age may shout out for Lochgelly's Bob McKinlay who holds the record for the club's most League appearances with a whopping 614 from 1951 all the way to 1969.

Another European Cup winner was Ken McNaught with Aston Villa in 1982 and indeed Ken scored in the Super Cup victory over Barcelona the following year. Ken's father Willie did play for Scotland during his time with Raith Rovers in the 1950s. Also at Villa and their appearance record holder was Edinburgh man Charlie Aitken, who played at left back from 1959 to 1976 for a total of 561 games. Another, beloved by those at Villa late in his career was Milngavie-born Andy Lochhead. Andy was a bustling centre forward who also played for Burnley in the 60s scoring 101 goals in 226 games. Andy once scored four goals against Manchester United on Boxing Day 1963.

Back up the road a bit to Dundee and two players from their 1961/62 League winning side; Bobby Cox was left back and captain to the side and time and time again is cited as a player that should have been capped but it was largely Eric Caldow of Rangers who kept him out of the national side. One of the stands at Dens Park is named after Bobby so revered was he there. Strike partner to Alan Gilzean, Alan Cousin is worthy of a mention too.

In the 70s, Dundee's free-scoring John Duncan came close to a cap on a number of occasions and would go on to play for Tottenham Hotspur. Across the road from Dens at Tannadice, home of Dundee United and from the League winning side of 1982/83 several of the team made it to the international stage including David Narey, Paul Sturrock, Richard Gough, Maurice Malpas and others but missing from the list would be Ralph Milne. Ralph had great pace and would often drive at defences before unleashing unstoppable shots but Jim McLean cites Ralph's lack of Scotland caps as one of his biggest failures, being unable to instil the right attitude into Milne.

Many of these players could have graced any Scotland side as could have a lot more I haven't mentioned. Of course had they played in more recent times many of them would probably be on 40 or 50 caps by now but alas they played in an era of truly great Scottish players as was the 60s, 70s and 80s.

149

ONE CAP ONLY

I was going to call this section 'One Cap Wonders' but I couldn't find enough to justify the title but there have been some notable players who have made their mark in the one game and others who surely should have gained more caps.

If you were to trawl through the early years of Scotland's line-ups you will find it littered with players that have scored goals and then disappeared altogether. This is partly explained by the SFA Committee's policy in the early days to spread the caps around; so if you lined up against England you were unlikely to play Wales or Ireland and vice versa; so players came and went pretty quickly at times. There are some players who have hit two or three goals and never returned to the international scene but there's also two who hit four goals each and suffered the same fate.

First up was Rangers forward Charles Heggie who scored his quartet of goals against Ireland in Belfast in 1886. Scotland with ten players making their debuts won 7-2; seven of the side would not play again! Two years later Scotland were to return to Belfast and record a 10-2 win over the Irish. William Dickson, then a forward with Strathmore would hit four that day and like Neil McCallum of Renton and Thomas Breckenridge of Hearts who scored one apiece this would also be his only appearance for the national side. Dickson would go on to play for Bolton Wanderers, Sunderland, Aston Villa and Stoke City in the following years.

The Wembley Wizards of 1928 are undoubtedly one of the greatest Scotland teams ever and at the heart of the defence was one Tom 'Tiny' Bradshaw, who stood at 6ft 1in and faced England's great goalscorer Dixie Dean. Scotland would win 5-1 but Bradshaw would be overlooked in the coming years, even after he moved from Bury to Liverpool, playing over 200 games for the Anfield club. Although he would play in several games for Scotland during the war years Sir Matt Busby only played one official game in 1933 against Wales at Ninian Park.

'Worse than East Fife' is quite often used as a derogatory term among Scottish club football fans but back in the post-war era from the late 40s through to the 50s East Fife were a team to be reckoned with, lifting the Scottish League Cup on three occasions. Several of their players were capped around the time but for Henry Morris and Charlie Fleming it was a bittersweet experience.

On 1st October 1949 Scotland played Ireland in a joint World Cup qualifier/Home International at Windsor Park, Belfast. Henry Morris would be the scorer of Scotland's first ever World Cup goal within two minutes and would add two more before the end as Scotland ran out 8-2 winners. However, when Scotland faced Wales at Hampden a month later Morris was nowhere to be seen. Team-mate 'Cannonball' Fleming was to suffer the same fate four years later when Scotland once more returned to Windsor Park for another dual purpose match. Scotland would win 3-1 with Fleming netting twice and like Henry Morris before him he was never again to grace the dark blue of Scotland.

Around the same time Hibernian and Hearts had players competing for titles and Scotland places alike. At Hibernian there was the 'Famous Five' who it was often cited never received their fair share of caps whilst across the city at Tynecastle Park it was the poor return for their 'Terrible Trio' of Jimmy Wardhaugh, Willie Bauld and Alfie Conn that was bemoaned. Bauld would win three caps in total scoring two goals, Wardhaugh was chosen twice but for Alfie Conn it would be a solitary cap won in May 1956 in a friendly v Austria at Hampden. Scotland would draw 1-1 with Conn scoring for Scotland. His son Alfie Jnr, would make two appearances for the national side in the mid-70s as a Spurs player.

The 60s had some of the greatest players ever produced playing for Scotland but there was a couple who perhaps could've won more. In

ALFIE CONN

his excellent book *A Scottish Hall of Fame* John Cairney selects 100 players to tell the story of Scottish football and in the middle of some very familiar names from the 60s there's Willie Hamilton. Who? Yes, that was my first reaction too but apparently Jock Stein rated him as 'the best player he'd ever seen'. Jock managed Willie during his time in charge of Hibernian and would give him his only cap in 1965 as Scotland faced Finland in Helsinki in a World Cup qualifier. Scotland would win 2-1 but Hamilton would not be chosen again; perhaps his skills and lifestyle were too similar to that other maverick Jim Baxter and the thought of the two of them in the same side would be chaotic.

All of the Celtic European Cup winning side of 1967 would win caps for Scotland but only full back Jim Craig would have one solitary cap to show, turning out for Scotland against Wales in 1967. Scotland did have a lot of good full backs back then but it was his Celtic left back counterpart Tommy Gemmell that kept Craig out of the national side by moving over to the right with the likes of Eddie McCreadie of Chelsea slotting into the left back spot.

Erich Schaedler of Hibs would be part of the 1974 World Cup squad but it was rather unusual in that such an inexperienced player would be chosen. Erich or Eric as he was more generally referred to at the time had been capped against West Germany for a friendly in Franfurt in March '74. This was to be his final cap but with competition such as Danny McGrain and Willie Donachie it is perhaps not surprising.

On 7th April, 1976 Willie Ormond was to give debut caps to seven players in a friendly against Switzerland at Hampden. Rangers' duo of Alex MacDonald and Bobby McKean, Tommy Craig of Newcastle and Hibernian's Des Bremner were never to play again. Bremner would go on to win the European Cup and Super Cup with Aston Villa in the early 80s. In fairness to Ormond he did give Alan Rough of Partick Thistle the first of his 53 caps that night and debutant Willie Pettigrew of Motherwell scored the only goal.

If there's a wrong time to win your first cap perhaps it's in a manager's last game; as is the fate that befell Ronnie Glavin and Joe Craig both of Celtic, on the evening of 27th April, 1977. Scotland would win 3-1 with Craig netting with his first touch after coming on as a sub but Willie Ormond quit to take up the post as Hearts manager a few days later and neither were to be picked during the Ally MacLeod whirlwind 18 months or so in charge.

MacLeod would cap one player who could count himself as unlucky to only reach a tally of one. Goalkeeper David Stewart had first come to prominence as an Ayr United player under MacLeod's guidance before moving to Leeds United in 1973 to be second choice to David Harvey. However, Harvey was to be involved in a car crash that saw Stewart take over in goals and indeed play in the 1975 European Cup Final. Luck would come into it again as David was given the chance to play for Scotland in a friendly v East Germany in September '77 as number one choice goalie Alan Rough had been dropped by club manager Bertie Auld and was not selected for the game. Stewart would have a fine game which Scotland lost 1-0 with David saving a penalty but he would see Jim Blyth take over as the second choice goalie and would not make it to Argentina '78 or play again for Scotland. He did however make it into the Panini World Cup stickers set and was featured on Tennent's Lager beermats to commemorate that tournament too.

The 1980s is a rather curious decade as but one player who was called up for Scotland in that era only ever played one game. Doug Rougvie of Aberdeen was a bit of a rough and ready full back for the Dons under Alex Ferguson and was capped against Northern Ireland in Belfast 1983 in what was to be the last British Championship. Scotland would lose 2-0.

In the more modern era, in particular in friendlies, caps are given away like confetti and in some matches four or five debuts can be made in the last 20 minutes or so. Murray Davidson of St Johnstone was his club's first capped player for over 80 years in 2012 but he only came on as a sub for Jordan Rhodes in the 89th minute against Luxembourg in a friendly.

However, not all modern one-time appearances are as minor as that. In March,

2004 highly touted John Kennedy of Celtic made his first appearance for Scotland under Berti Vogts in a friendly v Romania. John would be recklessly tackled by Romanian Ioan Ganea in the 14th minute and sustain an injury that would see him out of action for just under three years and ultimately rob him of his potential.

Final mention goes to Paul Wilson of Celtic who won his one and only cap coming on as a sub in the 75th minute in a Euro qualifier in Valencia, Spain in February 1975. In doing so Paul became the only non-white player to represent Scotland in the 20th century and the first Asian player to represent any of the four home nations at senior level. Paul said of his experience, 'I nearly scored but their keeper just got his hands to my effort. I was as sick as a dog. I was so proud to get my one cap.'

I hope that all of these players who probably merited more were equally proud.

WILLIE ORMOND

Willie will probably go down as one of the most affectionately remembered Scotland managers, leading the national side to the World Cup finals in 1974 and going about his job with a quiet dignity and determination.

As a footballer, Falkirk-born Willie had been one of Hibernian's successful 'Famous Five' forward line but was criminally underused by the national side gaining only six caps in total. His first five came in a flurry in the summer of 1954 with Billy Liddell of recently relegated Liverpool missing out on the left-wing position.

Ormond gained his first cap at the age of 27 facing England at Hampden in April, 1954. Allan Brown of Blackpool would open the scoring early on for Scotland and Ormond would add a second in the 89th minute and if England hadn't scored four in between it would have been a great day for his debut!

Willie held on to the number eleven shirt and scored in a pre-World Cup match in Finland as the Scots ran out 2-1 winners with fellow 'Famous Five' player Bobby Johnstone netting the other. He also played in both Scotland matches in the World Cup finals in Switzerland as they lost 1-0 to Austria and then as they succumbed to the heat and Uruguayan skill to lose 7-0 in Basle.

Ormond was one of the few players who were discarded by Scotland after the calamity in Switzerland and his only other cap would come in April, 1959 as Scotland lost 1-0 to England at Wembley.

After retiring from playing Ormond took over the reins from the departing Bobby Brown at St Johnstone in April, 1967. Brown was of course heading for the Scotland job and Willie would follow in his footsteps six years later after Tommy Docherty quit for Manchester United.

It has to be admitted that Willie did not have the greatest of starts to his Scotland managerial career. He would lose his first game on Valentine's Day 1973, 5-0 to England in a match that was meant to mark the occasion of the centenary of the founding of the SFA. The side he chose that night was made up of players that had been capped by Docherty and showed no real surprises.

Game two in May and Ormond took his side down to the Racecourse, Wrexham to face Wales in the first game of the Home Internationals. This side was peppered with players making their debuts including Danny McGrain and Jim Holton. He also reinstated David Hay to the side, moving him into midfield. Scotland would win 2-0 with goals from George Graham but then came a run of four defeats for Ormond although a certain Joe Jordan would make a late sub appearance for his debut against England as the Scots toiled at Wembley.

September '73 and Ormond faced the biggest night of his Scotland career thus far as his team faced Czechoslovakia at Hampden knowing victory would see them through to the World Cup finals in West Germany. Having lost five games out of his first six there's no doubt there must have been some nervousness for Willie and the fans on the terraces about the outcome of the match.

Ormond turned to veteran striker Denis Law who was having a good season with Manchester City to lead the line and also gave debuts to Celtic starlet George Connelly and Tommy Hutchison of Coventry City. Despite the loss of a soft goal to the Czechs, Scotland would go on to win with goals from Jim Holton and substitute Joe Jordan and so the World Cup awaited.

Willie would show a ruthless streak however in dropping goalkeeper Ally Hunter of Celtic from his side for the loss of the goal to Czechoslovakia and reinstated Leeds' David Harvey to the Scotland line-up following that game.

The 1974 Home Internationals started with defeat to Northern Ireland at Hampden but was followed by a 2-0 victory over Wales where Willie reintroduced Jinky Johnstone to the Scotland line-up. Jimmy would of course have his little boating escapade in the days between that game and the Scots facing England but rather than cast Johnstone aside like a number of the newspapers had demanded Ormond gave him the chance to redeem himself. Jinky took the game by the scruff of the neck and gave the English defence a torrid time as Scotland ran out 2-0 winners. Johnstone then famously gave the 'V' sign to the press box at the end of the game.

However, by the time Scotland reached their base in Germany, Johnstone along with captain Billy Bremner had been involved in another drinking episode on their pre-World Cup tour of Belgium and Norway. Johnstone would not be used for any of the games in the finals themselves and many surmise it was these discipline issues that saw Jinky denied an appearance at the World Cup. It may well be down to Ormond preferring Willie Morgan over Johnstone, as Jinky did have a side to him that was difficult to manage and he could be inconsistent too.

Ormond and his side of 1974 came home from Germany as the only unbeaten team in the tournament and are often looked upon as the Golden Generation to many a Scottish fan and perhaps our greatest side ever. However the side he assembled for the 1976 Home Internationals was arguably better and indeed Willie himself said so in an interview with Brian Moore on *The Big Match* stating that it was the best squad he ever had and that 'they had no reason to fear anyone'.

It was no easy task coming out of the World Cup and then rebuilding a side due to the loss of some major players such as Holton and Hay to injury as well as Bremner to indiscipline. No doubt there were some missteps along the way, notably defeat to Spain at Hampden in a Euro qualifier and the crushing defeat to England at Wembley in 1975, but by the Home Internationals of 1976 Willie had in place a midfield comprising of Archie Gemmill, Don Masson and Bruce Rioch plus a consistent goalkeeper in Alan Rough.

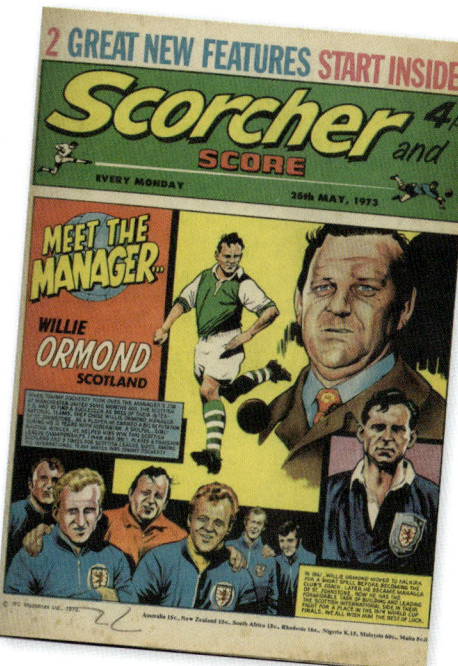

This team would make up the bulk of the side that Ally MacLeod would utilise in Argentina '78 but it is interesting to wonder whether Ormond would have done so or would he have read the signs that suggested the likes of Masson and Rioch had perhaps passed their peak.

Ormond would leave the Scotland job in May 1977 and take up a post with Hearts. Scotland defeated Sweden 3-1 in a friendly at Hampden in late April and Ormond had recalled Willie Johnston back into the Scotland fold after a seven year absence and so another piece of MacLeod's World Cup team was in place. With an eye to the future, he gave Dundee United's David Narey his Scotland debut that night too.

There's no doubt Ormond never really liked being in the spotlight and with another World Cup campaign under way he was probably quite relieved to take up the post at Tynecastle. However, you do wonder what he could have achieved in Argentina. His time at Hearts was not a great success and he was sacked in 1980 but would go back to his beloved Hibs for a season as manager before retiring due to ill health. Willie would pass away in 1984.

OVERLAPPING FULL-BACKS

The sixties saw some great full backs play for Scotland; from the unfortunate Eric Caldow of Rangers whose Scotland career was cruelly ended after 40 caps due to a broken leg suffered at Wembley in 1963 to the likes of Alex Hamilton of Dundee, Tommy Gemmell of Celtic and Eddie McCreadie of Chelsea but it would be the seventies pairing of Celtic's Danny McGrain and Sandy Jardine of Rangers that gets many a Scotland fan misty eyed at the thought of them running down the line and putting a cross in from deep; the archetypal overlapping full backs.

It was Willie Ormond who first put them together on the 30th May, 1973. Danny was on his third cap having been paired with Willie Donachie over the previous Home International games but was switched to left back to accommodate Sandy Jardine on the right, winning his fifth cap. Sadly, it was not a winning start as Scotland lost to England 1-0. Danny and Sandy were paired together for two more games that summer, which saw further defeats to Switzerland and Brazil. However, it was game number four that set Scotland alight and cemented their partnership as Scotland finally qualified for the World Cup by beating Czechoslovakia, on that unforgettable night at Hampden in September, 1973.

After missing a few games together, once more they were brought back for the big one in May 1974 as Scotland beat England 2-0 in front of a jubilant Hampden crowd which was wowed by the performance of Jinky Johnstone that day.

Then it was time for the 'Majors' with Sandy and Danny playing in all three of our World Cup games and as such are part of that elite squad among whom stood many of the giants of Scottish football; Bremner, Law, Dalglish et al. After the World Cup was over McGrain was diagnosed as having diabetes but he would come through to return to the Scotland team alongside Sandy but the 5-1 defeat at Wembley would see Jardine out of the team for just under two years, coming back as a sub in Willie Ormond's last game in charge.

Ally MacLeod would continue to use Jardine as a sub until it mattered when both Sandy and Danny lined up against Czechoslovakia in a World Cup qualifier in September, 1977. Scotland won 3-1 but McGrain would miss the next game at Anfield and indeed the whole of the 1978 campaign through injury. Sandy would flit in and out of the team and had slipped down the totem pole with Stuart Kennedy of Aberdeen being preferred but did in fact play in that nightmare of a game against Iran in Argentina.

So was that the end of the road for the Danny and Sandy show? Well no, there was one last hurrah. Jock Stein had chosen Sandy on quite a few occasions at the start of season '79-'80 and indeed made him captain for a few games. On 21st November, 1979 Danny returned to the fold to play alongside Sandy for the last time. Unfortunately it was against Belgium (do we ever beat them, even when they're ordinary?) and saw Scotland go down 3-1 at Hampden with the Belgians qualifying for Euro 1980.

Sandy won his 38th cap that night and had captained Scotland on nine occasions. Danny would go on to win 62 caps and captained the side on ten occasions. Danny would make two appearances at the World Cup in 1982 with the game against USSR being his final cap call.

Their record of playing together wasn't one of invincibility and indeed they only played 20 games as a pairing, but they were together on some of our greatest nights. It was the magic of having two great overlapping full backs in the side at the same time, which made those times so exciting. Even coming from either side of the Old Firm, they transcended the divide, as both were gentlemen and played with heart for their clubs and country and we loved them for it.

SCOTLAND GLORY, TEARS AND SOUVENIRS

We have had some decent full backs since, players such as Maurice Malpas, Stewart McKimmie, Tom Boyd and even latterly Gary Naysmith and Alan Hutton but none will ever match the glory of Daniel Fergus McGrain and William Pullar Jardine running down both wings.

PANINI, ME AND THE WILDERNESS YEARS

In the world of trading cards and stickers, Panini is of course, king, but for me they came around too late. They didn't really arrive on British shores or certainly Scotland until the mid to late 1970s, which meant I only ever completed one set of stickers before giving up collecting football cards/stickers for heavy metal music and vinyl record collecting. Prior to this, Panini had released British sets through the Top Sellers Company and there are a couple of nifty stickers with the likes of Tony Green and Alfie Conn in their Scotland colours at Wembley from these sets.

They did produce a 1974 World Cup set which as far as I am aware wasn't released in the UK and of course have celebrated each of Scotland's achievements in reaching, firstly five World Cup finals in a row and then two Euro Championships although there's nary a sight of those legendary curly-perms for the Argentina 78 set. Sadly for the enthusiastic tartan-wearing among us, Panini's World Cup and Euro collections also have the painful knack of reminding you if your team has once more failed to reach the finals of a major competition with the USA 94 being the first major sore point.

1998 brought lots of lovely collectables including of course, the Panini France 98 set but since then there's been diminishing returns for Scotland fans in a cartophilic sense. Of course that's nine consecutive major tournament sticker albums without Scottish interest but in the meantime we've had to collect stickers from countries such as Saudi Arabia, Senegal, Trinidad & Tobago, Togo, Honduras, Slovenia, Iceland and others with the 2016 European Championship one being particularly frustrating.

Panini also had the cheek to start producing the Adrenalyn cards for each tournament since South Africa 2010 and Scotland trading card fans have had to rely on the Futera Company for cards of the contemporary Scotland team with the likes of Darren Fletcher, James McFadden and Gary Caldwell and others being featured in sets down the years. There has also been a raft of retro cards produced – from Philip Neill's wonderfully drawn sets to JF Collectibles reproduced old photo sets.

And then came 2017 and all of a sudden Panini took pity on us forlorn Scots and produced three sets with the mighty football sons of

Caledonia featured in every one of them. First came the 'Five Home Nations' collection which had so many players in it including one or two who have never been capped such as Tony Watt [Charlton Athletic] and Jack Hamilton [Hearts]. Next appeared not one but two Road to Russia 2018 sets; one stickers, the other an Adrenalyn cards set. Incredible and also financially quite a burden for a 50-odd-year-old man never mind a wee ten-year-old.

Of course, these may have been somewhat contrived sets but then came a most deserved inclusion as the Scotland Women's side reached the Euro finals in 2017 and as such have their own fully-merited slot in a sticker album. These are wondrous times indeed!

PENALTY HEROES AND VILLAINS

It is a well-known fact that buried somewhere in every England fan and player's psyche is a fear of penalty kicks. As a Scotland fan I have looked upon their misfortune in countless shoot-outs with a great sense of Schadenfreude but I have to admit it is also tinged with a little bit of envy as Scotland have never reached that level, where a penalty shoot-out is needed to ensure our progress in a tournament, not even in a play-off.

However, we Scots too have our own penalty kick misery that has seen us lose out and ours begins way before England's.

On the way to the World Cup in Sweden 1958, Scotland played Spain at Hampden in a qualifier; with a few minutes remaining before half-time Scotland were awarded a penalty kick and so up stepped Charlton Athletic's South African-born John Hewie to score from the spot. This gave Scotland a 2-1 lead at the interval and two goals in the second half from Jackie Mudie sealed his hat-trick and Scotland's 4-2 win.

However, come the finals and in their third match needing a victory over France to progress, Scotland fell behind to a Raymond Kopa goal in the 22nd minute. On the half hour mark, Scotland were awarded a penalty and once more Hewie took it. By all accounts he hit an unstoppable shot that hit the underside of the crossbar and was unlucky to see it bounce out rather than in. Just Fontaine would score for France just before half-time on his way to a record thirteen goals in the one tournament that has never been bettered. A second-half goal from Sammy Baird gave Scotland some hope but alas it was not to be. Who knows how things would have transpired had Hewie scored from the spot.

JOHN HEWIE

Hewie would score from a penalty against Northern Ireland in 1959 but spot kick duty would then be passed on to a very reliable player. Right back to Hewie's left in all these games was Eric Caldow who would take over the mantle of taking penalties from 1960 onwards. Eric would score four out of four including one against England in the 88th minute at Hampden in 1962 that would seal a 2-0 win and Scotland's first home victory over the Auld Enemy since 1937.

Jim Baxter scored Scotland's next penalty at Wembley a year later, taking over the duty from Caldow who had suffered a broken leg in three places earlier in the match in a tackle from England's Bobby Smith. Baxter hit a double as ten men Scotland won 2-0.

On to the 1970s and to those returning heroes of the '74 World Cup playing against East Germany in a friendly at Hampden in October that year. Scotland were awarded a spot kick and despite the presence of Sandy Jardine who previously scored from the spot for the team, Tommy Hutchison of Coventry City took the responsibility and netted Scotland's opener in a 3-0 win.

A month later Scotland began their Euro qualifiers at home against Spain with Billy Bremner netting the opener in the 11th minute. Shortly after a penalty kick was given and once more Hutchison stepped up to take it. Spanish goalkeeper Iribar who had been at fault for Bremner's goal made up for it by saving the spot kick. Spain would take a fillip from this and would win the game 2-1. Scotland's Euro campaign more or less ended before it had barely begun as it would be this one result that saw them fail to qualify more than any other.

Bruce Rioch of Derby County would hit Scotland's next penalty at Wembley in May 1975; unfortunately England hit five in return but he would then go on to miss one against Northern Ireland the following year and handed the mantle on to Don Masson of QPR.

Don had scored two by October 1977, when he would hit the vital, though controversial penalty against Wales at Anfield to give Scotland the lead and put them on their way to Argentina. His next one would not go as well as Scotland looked to retake the lead in Cordoba, Argentina against Peru in the '78 World Cup. The rather eccentric Quiroga would save Masson's penalty and unfortunately for Don his Scotland career is blighted by this event and all too often people forget Masson's goals for Scotland including one against England in '76 and of course hitting that penalty at Anfield.

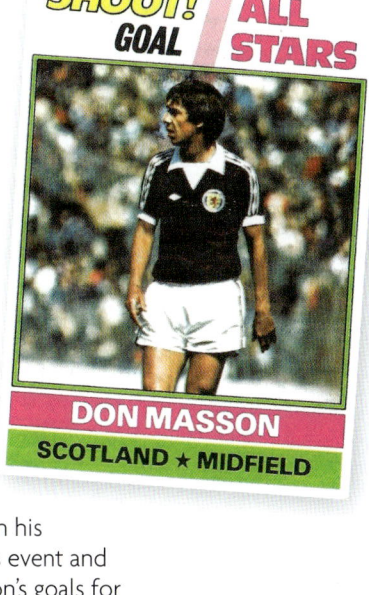

Just over a week later though the redoubtable Archie Gemmill would take over the penalty-taking reins and begin with one scored against Holland in Mendoza 22 minutes prior to his history-making moment at that '78 World Cup. Gemmill would score four from the spot and was then followed by the reliable John Robertson who tended to curl them in; hitting five in total including a winner at Wembley in '81.

For sheer coolness Davie Cooper would be next up to take a vital kick at Ninian Park, Cardiff in a World Cup qualifier v Wales in 1985. Scotland needed a draw to keep alive their hopes of reaching Mexico '86 and were trailing 1-0 when a perhaps 'fortunate' penalty was given for handball once again by a Welshman in the 81st minute. Cooper had only been on the park for 20 minutes but stepped up to slot the penalty away. Once more Scotland would [eventually] reach the finals at the expense of the Welsh.

This night however will always be tinged with sadness due to the death of Scotland manager Jock Stein shortly after the match.

Mo Johnston would take the responsibility for Scotland's next big penalty at Italia 90 to score against Sweden in the vital must-win game. Scotland won 2-1.

Gary McAllister would hit the third goal against the Commonwealth of Independent States as the crumbling Soviet Union was known in 1992, from the penalty spot in Scotland's 3-0 win in their final game of Euro 1992. Four years later and things would not go so well for Gary at Wembley '96. Uri Geller has suggested that his mindbending powers caused the ball to move slightly before Gary hit his spot kick against England on that fateful day, but we all know the truth; Gary didn't hit it as well as he could, David Seaman saved it and before you know it Gazza is up the other end putting the game beyond Scotland's reach.

This would not be Gary's final penalty for Scotland as he would score one against Belarus in Minsk as Scotland won 1-0 in a vital away match on their way to France 98.

France 98 would bring a wondrous moment from the spot as John Collins put away a penalty in front of millions of viewers around the world and 80,000 in the Stade de France to equalise against the holders Brazil in the opening game of the World Cup finals. Alas, our joy was turned to groans as Tom Boyd was unlucky to get in the way of the ball in a goalmouth scramble and see it land in the back of the Scottish net.

We've had some hits and misses since then but none that have really mattered in the end but just for once I would like to experience the ecstasy or agony of a penalty shoot-out in the near future . . . sometime.

PHOTOGRAPHS

Back in the 1970s very few people took cameras to Scotland matches – cans of lager and bottles of whisky perhaps, but seldom a camera. It was kind of frowned upon, a nerdy pastime which should be left to the official photographers. In addition, the everyday-use technology back then wasn't that great and so the likes of the Kodak Instamatic tended to be reserved for holidays and birthdays.

The 1982 World Cup finals in Spain was a sort of a holiday so it was perfectly acceptable to take snapshots of Jock Stein's boys in their duels against New Zealand, Brazil and the USSR. My 'arty', somewhat out of focus photos include Chinese lanterns adorned with the Brazil flag floating above the main stand at Seville's Estadio Benito Villamarin plus spot the ball action-shots against the Soviets in Malaga. You have to remember that it is extremely difficult to take award winning photographs when you are 'well-oiled'.

Despite having actively supported Scotland since 1971, it was 1984 before I first took a photograph at Hampden Park [Scotland v Wales in the British Championship]. I now had the 'novelty' Kodak disk camera with the end result being a really grainy-looking picture of Davie Cooper giving Scotland the lead from the penalty spot.

Stuart Clarke's groundbreaking 1996 publication *The Homes of Football* demonstrated that there was more to football photography than games and stadia. There were crowd scenes that included everything from waving flags to queuing for pies. There were also adjacent streetscenes with souvenir

SCOTLAND GLORY, TEARS AND SOUVENIRS

vendors, programme sellers and laughing policemen [sometimes] plus football-related billboard adverts and specially decorated bookmakers' front windows. A Konica Pop camera did the trick for me in the 1990s.

As well as making for souvenirs, football photographs also provide a great social record of ever-changing trends and fashions, from disappearing terracings to awful-looking away strips, from youthful-looking new recruits to the Tartan Army to grizzled, seasoned footsoldiers pretending to be youthful-looking new recruits.

The digital revolution has meant an improvement in quality as well as increased flexibility in the pursuit of photographic treasures. Increased travel mobility has also ensured that the post-1998 'Wilderness Years' have been well recorded – from Alicante to Zagreb with the likes of Bari, Kiev, Milan, Oslo, Paris, Prague, Stockholm and Warsaw in between. Memorable matches, wonderful cities and fabulous photographs.

Of course it would also have been nice to photograph Japan/South Korea in 2002, Portugal in 2004, Germany in 2006 etc etc.

PRE-MATCH AND HALF-TIME ENTERTAINMENT

In recent years much of what passes for pre-match and half-time entertainment is contrived, get the crowd worked up by a DJ, nonsense. But hey, one man's meat is another man's pile of pants.

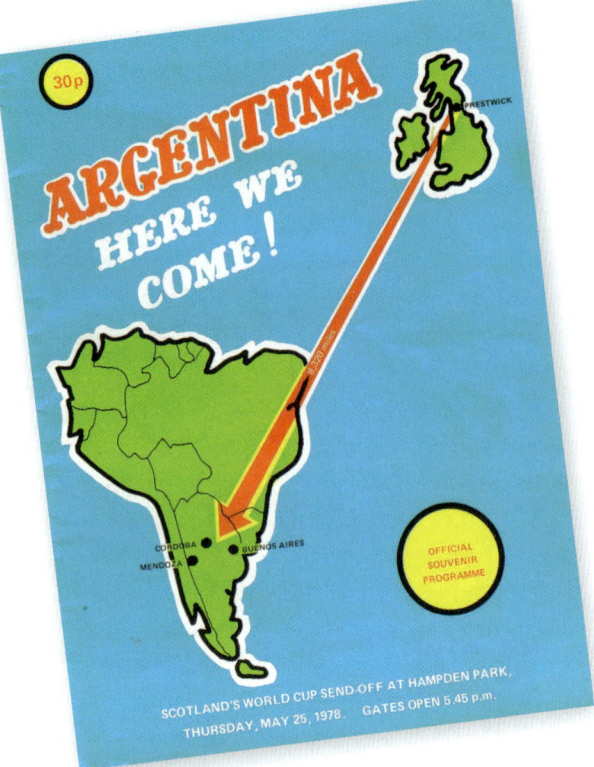

To be fair, times and tastes change although Pipe Bands seem to last forever. A look at some of the match programmes from the 1950s reveals that back then there was much emphasis on athletics, Scottish country dancing, gymnastics and keep-fit displays especially when England came to town.

In the 1960s and 1970s there were cycling events as well as Scottish musical megastars such as Andy Stewart [of 'Donald where's your troosers?' fame] and Dean Ford and the Gaylords [Ford would later front the more successful Marmalade]. We also got Majorette dancers which occasionally 'induced' some decidedly non-pc chanting from the terracings.

In June 1966 defending champions Brazil visited Hampden for a World Cup warm-up match and those spectators who arrived early were treated to the latter stages of the national youth competition final which included future Dundee United hero Hamish McAlpine. The final should have been played the previous Saturday prior to Portugal's World Cup warm-up match at Hampden but heavy rain put paid to that plan. One wonders what the groundsman thought about subjecting the playing surface to a Youth Cup Final just before a match involving illustrious guests such as Portugal or Brazil.

The pre-match entertainment for the 14th February 1973 Scotland-England centenary game included a decorated float featuring the winner and finalists from the *Daily Record* Glamour Soccer Fan competition with 'Miss Soccer Strip' throwing footballs into the crowd as she circled the stadium! It was the 1970s remember and it helped make up for yet another teenage year without a Valentine's card!

When Scotland played Portugal at Hampden in 1975 as part of the celebrations commemorating the 800th anniversary of the granting of Glasgow's burgh charter, at half-time the crowd of 34,307 were treated to a penalty shoot-out involving the Wombles [ie pointy-nosed, furry creatures who starred on children's television]. I have a sneaking suspicion however that they weren't the real Wombles but just out-of-work actors dressed up to look like the Wimbledon Common mutants.

The 1970s were also big on exhibitions of karate and kung fu although I don't think they managed to do the latter in slo-mo. I must mention the 'entertainment' that comprised the 1978 Argentina World Cup send-off at Hampden – complete with comedian Andy Cameron as compere, the players running to each end of the ground, followed by them boarding an open-topped bus and waving to the crowd as it went round the perimeter track before heading to Prestwick airport. Of course there was no actual football at Hampden that evening but technically it was pre-match entertainment in that it did take place prior to the kick-off versus Peru – just some nine days prior!

SCOTLAND GLORY, TEARS AND SOUVENIRS

In the 1980s and 1990s we tended to keep things simple [ie Pipe Bands – lots of them!] However, prior to the inauguration of new Hampden versus France in March 2000 the FIFA World Cup trophy was paraded around the stadium. [There doesn't appear to be any sign of it making a return visit.]

Into the 21st century and a considerable number of fixtures have come complete with pre-match pyrotechnics [does the SFA really have money to burn?] plus the occasional lone piper on the roof. Then there's the primary school kids playing six-a-side football, the halfway line goal challenge, karaoke and mascots [furry ones] on motorbikes.

I suppose it could be worse, there could be Morris dancers…

PROGRAMMES

Despite the ever-growing influence of the online electronic world, for many people purchasing a tangible, paper and print souvenir programme remains an essential part of the match-day experience.

That said, in recent years a number of Scotland's international programmes have been everything they shouldn't be – A4 sized, perfect bound and extending to over 80 pages bloated by touchy-feely [sometimes sycophantic] articles/interviews with players past and present. No-one takes a coffee table to the match and that's where these glossy magazines with the excessive use of photographs belong.

Programmes should be B5 size, 36 pages maximum [less is more] and be held together by staples. Rust is good – it's all part of the natural aging process for programmes and central defenders alike. The programme should actually include a programme of events which list timings and information relating to the gates opening, pre-match [and half-time] entertainment, kick-off and full-time.

Ideally, the front cover should be dominated by an action photograph of the two competing teams preferably with a Scots player winning the ball or celebrating scoring a goal. Looks of frustration, angst or crushing disappointment on the faces of the opposition footballers are also desirable. Some recent Scotland programme covers

have consisted of bland, abstract imagery and ok, so maybe it would be too much to expect a Jack Vettriano-esque design but please don't give us boring – we get enough of that on the pitch with many of our friendly matches.

There should be pen pictures with associated photographs [head and shoulders only] of both squads of players plus the manager/coaches. Statistical information should include number of caps won, first cap, last cap, goals scored [or for goalies, shut-outs achieved], height and weight. Football anoraks, like dieticians, need to know if our strikers are putting on the beef. Background information on the match officials should also be included for it's important that their decisions can be questioned in the correct language and in the knowledge that one or more of them may also be qualified lawyers.

Also as in years gone by, programmes should include adverts for Scotland strips [but not the pink one], alcohol, confectionery [not just the sponsor's chocolate] and rainwear products because in Scotland we will always enjoy wearing the colours,

supping an ale and munching a packet of crisps etc – especially when it's chucking it down. Other nods to yesteryear should be in the shape of a feature on the type of football being used, a topical cartoon and a cover price that is less than the cost of a pint of beer.

Staying with the cover price, throughout most of the 1950s it was sixpence in pre-decimalisation money [ie 2.5 pence] with the regular exception of the England match for which the programme cost one shilling [5 pence]. In the 1960s most Scotland programmes cost 5 pence whilst throughout the inflation-prone seventies it was 10 pence, 15 pence, 20 pence, 25 pence, 30 pence and 40 pence.

It hit the 50 pence mark in May 1980 for the visit of England in the last years of the British Championships whilst by the close of the decade it cost £1.00. By the end of the 1990s its regular price was £2.00 before hitting the £3.00 mark in March 2003 when Iceland came to Hampden on Euro qualifying business. The programme held steady at £3.00 until the SFA lost the plot in October 2014 and started charging a fiver throughout the Euro 2016 qualifying campaign before dropping back to £3.00 for the Russia 2018 malarkey.

In conclusion, and despite the BREXIT vote, it would be courteous if the Scotland programmes also included a couple of articles in the language of the opposition team although Switzerland with its four national languages could be a bit space-consuming.

That said, let's not confuse matters by following the example of the Football Association of Wales who now produce a completely bi-lingual programme [in English and Welsh] – unless of course it's sold at half the usual price....

QUEUING FOR TICKETS

This is a guilty pleasure from the past which is now gone due to membership of the Scotland Supporters Club and online technology whereby from the comfort of your home [or workplace when the boss is away] you can order your match tickets and even choose specific seats – just like a night out at the theatre.

Back in the day you had to queue for the briefs and the ticket outlets tended to be Hampden Park and the offices of the SFA or the Scottish Football League [all in Glasgow of course], plus a number of travel agents and/or sports shops scattered throughout Scotland. There was a real sense of achievement however, a real thrill when you eventually got your hands on the tickets – like getting past the bouncers at the entrance to the Dancing when you were well pished!

In more recent years tougher supporters than I have derived even greater satisfaction from queuing overnight for Scotland tickets [often in cold, wet weather] outside Hampden or Safeway Superstores. Apparently there's a real sense of 'we're all in it together' camaraderie with banter, sing-songs and sharing of strong liquor – mostly for 'central heating' purposes. It can bring out the best in people – like superstore managers offering free coffee or hot orange and a doughnut. Even stewards at Hampden have been known to open the doors early to provide shelter from the latest monsoon that was sweeping across Mount Florida.

So maybe queuing is a young person's adventure and applies to queuing for tickets only. Queuing for half-time pies and bovrils is a different experience altogether – often one in which the law of the jungle takes over!

SCOTLAND GLORY, TEARS AND SOUVENIRS

RANKINGS

The FIFA World Rankings were introduced in December 1992 and as at the end of December 2016 only eight teams have held the number one spot – Argentina, Belgium, Brazil, France, Germany, Italy, the Netherlands and Spain. Obviously, if the rankings had been introduced earlier – like in 1884 when Scotland won football's first-ever international tournament [the British Championship] – then Scotland would have been top of the pile right at the outset. I acknowledge that FIFA didn't exist until 1904 but you get my drift.

Going off at a tangent, I understand that something called the World Football Elo Ratings [which are named after its creator, Arpal Elo, a Hungarian-born physics professor] indeed has Scotland at the number one spot for almost 6,000 days between 1876 and 1892 with further 'chart-toppers' in 1904 and 1925.

More recently, [ie subsequent to the SFA re-joining FIFA in 1946] when Scotland returned undefeated from the 1974 World Cup finals in West Germany surely that would have earned us ninth spot at least. Argentina 78 might have produced something even better – for in defeating the Netherlands we bested the team that would eventually finish runners-up to champions Argentina!

Back in 1957 West Germany were the reigning world champions when Scotland trumped them 3-1 in a friendly in Stuttgart – and let's not forget that in 1967 Scotland defeated the then world champions England at Wembley in a British Championship/ Euro qualifier double-header. We also beat the 1986 World Cup winners Argentina, 1-0 in a friendly at Hampden in March 1990 plus there's our 3-1 win over Czechoslovakia in a World Cup qualifier in 1977 when they

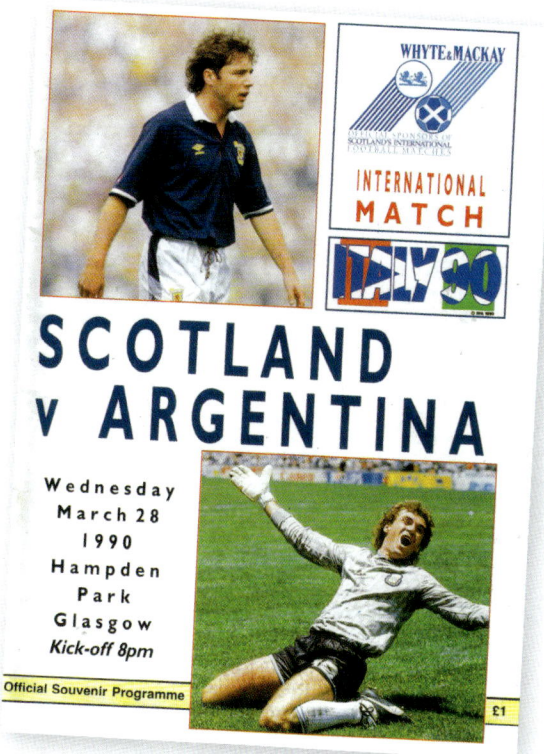

were the reigning European champions. Surely these prestigious results would have done us a power of good had there been a FIFA rankings system in place at the time?

In the real FIFA [ie post 1992] world however it transpires that our best official ranking came about in October 2007 when we were placed 13th following a winning run that included victories over France in Paris and the Ukraine at Hampden in Euro 2008 qualifiers. Conversely, Scotland's lowest-ranking position to date is 88th which was 'achieved' in 2005 when Berti Vogts was guiding us towards undreamt of depths. On the positive side as there are over 200 FIFA members, 88th still meant that we were in the top half of the table!

I wish I could say that the only rankings which really matter are those which saw Scots tennis ace, Andy Murray, claim the coveted number one spot in 2016. However, the FIFA rankings, accurate or otherwise, affect the seeding arrangements when the draw for the qualifying groups are being made. Haste the day then, when geographical/confederation barriers will be removed and our World Cup qualifying group could include Costa Rica, Peru, Morocco, Iran and the Cook Islands... with Wales as the top seed!

REPUBLIC OF IRELAND

Following the partition of Ireland in 1921 there was created the Dublin-based Football Association of Ireland [FAI] which is the football governing body for what became the Republic of Ireland [ROI]. [See also Ireland/Northern Ireland.] Although there had been inter-league representative matches between our two nations since 1938 it was not until 1961 that Scotland played the ROI when they were drawn together in the same World Cup qualifying group – with ultimately Czechoslovakia making it through to the finals. Scotland and the ROI were also drawn together in the qualifiers for Euro 1988 and Euro 2016 and on both occasions the Irish made it through to the finals whilst Scotland did not.

Like Northern Ireland [but unlike Scotland] the Republic have also made it beyond the group stages at the finals of major competitions [1990, 1994 and 2002 World Cups plus the 2016 European Championships].

ROI thorns in Scottish sides have included Noel Cantwell, Johnny Giles, Mark Lawrenson, Liam Brady and Robbie Keane. Arguably more painful however, were the relatively recent decisions of James McCarthy and Aiden McGeady to choose Ireland over Scotland for their international careers.

Let's not be churlish however, so here's to Hearts midfielder Gary Mackay – scorer of the Republic's most important goal ever...

ROUS CUP

In 1985 England and Scotland kind of did the dirty on Wales and Northern Ireland by abandoning the 100 years old British Championship before introducing to a largely disinterested world.... The Rous Cup. [Tah-dah!] Named after the former FIFA President Sir Stanley Rous, the competition lasted only for five years and mercifully I don't see a Blatter Cup coming along anytime soon.

Anyway, in both 1985 and 1986 the Rous Cup comprised of one-off matches between the old enemies whilst from 1987 to 1989 the competition was a triangular tournament involving Brazil, Colombia and Chile respectively with the final arithmetic being that there were eleven Rous Cup matches in total – five hosted by England and six by Scotland.

SCOTLAND GLORY, TEARS AND SOUVENIRS

In the inaugural game on 25th May 1985 and in front of a crowd of 66,489 at Hampden Park, Scotland lifted the trophy thanks to a headed goal from Dundee United's Richard Gough. It was to be Jock Stein's last home game in charge before Reykjavik then Cardiff…

For the second edition of real football's answer to the Calcutta Cup, Scotland, with caretaker manager Alex Ferguson in charge, went to Wembley on Wednesday 23rd April 1986 and lost 2-1 with 68,357 watching on. Terry Butcher and Glenn Hoddle gave the home side a 2-0 advantage at half-time before Graeme Souness converted a penalty after Butcher had hauled down and injured Charlie Nicholas. By all accounts it was a bit of a rough-house World Cup finals preparation match for both sides.

Incidentally, the 1986 tie was also the first time Scotland had played a match on St George's Day – the irony being that the first ever international was played over a century earlier on St Andrew's Day, albeit on a cricket ground.

In 1987 the competition opened on 19th May with England and Brazil drawing 1-1 at Wembley – Gary Lineker netting for the home side and Mirandinha equalising for the South Americans. Four days later Scotland [managed by Andy Roxburgh] and England slugged out a 0-0 draw at Hampden with Leicester City's Ian Wilson debuting for the Scots in front of 64,713 – this was only the third occasion in which this fixture had finished goalless. On 26th May Scotland and Brazil then went toe to toe at Hampden to see who would win the World Cup, sorry, I mean the Rous Cup. Only 41,384 witnessed Scotland spurn first-half chances before Rai and Valdo beat the Scots keeper Andy Goram of Oldham Athletic to give Brazil a 2-0 victory and so the trophy left Mount Florida bound for Rio.

In 1988 the South American guests were Colombia who opened the competition on 17th May with a 0-0 draw at Hampden. This time only 20,487 came along to see the likes of Carlos Valderrama with his superlative midfield skills and massive blond Afro-hairstyle – a proper curly-haired bossman. Also, in goals was the eccentric Jose 'El Loco' Higuita. However, I don't recall any scorpion-kick clearances that evening.

Four days later 70,480 saw Scotland lose 1-0 to England at Wembley with Peter Beardsley scoring in the 11th minute, and three days after that the English won the trophy by drawing 1-1 with Colombia. Only

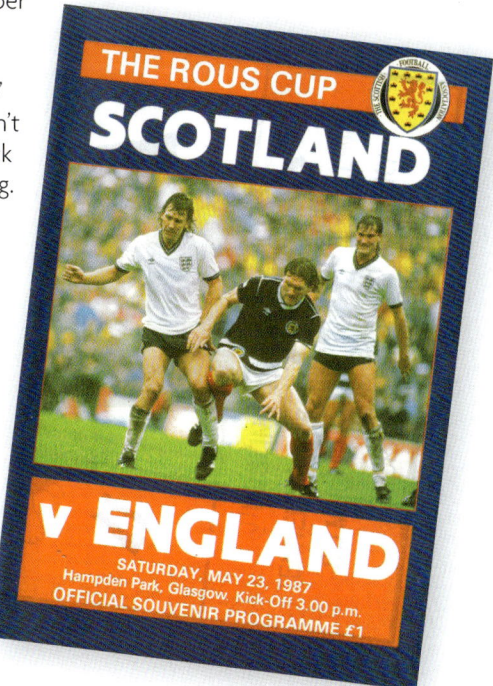

165

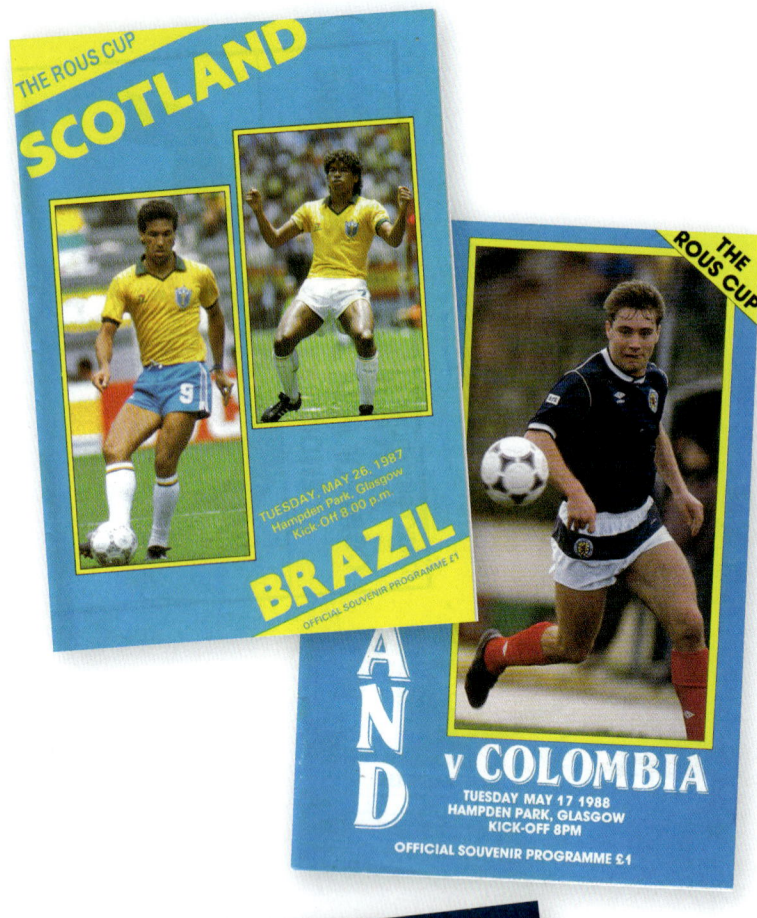

25,756 were at Wembley to see goals from Gary Lineker and the ill-fated Andres Escobar.

Apathy [and some street violence] reigned at the 1989 tournament which began with a Wembley attendance of just 15,628 on 23rd May for the goalless draw involving England and Chile. Four days later England travelled north and won 2-0 at Hampden with Chris 'man of many bad hairstyles' Waddle and Third Division player Steve Bull doing the damage in front of 63,382. Clucking bell!

On 30th May 1989 the curtain came down on the Rous Cup [it was never going to rival *The Mousetrap*] when an audience of 9,006 at the Hampden Theatre of Echoes saw Scotland beat Chile 2-0 thanks to goals from Aston Villa's Alan McInally and Murdo MacLeod of Borussia Dortmund. Thank you and goodnight…

ROXBURGH, ANDY

Or the Rise of the Glaswegian Schoolteachers as this period should be known with Roxburgh being followed by Craig Brown, both of whom were primary school teachers before moving into coaching full time.

Indeed it was a bit of a surprise when Andy Roxburgh took over from caretaker manager Alex Ferguson after the World Cup in Mexico 1986. Roxburgh had held the post of the SFA's Director of Coaching since 1975 and had won the UEFA Under-18 Championship in 1982 with Scotland and also had some measure of success in the 1983 FIFA Under-20 World Cup in Mexico with his side topping their group. However to the average Scotland fan he was still a bit of an unknown quantity and lacked the charisma and presence of a big name but for all that Andy's time as Scotland manager can be called successful in the main.

It did start unimpressively though with a poor opening to the 1988 Euro campaign. Scotland started with two blank draws but Roxburgh did recall Mo Johnston immediately to the squad; a move that would pay big dividends for the following World Cup campaign. Roxburgh did however achieve something very few Scotland managers have before or since; he managed to beat Belgium in a Euro qualifier with the Scots running out 2-0 victors in October 1987 at Hampden with goals from Ally McCoist and Paul McStay. He would also achieve the low of playing out a

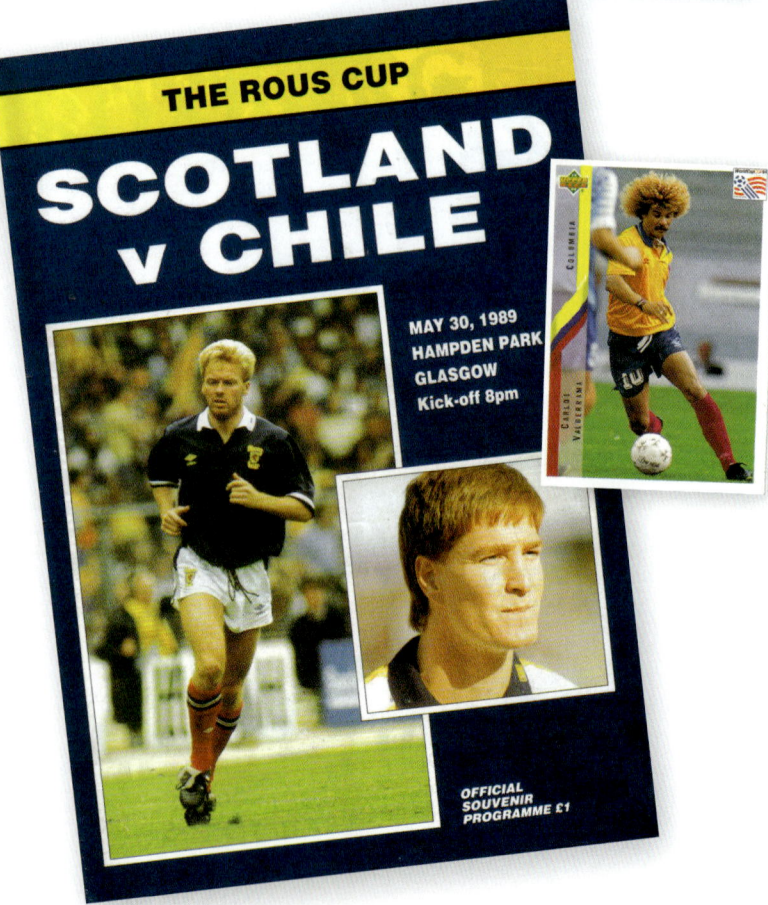

blank score draw with the not-so-mighty Luxembourg but with the win against Belgium and indeed a victory away to Bulgaria there were some signs of progress towards the end of the campaign.

1988 started off with a number of draws and out of eight games Scotland would only achieve one win. However, it was a vital one with Scotland winning their opening game of the 1990 World Cup campaign away to Norway 2-1 with Mo Johnston hitting the second goal. Mo would score six in five games to help give Scotland wins against Cyprus, home and away as well as a memorable double against France at Hampden.

These early gains meant that Scotland could afford to lose their last two away games to Yugoslavia and France before drawing with Norway at home to qualify as group runners-up. Aberdeen's Willie Miller would be injured in this game and it would ultimately see him retire early from playing and there's no doubt he was a big loss to the Scotland side in terms of experience.

Roxburgh is still the only Scotland manager to receive the Scottish Football Writers' Association Manager of the Year award – for season 1989/90 – and just like any monthly management award it seems, it of course subsequently saw a downturn in results for Roxburgh and Scotland. There was a high of beating world champions Argentina at Hampden in March 1990 but Scotland were to find that they had peaked in qualifying; an all too familiar story as Johnston's goals were to dry up and Roxburgh struggled to find his definitive line-up either in defence or up front. The Argentina game had yielded Everton's Stuart McCall who would become a pivotal part of the Scottish midfield and Roxburgh did try to experiment by having a 'B' match and a full international against East Germany on consecutive nights but these didn't bring forth anyone else to stake a major claim for a place in the World Cup squad.

His final friendly match before Italia '90 saw Scotland defeat Malta 2-1 with Alan McInally of Bayern Munich scoring both goals. Roxburgh chose McInally and Mo Johnston to start against Costa Rica in Genoa. Unlike Ally MacLeod in Argentina there is no doubt that Roxburgh would have had a full dossier on all his opposition and indeed tactically would have laid out his plans to his players but fundamentally could he inspire? Not enough to get a result against Costa Rica in what was a poor display devoid of any creative ideas. Scotland lost 1-0 and I would also question the decision to play in the away kit that day [ie mostly white with yellow horizontal stripes] when to my mind we should always start in the dark blue strip every time when we can. Please note the term dark blue.

Scotland would, of course, come out with all guns blazing for the Sweden game and win 2-1 thanks to goals from McCall and a penalty from Mo Johnston. Sadly for the final game Scotland once more lacked any cohesion or penetration and lost to a soft goal from a poor Brazil late in the game.

However, Andy would achieve something that Bobby Brown, Willie Ormond and Jock Stein could not do before him and qualify for the European Championships and yet it didn't look so good 13 minutes into the first game as Scotland went 1-0 down to a strong Romanian team in front of a paltry 12,801 crowd at Hampden.

Scotland recovered though to win 2-1 and would do so likewise a month later against Switzerland. They would only lose once, to Romania in Bucharest and were able to count on a few players to score the goals and had goalkeeper Andy Goram initially of Hibernian and then Rangers in imperious form throughout qualifying and indeed the finals itself.

Given there was only eight competitors in the finals in Sweden '92 it's not surprising the high level of opposition Scotland would face but they were unlucky to come away without a point in games against the Netherlands and Germany. However, Scotland were to finish on a high with a convincing 3-0 win over the

CIS or to give them their full name the Commonwealth of Independent States as Russia and some remaining satellite states were known at that point.

World Cup 1994 was going to be in the United States [of America] and in many ways was the tournament everyone wanted to take part in. Unfortunately for Scotland the wheels fell aff the Andy Roxburgh wagon and he would eventually jump ship to a post with UEFA. (Transportation geeks please note I know you can't jump ship from a wagon.) To be honest except the horror of a 5-0 defeat away to Portugal the real problem for Scotland was a lack of goals and failure to win any home games against Portugal, Italy and Switzerland instead playing out nil-nil draws in two and a one each in the other.

Following the shocking defeat in Lisbon Roxburgh dropped three Rangers outfield players who had been mainstays of his side for a number of years in Richard Gough, Dave McPherson and Stuart McCall and indeed would not play any of them again.

Scotland still had five qualifiers to complete which saw them gain wins home and away to Estonia and a draw with Switzerland. Andy would quit before the penultimate game against Italy in Rome but a ready-made replacement was in place in Craig Brown.

Andy Roxburgh may not have been the most charismatic of Scotland bosses and apparently at times treated his charges as boys rather than men but given his youth-side background perhaps it's not surprising, particularly as many of the players he utilised had progressed through the youth system under Andy himself. Mr. Roxburgh also achieved the distinction of having guided Scotland to two major finals.

SCOTCARDS 1972

After their failure to reach the 1970 World Cup finals Scotland seemed to slump rapidly. Bobby Brown who had begun his management of Scotland with that famous victory at Wembley in 1967 saw his side repeatedly depleted through injury, loss of form or an unwillingness of the big English clubs to release their players and so he gave up the ghost by the end of the summer of '71.

Tommy Docherty duly arrived and brought a freshness to the international scene, talking up the Scotland team and their players which saw some of the previous apathy abate and supporters return to the terraces of Hampden to support their team. Of course some victories in among that lot helped too.

The *Scottish Daily Express* bought into this and released a series of postcard size footballer cards at the start of the 1972/73 season. The cards themselves are artist drawings but they are colourful and look like the players they represent unlike the horrible set *The Sun* newspaper released in 1978.

The players the *Express* chose did represent the current Scotland line-up under the Doc with players new to the international scene such as Asa Hartford, Archie Gemmill and even Bob Wilson – the English-born Arsenal player who played for Scotland on two occasions. There are of course established Anglos such as Billy Bremner who in card #1 looks as though he's ready for a fight with a referee perhaps or an opponent maybe or possibly no one in particular.

Although it was only the Anglo players that were in Scotland colours, the set also included players from less fashionable clubs who Docherty had selected for various Scotland squads and in particular the previous summer's 'Mini World Cup' [Brazil Independence Tournament]; so we also have the likes of Kilmarnock's Ally Hunter, Dundee's Iain Phillip and Alex Forsyth of Partick Thistle.

There are only 24 to collect but they are well worth looking out for if only as evocative mementos of a time when Scotland had a manager who could perhaps have taken Scotland to the heights – if only he hadn't buggered off to Manchester United!

SCOTLAND GLORY, TEARS AND SOUVENIRS

SCOTLAND SUPPORTERS CLUB

The forerunner of the Scotland Supporters Club [SSC] was the Scotland Travel Club [STC]. The STC was founded in 1980 with the expressed purpose of encouraging responsible behaviour by fans. Members were guaranteed one ticket for all home matches plus the opportunity to apply for tickets for away matches. The STC was re-named the SSC in 2005 with membership usually restricted to around 30,000 and sometimes there is a waiting list – yes really!

Being 'in the club' so to speak has other bonuses, a faintly sad but personal favourite was receiving a Christmas card containing photocopy images of squad and management autographs. Christmas 2003 was particularly special as it included scrawls from the likes of Berti Vogts, James McFadden, Darren Fletcher, Barry Ferguson and Lee Wilkie! These days SSC members receive an electronic Christmas card from the SFA by email – which is just not the same.

Membership renewal every two years has brought a whole host of Scotland collectables such as pin badges, kilt-pins, beanie-hats, scarves, t-shirts, ties, key-rings, DVDs, CDs, booklets and discount vouchers covering coaching courses and physiotherapy treatment.

Before we all went on-line an occasional and somewhat quirky SFA-produced collectible were the fold-up, pocket-sized travel guides that were provided for supporters heading to away games. They were formulaic but helpful including as they did a city map/stadium location plan; some recommended restaurants, pubs, and nightclubs; useful tips on transport, health, safety and security, etc., as well as some suggestions on things to do and see [ie castles, cathedrals and museums but no shebeens, bordellos or knitwear shops].

My one criticism was that within the section on useful foreign words and phrases there was a tendency to include local translations for stereotypical scenarios such as 'My mate is a bit crazy but he's harmless' and 'I am drunk please let me into my hotel room.' Then again maybe I'm just an over-sensitive ex-lush!

It has to be said that by and large the STC/SSC staff have done a great job over the years not only in the processing and distribution of match tickets but also by acting as tour guides, medics, and 'Agony Aunts' to the Scotland support. There has of course been the occasional hiccup, eg delays in the allocation of 'spot-check' tickets at away venues such as at the Gibraltar game in the Algarve in October 2015 which meant that a considerable number of us missed the kick-off but we'll let that go.... for now.

By way of 'further assistance', in 1985 the SFA introduced Scotball Travel & Leisure Limited and invited supporters to 'Come fly with us – The Scotland squad does'. Unfortunately Scotball's package deals were never particularly competitive and the advent of budget airlines hastened the demise of the SFA's travel agent. Another contributory factor I reckon was that there probably weren't enough supporters out there who wanted to pay extra money just for the privilege of being on the same plane as and perhaps partaking in a dry sherry or two with the likes of Frank 'Where's the burdz?' McAvennie and Alan 'Rambo' McInally.

SEASIDE PREPARATIONS

For a good number of years, in preparation for home matches, Scotland squads would meet and train at small seaside towns in Ayrshire – usually Largs or Troon where the associated junior football grounds could be 'borrowed' for plotting the downfall of the likes of England. Seamill was another favourite seaside haunt of Scotland managers, particularly Jock Stein. There's nothing wrong with a *Chariots of Fire* type run along the beach dodging a freezing-cold incoming tide, award-winning sand-sculptures, over-excited dogs, greeting weans, obnoxious kite-fliers, seaweed and jellyfish. It's character building....

In their 20th century heyday Ayrshire coastal resorts were a magnet for Scottish holidaymakers and Scottish international footballers alike. The Queen's Hotel in Largs was the base for Scotland during the 1974 British Championships and it was from the adjacent beach that a somewhat 'refreshed' winger Jimmy Johnstone was 'encouraged' by some of his equally refreshed team-mates to try rowing to America. The coastguard duly rescued Scotland's wonder winger/drunken sailor and a couple of days later, the invigorating sea-air inspired wee Jinky and his colleagues to a 2-0 victory against the Old Enemy at Hampden.

In more recent times our international players are 'holed up' at the likes of the five star Cameron House Hotel – a plush country house hotel overlooking Loch Lomond or Mar Hall Hotel in Bishopton – a luxury spa hotel on a 240 acre golf estate overlooking the River Clyde. Between them they offer a combination of posh rooms with high-speed internet access and entertainment systems plus high-thread-count sheets, four-poster beds and claw-foot tubs. Rainfall showerheads and designer toiletries plus indoor pool and beauty treatments for our pampered, manicured and yet ultimately unsuccessful footballers. I can't help but wonder what a genuine working-class hero such as Jock Stein would have said about it all.

Remember all this is prior to home qualification games – it is not hard-earned, well- deserved luxury in readiness for competing in the finals of the World Cup or European Championships.

In my humble opinion there should be no more ostentatious luxury for our players until we qualify again for the finals of a major tournament – so get your under-achieving arses back down the Firth of Clyde to a modest, but adequate hotel [or B & B] in Troon, Largs or Seamill! Rant over.

SMITH, WALTER

When Lanarkshire-born Walter Smith was chosen as the new Scotland manager he perhaps wasn't fully embraced by some fans due to his time in charge of the all-conquering Rangers team of the nineties but Walter would soon prove himself to be amongst the most adept and outstanding of Scotland managers. Although for a lot of us a manager that was not Berti Vogts would suffice, such was our despair at the time.

There is no doubt the Scotland side had become shambolic under Vogts and Smith needed to steady the ship. He would name Ally McCoist and Tommy Burns as his assistants which some saw as rather astute given their Rangers and Celtic backgrounds. However, Smith saw

SCOTLAND GLORY, TEARS AND SOUVENIRS

them as a good fit for the job. Burns had been caretaker manager for one match after Vogts' departure; a resounding 4-1 defeat to Sweden at Easter Road.

Smith's first game in charge was against Italy in Milan in March, 2005 and he would recall David Weir to the line-up as well as give a debut cap to Paul Hartley of Hearts. Hartley had been completely overlooked by Berti Vogts who used over 60 players in his time in charge. Paul would be a regular in Smith's side in midfield and starting alongside him in Milan was Lee McCulloch of Wigan Athletic in only his second Scotland appearance. Scotland would lose with both goals being scored by Andrea Pirlo but they looked fairly solid for most of the match and it seemed to be a decent start.

In his first home match in June 2005, Scotland defeated Moldova 2-1 with Christian Dailly and James McFadden netting which was followed by a draw away to Belarus a few days later. September would see Scotland draw with Italy at home and beat Norway 2-1 in Olso. Kenny Miller had hit a rich vein of form at the time, scoring in the first and hitting a brace in the latter and had he not been injured before half-time you would not have bet against him hitting a hat-trick that night.

However, as with all Scotland stories nowadays, there has to be a moment of misfortune and for Walter it was in the game against Belarus at Hampden a month later. A calamitous gifted goal to Belarus five minutes into the game gave an indication of how the day would go with Scotland inept throughout and lucky not to concede more and as the rain monsooned down on Hampden the home side's chance of a play-off spot was washed away.

Four days later and Smith's side produced one of the best Scotland displays away from home for many a year with a 3-0 crushing of Slovenia in Celje with delightful goals from Darren Fletcher, James McFadden and Paul Hartley. This win would garner more ranking points that any other international played that season and Scotland would begin to rise up from the plummeted depths of the low 80s and would eventually see Walter push their ranking up by 70 places before he would depart. I have no doubt that had Smith begun that 2006 World Cup campaign in charge a play-off place would have been achieved.

Scotland would of course win a cup under Smith's tutelage and with some style. Scotland were invited to take part in the Kirin Cup in Japan in May 2006 and started it off with aplomb with Rangers players Kris Boyd and Chris Burke hitting two goals in a 5-1 thrashing of Bulgaria in Kobe. They would gain a draw with the host nation to win the cup outright and we all started looking forward to the 2008 Euro qualifying campaign with some hope and with some trepidation given the teams in our group.

Scotland were seeded fourth in the draw and were unlucky to have France, Italy and Ukraine all in their group but some magical moments and heartbreak were awaiting us in the months to come. Scotland came out of the traps unusually fast, crushing the Faroes 6-0 at Celtic Park scoring five goals in the first half. They followed this up with a 2-1 victory over Lithuania in Kaunas which set them up nicely for the visit of France at Hampden in October 2006.

The French turned up at Hampden confident of getting a result and with players of the calibre of Henry, Vieira, Ribery and Trezeguet they were expected to leave with all three points. They did pummel the Scotland goal throughout the match but Gary Caldwell of Celtic would be the unlikely hero of the day in scoring the game's only goal. It was a moment of utter joy to be there and at the end of the game to be singing along with thousands of others to a tune written by an American and performed by an English band. Belting out Status Quo's 'Rockin' All Over The World' remains one of my great Scotland memories.

And so the Walter Smith bandwagon was rolling on with three wins out of three but four days later a defeat in Kiev to Ukraine saw it slow down a bit and then in January 2007 it would come to an abrupt end. Rangers were in freefall following the appointment and hastened departure of Paul Le Guen and so turned to Smith to rescue their fortunes. The SFA were reluctant to let him go but soon Walter was Ibrox bound.

It was a sad end for Walter and Scotland as he was putting together a good side capable of getting results both at home and away. I do believe Smith when he has stated that no other club would have tempted him away from the Scotland job, unlike his successor who jumped ship at the first opportunity. Although Alex McLeish would take over and the team would continue to progress, Walter's departure still rankles with a lot of supporters and was seen by some as a betrayal at the time. Overall, though, Smith was as good a manager as Scotland has had in this millennium and he left the team in a much healthier state than when he arrived.

SPONSORSHIP AND PARTNERSHIPS

When Scotland played Luxembourg in a Euro qualifier at Hampden Park in November 1986 it was an historic occasion. Not only because Kenny Dalglish made his 102nd and final appearance for Scotland but due to the fact that it was the first football international to be sponsored in Britain. The sponsors were Whyte & Mackay Whisky Distillers but as far as I can recall there were no free samples being handed out, certainly not to those of us who occupied the freezing cold, uncovered East Terracing that evening!

Anyway, Scotland turned in a dramtastic performance and won 3-0.

Of course prior to this there had been many ad-hoc, individual sponsorship deals, some of which were linked to qualifying for the World Cup finals. For example, in the run-up to the 1974 finals in West Germany, the car-makers Vauxhall offered up 28 vehicles on a free loan for a year for distribution to players and officials. Much squabbling regarding the distribution

resulted however and to make matters worse many of the players were under the misapprehension that the cars, which had the driver's doors monogrammed with their initials, were theirs to keep. Just a thought but maybe it's just as well that Celtic midfielder Vic Davidson didn't make the squad.

Anyway, the Whyte & Mackay 'match' deal ended in March 1994 when Scotland lost 0-1 to a Netherlands side that boasted Frank Rijkaard, Dennis Bergkamp and Marc Overmars in a friendly match at Hampden. So much for Dutch courage that evening but the Water of Life did help Scotland reach the 1990 World Cup finals as well as the finals of Euro 92.

Four years later in March 1998 when Scotland faced Denmark at Ibrox Stadium in preparation for going to the World Cup finals three months later, Scottish Gas became the first official sponsors of Scotland's international football team. Brian Laudrup [then of Glasgow Rangers] scored to give the Danes a 1-0 victory and post-France 98, Scotland's international gas has remained at a peep.

In 2002 Berti Vogts arrived and so too did a sponsorship deal with Safeway [the supermarket chain] which included match tickets, competitions, merchandising and a range of promotional offers being available at stores throughout Scotland. Unfortunately, some of Scotland's performances under the

SCOTLAND GLORY, TEARS AND SOUVENIRS

stewardship of the bold Berti were so bad that it became more embarrassing for blokes to ask for match tickets in store than it was for us to enquire about female hygiene products.

In the UK, Safeway was acquired by Morrisons in March 2004 and a rebranding/sell-off exercise followed. The Safeway name disappeared from the UK in November 2005 whilst Vogts disappeared from Scottish High Streets a year earlier.

So Morrisons took over the sponsorship deal in time for Walter Smith's first home game in charge, a World Cup qualifier against Moldova in June 2005 which Scotland won 2-0. Morrisons' motto was 'Proud to serve Scotland' and so was Walter Smith until Rangers came a-calling in January 2007 but that is another story.

By the time the Euro 2008 qualifiers started in August 2006, the Nationwide Building Society were the 'Official Partner of the Scotland Football Team'. Pride, Passion, Belief was their tagline. Nationwide also had sponsorship deals with the England, Northern Ireland and Wales Football Associations.

Just to confuse matters however, in the programme for the home Euro qualifier against France in October 2006 [which we won 1-0, Zut alors!] Tennent's Lager announced they were sponsoring the national team. This time the catchphrase was 'We'll never stop following Scotland....wherever it takes us, whatever it takes'.

After Scotland's failure to make the finals of Euro 2008 the mantra changed to 'Never stop dreaming'.

By 2010 the Scottish FA's partners included McDonald's [the fast food chain] and Mars [the chocolate manufacturer not the planet].William Hill Bookmakers later joined in the fun and are considerate enough to regularly remind us that when the fun stops, stop. [Hopefully someone will let us know when the fun is about to start]. In addition, Taggarts Motor Group and Jaguar were the official suppliers of executive cars to the SFA and the SFL whilst Marks & Spencer were the official tailors to the SFA. M&S or S&M? You pays your money etc etc...

Since 2011 our old friends Vauxhall Cars have been the Scotland team sponsors although Tennent's Lager proclaim that they are a Proud Scotland Supporter. A quick look at the SFA website meanwhile reveals a whole plethora of sponsors and partners. All those big names, all those monies coming into the game – Scottish football must be doing really well, eh?

173

STADIA – AWAY GAME DELIGHTS

Following Scotland away from home has offered groundhoppers like myself some wonderful opportunities to visit some marvellous [and some not so marvellous] stadia.

Old Wembley Stadium [for which the people of Glasgow contributed £105,000 to the original 1921 appeal fund] had a capacity of 100,000 and with its twin towers [and drainpipes for assisting the ticketless], provided many great memories. New Wembley is a magnificent replacement stadium [90,000] but so far there are no great memories although Kenny Miller's goal there in 2013 was a belter.

Cardiff's Millennium Stadium [74,500] is a wee bit special too but a 4-0 stuffing there in 2004 kind of spoiled things a bit. Dublin's giant greenhouse [aka the Aviva Stadium [51,700]] is another favourite with its roof undulating in a wave-like manner so as to avoid blocking light to nearby houses. That's what I call considerate. Scotland won two out of three Carling Nations Cup matches there in 2011.

We've not even reached mainland Europe yet and you can see that dear old Hampden has been left behind a bit in terms of artistic merit and features such as retractable roofs, spacious toilets and better than average catering facilities.

Warsaw's Stadion Narodowy [58,000] is another modern-day beauty. Its silver and white façade resembles a waving flag of Poland and it was in this magnificent arena in October 2014 that Scotland played some pretty good football, drew 2-2 and raised our hopes that we would be heading to Euro 2016.

Conversely when I visited Kiev's Olympic Stadium for a Euro qualifier in 2006 it was a badly-lit hovel. Six years later and following extensive renovation works including the construction of a new roof it hosted the final of the 2012 European Championships.

Bari's Estadio San Nicola [58,000] and the Estadio Algarve [30,000] are architecturally very pleasing to the eye. The former resembles a giant flower whilst the latter features two facing roofs which give the illusion of giant sails. The big problem was their out of town, middle of nowhere locations making transport to and from the matches against Italy [2007] and Gibraltar [2015] a bit of a nightmare. Those Scotland supporters who wanted to re-locate our own national stadium to somewhere in Strathclyde Park please note.

For a sense of footballing history, it's difficult to beat the Giuseppe Meazza Stadium [aka San Siro] in Milan [80,000 capacity, 11 large cylindrical towers and a distinctive wrap-round series of ramps]. It's also difficult to beat Italy on their own turf and we lost a World Cup qualifier there in 2005.

Over the years Scotland have of course played at some of the most iconic football stadia in the world including the Amsterdam Arena [two sore ones in 2003 and 2009], the

SCOTLAND GLORY, TEARS AND SOUVENIRS

ESTÁDIO MÁRIO FILHO (MARACANÃ)

Maracana Stadium, Rio [a narrow 1-0 defeat by the hosts in the 1972 Brazil Independence tournament] and the Westfalen Stadion, Dortmund [two undeserved defeats in 2003 and 2014]. We have however excelled at the likes of the Estadio Boca Juniors, Buenos Aires [Argentina 1 Scotland 1 – June 1977 but we were arguably the better team] as well as at the Bernabeu Stadium, Madrid [Spain 2 Scotland 6 – June 1963 where we most certainly were the better team].

Incidentally, the formal title of the Maracana Stadium is the Estadio Mario Filho, named in honour of a former journalist. So which Scottish journalist would you re-name Hampden Park after – Hugh Taylor, Alex Cameron, James Sanderson, Bill Leckie, Keith Jackson or Graham Spiers?

STEIN, JOCK

There is no doubt that as a Scottish manager, Lanarkshire's Jock Stein is among the greatest along with the likes of Matt Busby, Bill Shankly and Alex Ferguson but as a Scotland manager there is perhaps a sense of under-achievement given the talent he had at his disposal with great players like Dalglish, Souness, Wark, Hansen, Strachan and many others. Ultimately his untimely death also leaves us with a feeling of an unfinished job.

Jock actually had two shots at being Scotland manager. His first came in May 1965 when he took over from the departed Ian McColl on a caretaker basis shortly before a World Cup qualifying away double header. Scotland came back with a 1-1 draw in Chorzow, Poland and a 2-1 victory in Finland.

Although initially it was only for the two games, Jock stayed on until the completion of the qualifiers. Ultimately a costly defeat to Poland at home, meant Scotland would not progress any further but the 1960s was a different era for a coach. Jock obviously named a side that would aim to beat Poland that night and when Billy McNeill put them ahead after 14 minutes things would have looked good. He may have asked for a bit more caution in the second half but he didn't have the opportunity to replace a forward with a deep-sitting midfielder or an extra defender as there were no substitutions allowed and so with the loss of two late goals, Stein was in many ways helpless to prevent them.

There would however be the experience of beating Italy at home with John Greig providing that moment of ecstasy at the death. For the final match in Naples, the Scotland side was so depleted that Stein resorted to picking Ron Yeats of Liverpool as his number nine but even with that extra defender Scotland went down 3-0.

And so it would be almost another fourteen years before he was to return to the Scotland post full-time following the departure of Ally MacLeod. Jock's first two years in charge did not make for good reading and up until September 1980 he had been in charge for 17 games, winning five (including two v Norway), drawing two and losing ten. No Scotland manager today could survive that record and with a World Cup qualifying group about to start which included Sweden, Portugal, Northern Ireland and Israel it was not going to be easy to qualify.

Jock's teams seemed to be built around a cautious approach, the cavalier style of Ormond and MacLeod that embodied British teams was replaced by a more modern, European, possession style of play which infuriated a lot of us on the terraces as we longed for the Scotland of old who piled on attack after attack. Jock would also utilise a third central defender in midfield so you would see line-ups with the Aberdeen pairing of Miller and McLeish but also have the likes of David Narey, Paul Hegarty and Alan Hansen in the mix too.

Scotland managers at the time were allowed to fail to qualify for the Euros as it was seen as secondary to the World Cup which was the be all and end all although defeating England was also still seen as

JOCK STEIN
SCOTLAND

Year of Birth — 1922
Managerial Experience — 25
Record Signing — n/a
Trophies Won — 29
Teams Managed — 5
Fans Friend — 16

John 'Jock' Stein will remain one of the most notable managers in British football history. Without doubt, he will be best remembered for winning a consecutive 9 Scottish league championships, 11 in total, and a similar number of Scottish Cups. Having gone 8 years without a trophy Celtic brought Jock Stein to the helm in March of 1965 where he made an immediate impact by winning the league in his first full season in charge. Following an illustrious 19 years in charge of Celtic, of which the highlight was a 1967 European Cup victory against Inter Milan, he moved on to achieve relative success in charge of Scotland following the briefest of times at Leeds United.

important. Scotland did qualify for Spain 1982 but it was ground-out due to some poor home form and ultimately it was two away results that got Scotland through.

Scotland would win 1-0 in both Stockholm and Tel Aviv with the success in Israel being quite precious as no other side left there with full points. It might not have been pretty but Jock's methods did ensure that points away from home were garnered. However, at Hampden there were some dour matches with a blank draw against Portugal being particularly dismal. Scotland gained qualification in a tight, tense match at Windsor Park, Belfast that ended with a 0-0 draw but the Irish would still qualify as runners-up and would have a memorable Spain '82. In between qualifying Scotland achieved a win at Wembley in May 1981 thanks to a penalty from John Robertson of Nottingham Forest.

Willie Ormond often talked about getting the right blend of players and as Jock approached Spain '82 it seems that he chopped and changed the defence in particular quite a lot. He starts off that year with an Alan Hansen and McLeish pairing followed by the introduction to international football of Allan Evans from Aston Villa pairing with Miller in the next. In the Home Internationals we see Evans / McLeish for the Irish game, Narey and Hansen for the Welsh game and then finally Evans and Hansen for the English game. This final pairing would start the World Cup but some slack play against New Zealand in the opening tie saw the pairing of Hansen with Miller line up against Brazil and also in the USSR game and we all know how that one finished.

Many a lesser manager than Jock might not have had the courage that Stein did in naming Miller and Hansen as his defensive pairing following their mishap in Spain for the games following the World Cup but Jock chose to show belief in his players by doing so. However, Scotland did not have a great Euro qualifying campaign 82/83 and once more failed to reach the finals.

However, when the World Cup rolled around again Scotland were on better form; a startling 6-1 friendly victory over Yugoslavia was followed by World Cup wins against Iceland and Spain and with the emergence of Maurice Johnston, it seemed Jock finally had a striker who had goals in him and would complement Dalglish up front.

Two defeats were to follow though; a not unexpected one to Spain in Seville as the Scots lost 1-0, but defeat to Wales at Hampden saw Scotland's chances of progression slump. They would need to win in Iceland and then a draw with Wales away could still see them through but first there was the little matter of the inaugural Rous Cup against England at Hampden.

Richard Gough of Dundee United would win the cup with his headed goal in the 68th minute at Hampden in May 1985. Scottish fans would wait longer for the Icelandic goal to be breached in Reykjavik three days later as Jim Bett of Belgian club Lokeren would score his only Scotland goal in the 86th minute to give Scotland the points.

The loss of Jock Stein at the end of the game against Wales with Scotland having qualified for the play-offs left the nation bereft and it was with a heavy heart that we moved on to play the matches with Australia. Alex Ferguson who had taken up the role of Jock's number two took over as caretaker manager through to Mexico '86.

It is hard to say how Scotland would have performed in Mexico under Jock. I don't think he would have taken Hansen having only used him as a sub on one occasion since 1983 but with his man management skills honed over the years would he have handled Mo Johnston differently and included him in his squad? Would he have been able to get that wee bit extra out of the players and perhaps gained that win against Uruguay which would have taken Scotland through to the knockout stage? Alas, we will never know.

TARTAN ARMY

The 'Tartan Army' is of course the modern-day collective term for supporters of the Scotland football team, ridiculous court cases regarding copyright and trademarks notwithstanding! Once upon a time however [ie the 1970s] 'The Tartan Army' included a number who were drunken 'causebothers' – especially on the London Underground [and other locations] every time we visited the English capital to see Scotland take on the Auld Enemy at Wembley Stadium. Nowadays however we are a self-policing entity who travel to international matches throughout Europe raising money for local charities and endeavouring to be friendly and respectful to everyone we meet. So how did that transformation come about?

One theory is that it stems from the early 1980s and our desire to differentiate ourselves from England fans, particularly those England fans that liked to throw tables, chairs, bottles and punches at rival supporters when travelling abroad.

As for the composition of the Tartan Army, well it's reckoned that the proportion who are also Rangers supporters, arguably the original backbone of the Scotland support, has declined considerably since the 1980s whilst the proportion that are Celtic supporters remains disappointingly low. This may be due in part to the fact that Celtic and Rangers supporters also regularly have European club football on which

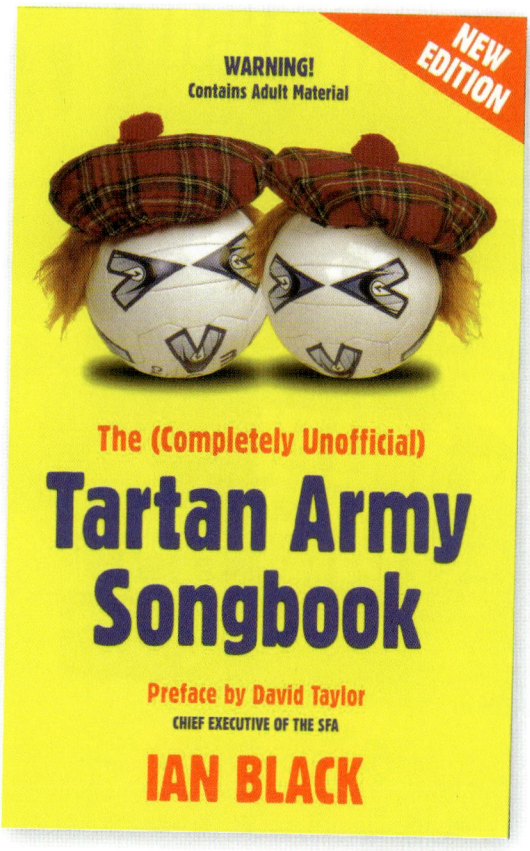

to spend their financial resources. Speaking as a Partick Thistle supporter my financial resources seldom have this problem to worry about and as such travelling to Scotland away games can take preference. Paradoxically, our friends in the north-east [who are sometimes accused of being 'careful with their money'] probably spend more than most traipsing across Scotland and continental Europe supporting club and country.

There may be other political, cultural or even religious reasons why some sections of the population feel 'disenfranchised' from the national football side, which is a great pity for the Scotland team are there for everyone to enjoy and endure! On the plus side, the number of female supporters appears to have increased.

The Association of Tartan Army [Supporters'] Clubs [ie ATAC] was formed in 2000 to act on behalf of fans of the national football team. ATAC directly represents members of affiliated clubs throughout Scotland and beyond but does not claim to represent the Tartan Army as a whole. Examples of TA clubs include the West of

Scotland Tartan Army [WESTA], Lunnain Albannaich [The Tartan Army in London] and the International Tartan Army [INTA].

So once upon a time the Tartan Army were feared and then we became recipients of awards for impeccable behaviour [eg at Euro '92 in Sweden and at the France '98 World Cup finals] – all of which is good. The Tartan Army have also inspired books and songs and have produced their own magazine and unofficial match-day programmes. It is just the occasional self-adulation or the patronising comments that are difficult to bear.

Again, once upon a time relatively few of us wore kilts to Scotland matches, so once upon a time chafing of our nether regions wasn't a significant problem especially for us lowlanders. And once upon a time, the colourful but appropriately-dressed Scotland support wouldn't be seen dead in pink replica jerseys!

I also have to say that the chant of 'No Scotland, no party' and the away trip saying 'Win or lose we're here for the booze' doesn't do it for me. The rest of the world does indeed know how to party – a recent example being the 2016 European Championships in France. Most supporters had a whale of a time, especially those from Iceland [sorry]. We were not missed and indeed it could be argued that we are in danger of becoming the Forgotten Army at least in so far as the finals are concerned.

As for these away trips, I won't deny that I am partial to sampling the local brew [or seeking out an Irish Bar where I can order some dark beer] and I also enjoy the sightseeing. However, the primary objective will always be to cheer on Scotland at the football. I'd willingly embrace sobriety and celibacy [for a few months] if it would somehow guarantee an away win in the likes of Georgia! The off-field camaraderie and crack are admittedly something special however and as such I would recommend that a Scotland away-trip should be on most football-lovers' bucket-list.

This is of course a simplistic and at times highly personal overview but we can't have an A to Z and not include something on the TA.

TEA FOR TWENTY-TWO

You only get 'oo' with Typhoo – apparently.

Anybody that has collected cards over the years will have no doubt at some point come across all those cards that Brooke Bond Tea published whether it is sets such as Famous People, the History of Aviation or even British Butterflies but they only ever released one football set and that was in 1976. They published the 40 Ways to Play Better Soccer set but if you were a Scotland fan then being shown how to play better soccer with only pictures of England players was a bit of a disappointment as well as an insult, although England had horsed us 5-1 at Wembley in 1975 when the set was probably being commissioned.

My family collected Brooke Bond cards in the late 60s but had I known that Typhoo had such great sets in the 60s I would have begged for a change of tea. Mind you, we were one of those strange families that didn't take to ITV with vulgar adverts and comedies and only watched BBC, so changing tea companies might not have gone down well.

The Typhoo sets had cards on the side of the packet and tokens you saved up to get 10" x 8" colour photos of initially teams and then later players. There are lots of Scots players to collect in all three players' sets. In set one there's Willie Henderson of Rangers, Joe McBride and Billy McNeill of Celtic and among the Anglos Jim Baxter of Sunderland and Eddie McCreadie of Chelsea. Later sets would see the likes of Chelsea's Charlie Cooke, Billy Bremner of Leeds United and Ian Ure of Arsenal but the 1973/74 set would have Coventry City's Colin Stein resplendent in a Scotland strip. It's

just a pity that Stein made the last of his 21 appearances for Scotland in season 1972/73.

Edinburgh Company Melrose Tea released an all-Scottish set of 28 cards for the 1986 World Cup but I have never been able to source any of these. However, much easier to find is the set by PG Tips which was for the 1998 World Cup and featured plenty of world stars such as Zidane, Bergkamp, Romario, Beckham and Colin Hendry.

At an age where I drink a lot of tea can I ask for just one company to release another set of cards preferably with lots of Scottish interest, so maybe not a World Cup finals set then.

TEAM PHOTOS

I have been getting a wee bit obsessional of late with Scotland team photos. It used to be quite a regular thing down the years for football magazines to publish

a Scotland team pic every season. Little did people know, that years down the line people like myself would slavishly study them trying to pinpoint the exact game the picture was from or for what squad.

There's a lot from the 1950s that can be hard to get as I don't always recognise the players. Okay big George Young is easy to spot but then there's players that only played a handful of games; so you spend your time on your computer bringing up differing images of who you think it could be. If you're lucky you spot someone quite distinctive and begin to mix and match. Oh aye he played with him four times but only three times with him and they two only twice and suddenly, bingo, you have it.

Of course, it's even better when you come across some guy who played the once and get him straight away.

The team strip also gives it away but it was still a bit of a surprise recently when I came across a team photo from 1955 of the Scotland side lining up to play Yugoslavia in Belgrade and the strip was unrecognisable as it was white with black or blue trimmings. Turns out a lot of people hadn't seen it before and it was blue trimmings with blue shorts and red socks. In the modern era strips change that quick that it is hard to keep track but sites such as the Historical Football Kits come in handy with such titbits as Scotland wore their 1980 to '82 change strip only once, with red socks, in Tel Aviv, Israel on World Cup duty.

A lot of the 1950s photos came from annuals – not the Christmas type though but more like the hardback equivalent of the *Scottish Wee Red Book* which normally came out just before the season began, listing club and international fixtures and so they tended to be quite small. Of course, as production values rose in the 70s and 80s the magazines produced the glossy single and double page versions, but nowadays not so much, although *Match of the Day* magazine published the team lining up before the friendly against Canada in March, 2017.

Trading cards and stickers over the years have also contained team photos but of

The Scottish team, with George Young carrying a bouquet of flowers, lines up before the Belgrade clash with Yugoslavia.

SCOTLAND GLORY, TEARS AND SOUVENIRS

It's a fine tradition being able to watch the football in the comfort of your own home either by yourself or in the company of family and friends. An armchair in your living-room is far more comfortable than an armchair in a 'Wetherspoons' pub. Furthermore if the result goes badly, it is your own ornaments that get broken, course with the stickers it can be hard to see if it's a Scotland team, never mind who's playing especially as my eyes get that wee bit older. Every now and then with new sponsors there seems to be produced team postcards which are quite collectable although not valuable and there's also a few 'Best Wishes' team cards which have been printed by the SFA from time to time.

Finally you can go for the expensive end of the market and buy a team photo signed by one or two of the players themselves, most of which seem to go for over a tenner. Anyway, here among this lot are some for you to do your own detective work with. Enjoy.

TELEVISION AND PUNDITRY

All coverage of Scotland matches – full game live or highlights – should be available on terrestrial television as used to be in the good old days before satellite and cable etc muscled in on the act. Anything else is unfair, undemocratic and quite often, a complete pain in the arse!

your own cat that is kicked. [Not that we would recommend cruelty to animals.]

It might come as a revelation to some people but not all Scots like frequenting pubs to watch a football match especially those pubs which advertise that they are 'showing' the game but on the day do not include sound! Watching Scotland play football without a commentary can sometimes be akin to watching an episode of the gloriously inept *Keystone Kops* from the days of the silent movies.

With regards to the commentary, it is also essential that the commentator and his assistant [match-summariser? hanger-on?] are both Scottish and that there is a link to a television studio in Glasgow or Edinburgh. We're not over-keen on patronising comments and commentary from our

neighbours, thank you very much. When it comes to their own national team, habitual referring to 1966 also rips my knitting. I always think 1066 is more significant. These issues are particularly important especially when it comes to including Scotland match highlights in video and DVD compilations.

Furthermore, wall to wall coverage of football in general is not TV heaven – there has to be a balance. As such my 'British' TV heaven XI would read as follows – *Football Focus, Dr. Who* [Tennant or Capaldi], *The Two Ronnies* [with Corbett excelling], *Sportscene, Scotsport, The Benny Hill Show, Taggart, Sportsnight* with Coleman, *Are you being served?, Top of the Pops* and Glen Michael's *Cartoon Cavalcade*. A winning line-up that can accommodate both Bob Wilson and Mrs Slocombe's pussy! 1970s dinosaurs are us! I digress.

There are of course some modern-day developments which are welcome – large TV screens, better quality of picture and various camera angles for viewing or re-playing the action. Extensive coverage of other international matches [especially qualifiers] is also to be welcomed. Pay per view television should have ended however when they did away with slot TV.

And finally, a word about Pundits – aerosols I hear you say – but no, for some of them are quite good at what they do. I remember that during the 1974 World Cup finals ITV duly enlisted the services of Brian Clough [then manager at Brighton and Hove Albion FC] plus Malcolm Allison [then manager of recently relegated Crystal Palace FC] – which brought the response 'Now let's hear from our panel of third and fourth division experts' – however, that dynamic duo certainly made for an interesting and lively debate.

I suppose it's the old story of one man's meat is another man's poison. I can just about manage to endure Gary Lineker's puns and attempts at humour in his regular Saturday night *Match of the Day* slot but when World Cup or Euro Championship finals come a-calling every second summer I'm all for bringing back capital punishment for lesser offences such as 'Talking absolute bollocks about England's prospects and being disrespectful to other nations'.

I never thought I'd say this but I miss Alan Hansen [26 Scotland caps, no goals and one memorable collision] – a friendly sage in a sea [or at least an English Channel] of blinkered babblers. That said I'm also quite fond of TV talking heads Danny Murphy [nine England caps and one goal between 2001 and 2003] and of course Pat Nevin [28 Scotland caps and five goals between 1986 and 1996] – the Melvyn Bragg of Scottish football!

TESTIMONIALS
Testimonial matches used to occur all the time in the 60s, 70s and 80s but these days with such high player turnover even at small clubs it's rare for a footballer to be given one. After all, who now spends ten years at the one club? Of course, there are some among the football elite such as Steven Gerrard, Ryan Giggs etc but there's often controversy attached to these fabulously wealthy players being awarded a testimonial.

Over the years though there was the odd turnout of a made-up Scotland XI for players that were worthy of such a match; some for great service and some like the tragic John White were benefit matches to raise funds for his family.

John White lost his life on 21st July, 1964 after being struck by lightning on Crews Hill Golf Course in Enfield. John had been part of Tottenham's great double winning side of 1960-61 and had made 33 appearances for Scotland from 1959-64. Four months later there was a memorial match played between Spurs and a Scotland XI to pay tribute to John who like Jim Morrison, Janis Joplin, Kurt Cobain and others, had lost his life at the age of 27.

If you turned up at White Hart Lane on 10th November, 1964 expecting to watch the John White Memorial

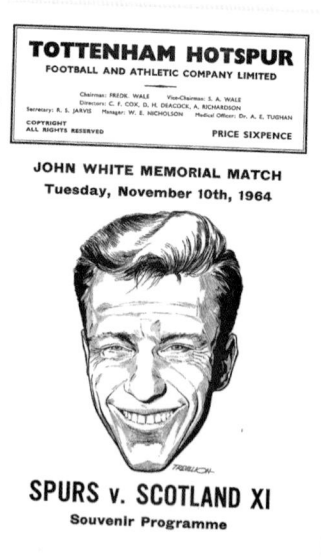

Match, then you wouldn't have seen much as it was a foggy night in old London town and indeed for most of the country and so the game was postponed for 24 hours.

The Scotland line-up the next day [with national manager Ian McColl in charge] would comprise of Jim Cruickshank (Hearts), Alex Hamilton (Dundee), Jim Kennedy (Celtic), John Greig (Rangers), Ron Yeats (Liverpool), Jim Baxter (Rangers), Neil Martin (Hibs), Alan Gilzean (Dundee), Willie Wallace (Hearts), Ian St. John (Liverpool) and Davie Wilson (Rangers).

Among the Spurs players was Scotland's Bill Brown in goals, with Alan Mullery, Jimmy Greaves and John's brother Tommy White of Hearts up front. Scotland would win 6-2 with Alan Gilzean making an impression on the Spurs fans and management that would soon see him move from Dundee to White Hart Lane.

Over at Leicester in May, 1966 and Alex Dowdells who had been a trainer with the national side [and Celtic] before moving to Filbert Street was given a testimonial. Scotland manager John Prentice was denied a number of first choice players however so the side resembled a Scotland league select and included the likes of Ally Shewan of Aberdeen and David McParland of Partick Thistle although full international players such as Dundee's Alex Hamilton, Willie Wallace of Hearts and goalkeeper Bobby Ferguson were included too. Other players such as Jim Scott and Pat Stanton of Hibs, Dundee's Andy Penman [who would score Scotland's goal in a 1-1 draw], and Dave Smith of Aberdeen were all to make their full Scotland debuts a week later in a 3-0 defeat to the Netherlands in a friendly at Hampden.

March, 1976 and former England midfielder Alan Mullery was given a testimonial by Fulham with a Scotland XI playing the Rest of the World XI but this was a bit of a mish-mash with a 'whoever turns up can get a game' mentality but among the Scotland side were Leeds United players David Harvey and Peter Lorimer. I believe their English clubmates Norman Hunter and Terry Cooper also turned out for the Scots. QPR's

183

Scotland's Leigh Griffiths celebrates scoring his side's second goal of the game against England during the 2018 FIFA World Cup qualifier at Hampden Park.

SCOTLAND GLORY, TEARS AND SOUVENIRS

Frank McLintock and Don Masson appeared as well as, apparently, Graeme Souness.

Non-Scots playing for Scotland was not that unusual however with Bobby Charlton noted in a Scotland strip for a testimonial match for English League secretary Cliff Lloyd in May 1981.

Three giants of the Scottish game; John Greig [Rangers], Alan Rough [Partick Thistle] and Kenny Dalglish [Celtic and Liverpool] were given testimonials with Scotland sides represented.

In March, 1978 Ally MacLeod took along to Ibrox Stadium a makeshift Scotland side that did include the likes of Don Masson, Bruce Rioch, Archie Gemmill, Jim Blyth and others such as John Brownlie of Hibs and Brian Whittaker of Partick Thistle. Rangers, who would win the treble that year, took it a wee bit seriously and walloped Scotland 5-0 in front of a jam packed crowd of 65,000.

Alan Rough was given a testimonial in May 1982 with a Scotland XI playing Celtic. The Scotland side contained such players as Asa Hartford, Paul Sturrock, Alan Brazil and Kenny Burns in their number. Celtic won 8-3, with Roughie a bit dodgy at one or two of the goals. Maurice Johnston who was with Thistle at the time came on in the second half to 'represent' Scotland for the first time.

Kenny Dalglish, to commemorate his 100th appearance for Scotland, was given a testimonial match that saw a Tommy Docherty XI play an Alex Ferguson XI in May 1986. Docherty who gave Dalglish his first Scotland cap had the likes of Kenny and Liverpool team-mates Souness, Hansen and Nicol all in his side whilst Ferguson had the likes of home based players Malpas and Narey of Dundee United, MacLeod, Aitken and McStay of Celtic as well as Cooper and McCoist of Rangers. Docherty's side won 5-2 in front of a crowd of just under 25,000 at Hampden.

There may well be other such matches over the decades that have been forgotten about. However, I doubt there will be too many in the years to come, which in some ways is very sad and says a lot about the loyalty of football players and clubs in these days of financially driven mindsets.

THE TOEPOKE

When Jimmy Hill described David Narey's goal against Brazil at Spain '82 as a toepoke it outraged a nation. So pejorative was such a term that it was seen as an insult to describe it as such. Growing up in the West of Scotland in the 1970s anytime you played such games as 'Heidy Kick' or 'Wan n Aff' there would always be someone who would cry out 'n nae toebashers'. For to toebash [or toepoke] the ball was to blaspheme against the football gods; you could handle the ball, you could hack your opponents but to toebash was unforgivable and meant an automatic disqualification of a goal. Me, I toebashed and toepoked my way through many a game.

As to David Narey, for most people the toepoke in Seville is the standout moment on his footballing cv but there was so much more to the man than that. Narey's 35-cap Scotland career began in April, 1977 when he replaced John Blackley of Hibs in the 76th minute of a friendly against Sweden at Hampden to become the first Dundee United player to turn out for the national side. Many would follow in his footsteps including his team-mates at the time such as Paul Hegarty, Paul Sturrock, and Eamonn Bannon. Scotland won 3-1 that night but it would mark the end of Willie Ormond's tenure as Scotland manager as he would depart to manage Hearts shortly after. It also marked

SCOTLAND GLORY, TEARS AND SOUVENIRS

the end of John Blackley's seven-match career for Scotland which included the first game of the 1974 World Cup against Zaire.

Ally MacLeod's whirlwind eighteen months in charge of the Scotland side would come and go with nary the sight of Narey in his team. Jock Stein though would recall David back into the side for his second game in charge; a 1-0 defeat by Portugal in Lisbon. But Narey would remain in favour over the next few years and he would take part in the 1-0 win at Wembley in 1981 and then came the World Cup finals in 1982.

David would only appear in the last few minutes in the opening match against New Zealand in Spain as Scotland played out a 5-2 win but was to start against Brazil in place of Danny McGrain at right back. What he was thinking as he hit that wonderful strike into the back of the net in the 18th minute, goodness knows but maybe he did offend the football gods. After all, this was the Brazil side of Socrates, Falcao and Zico. Forever known as one of the greatest teams to never win a World Cup, the Brazilians put Scotland to the sword with four goals once they recovered from the shock of going behind. Incidentally, it was the Scotland defender's only goal for his country.

Narey would also play in Scotland's final game at the Spain World Cup which saw us go out after drawing 2-2 with the USSR.

Come 1984 however he was out of Jock Stein's plans for the side as they started to build towards the World Cup in Mexico '86.

Having not played for Scotland in either '84 or '85 Narey was brought back into the side in 1986 by Alex Ferguson who had taken on the role of caretaker manager following the tragic death of Jock Stein. Narey would play in two of the three games in the Mexico World Cup and although he would only be used sparingly after this by the new incumbent manager Andy Roxburgh, his final cap would come in February, 1989 as Scotland beat Cyprus 3-2 in Limassol in a World Cup qualifier for Italia 90.

David would win quite a few honours [and set a few records] with Dundee United including a championship winners' medal in season 1982/83 before going on to finish his career at Raith Rovers where a famous League Cup Final victory for the Kirkcaldy club against Celtic awaited him in 1994/95.

TICKET STUBS AND TICKET PRICES

Match tickets are perhaps the most personal example of a football collectable. It's also a more expensive souvenir than programmes, badges or scarves, etc., and perhaps it's a souvenir that you have also had to invest a considerable amount of time in obtaining [eg an overnight queue]. Match tickets are often poignant reminders of exactly where you were in the stadium on the day that Scotland pulled off a memorable win against all the odds or alternatively snatched defeat from the jaws of victory.

187

Unfortunately, for many of the Scotland matches at Hampden during the 1970s the arrangement was that you surrendered the ticket in its entirety especially if it was for the standing areas at the ground. I suppose we could have kept a photocopy as a souvenir but that's just not as good as the real thing.

It was around 1978 that the SFA started producing terracing tickets for Scotland matches in which only a portion of the ticket was surrendered but throughout the 1980s this meant that you lost half of the match details and were left with souvenirs that read Scot v. Switz - Wednesday 30 or land v. land - ember 1984.

Another annoying feature are those tickets that don't name the teams involved. World Cup finals tickets for Spain 82 and Italia 90 were nameless although thankfully for Euro 96 and France 98 the word 'Scotland' does appear in print alongside that of our opponents. [There is no truth in the rumour however that a security watermark reads 'Enjoy it whilst you can'.]

I think it somewhat ironic that for some of the older match tickets, dealers are asking for considerably more than the original cover price – and they come without the benefit of admission to a game of football!

Of course in recent years the advent of all seated stadia has meant that tickets are now the rule rather than the exception and in many instances no part of the ticket has to be given up. Furthermore, electronic scanning of briefs has made turnstile operators something of a scarce commodity.

At the same time however, the ticket artwork has become increasingly imaginative in that instead of merely having the fixture details printed on a plain background we now have aerial photographs of stadia, crowd scenes and player celebrations as more eyecatching backdrops. This is all in addition to international crests, tournament logos and trophies and a plug for the sponsors, naturally. Why not go further though and include on each ticket an iconic but relevant image, such as that of Kenny Dalglish putting the ball through Ray Clemence's legs on a Scotland-England ticket or David Narey's toepoke on any future Brazil brief?

Meantime however the reverse of the ticket tends to be given over to a seat/stadium location plan and/or extracts from government legislation reminding us all not to come to the game pissed as a fart and to refrain from bringing the likes of fireworks into the stadium. I love those foreign tickets though which use signage to tell us that the likes of dogs and large

SCOTLAND GLORY, TEARS AND SOUVENIRS

umbrellas are also banned. Quite right too for it's a real pain having a seat directly behind a German Shepherd and its golf brolly.

Football tickets may still have something to learn however from their rock and pop counterparts when it comes to generating advertising revenue. For example, the reverse side of the ticket for a recent Roxy Music concert at Glasgow's Clyde Auditorium contains a full colour advert of The Krankies and John Barrowman in the pantomime *Aladdin*. To us saddos who collect and salivate over match tickets it's all just Fan-dabi-dozy! [sorry].

And finally, a quick review of ticket prices. For the June 1973 Scotland v Brazil centenary celebration match the price of tickets in the north and south stands ranged from £1.65 to £3.30 whilst for the terracings and enclosures – which were pay at the gate – it cost 55 pence, 66 pence and 77 pence.

Fifteen years later at the Scotland v Yugoslavia World Cup qualifier a ticket for the north enclosure cost £5.00. However, by the time the north enclosure had become the north stand and the Netherlands were the visitors for a friendly match in March 1994 the price had gone up to £12.00.

During the Euro 2004 qualifying campaign it cost £12.00 for a north stand ticket to see the Faroes or Lithuania but £25.00 to see Germany or the Netherlands. For the 2010 World Cup it was £30.00 for north or south stand tickets irrespective of whether the opposition was the Netherlands or the Former Yugoslav Republic of Macedonia.

And so to the qualifiers for the Russia 2018 World Cup and a Scotland Supporters Club £180 'five-game season ticket' means a south stand ticket for the Scotland-Malta game equates to £24 whilst the equivalent brief for the Scotland v England match works out at £54. There are other discounts available for families and children but unfortunately no refunds for crap performances which I think should be a given.

TOPPS TRADING CARDS

With the demise of A&BC, American company Topps Chewing Gum took over the production of Footballer cards and if you thought they would have brought a more professional look to things; think again. There would still be those painted-on strips and repeated images but as far as I know at least they did get the players' names attached to the right picture.

The first set is quite a quirky one, published for the 1975/76 season with only 88 cards; it has some very colourful images and with shaded borders looks quite attractive. As for quirkiness, well, there's nine Clyde players in the set and only four from Celtic.

Card number one has Danny McGrain in a painted on green tracksuit. I didn't realise it was painted-on until I looked at the set from 1977/78 when you see what was the original picture and Danny was actually wearing a Scotland tracksuit at the time. With a small bit of detection which includes looking at the Derek Parlane card in the 75/76 set, you

see the same background stadium and you can work out it's from May 1973 at the Racecourse Ground, Wrexham. Scotland beat the Welsh 2-0 that day with Manchester United's George Graham getting both the goals in what was Danny and Derek's debut match.

Further on in the set there's Derek Johnstone resplendent in his Scotland colours with a dodgy luminous green background trying to convince us that it's an all-new card when really it's just a rehash from the A&BC set from 1973/74. The English equivalent set includes a Great Britain Select Eleven which is really nine Englishmen, one Welsh player and Billy Bremner with Northern Ireland getting 'neel pwoi' for that one.

The 1976/77 set is a fine one with quite a few action shots though still one or two paint-on jobs and Jim Stewart of Kilmarnock is listed as Jim Steward. There are some cards of later Scotland greats including a rather spotty Gordon Strachan [Dundee] and David Narey [Dundee United] with a page-boy haircut.

There is one player in his Scotland colours and that is Eric Schaedler. Schaedler's given name was Erich but it was more common at the time to see it written as Eric. Erich's father was a German POW who remained in Scotland after the war, marrying a Scots girl. Schaedler was a big part of the Hibernian side in the early 70s known as Turnbull's Tornadoes and was known for being a fast running, full-on full-back with crunching tackles. Erich represented Scotland once in March, 1974 playing in a friendly against his father's homeland team of West Germany in Frankfurt. Erich would also be part of the squad for the 1974 World Cup. Sadly Erich would take his own life on 24th December, 1985 in the Cardrona Forest in the Borders area of Scotland. Erich was 36 at the time and was still playing football for Dumbarton.

The English set had a section of *Shoot!/Goal* All Stars which did include a number of Scots such as Sandy Jardine, Kenny Dalglish and Billy Bremner. Bremner is

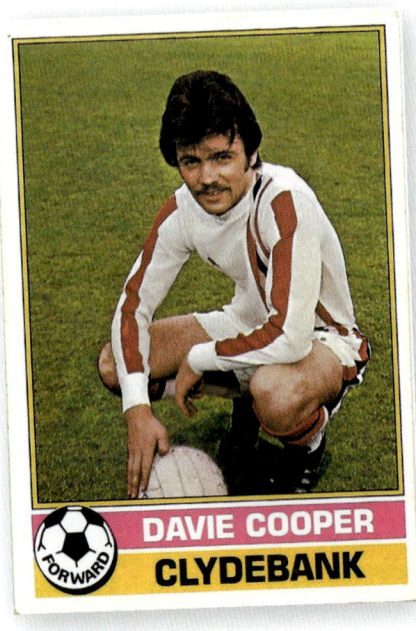

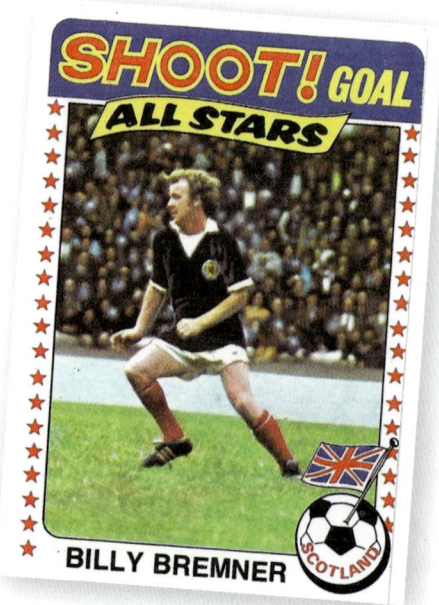

SCOTLAND GLORY, TEARS AND SOUVENIRS

seen in Scotland colours despite the fact he received a lifetime Scotland ban from the SFA in 1975 for a drink-fuelled escapade in Copenhagen that year.

Similarly the 1977/78 and 1978/79 sets have All Stars in both the Scottish and English collections with some strange choices among the Scotland sets such as Willie Gibson of Hearts but there's also some classic colouring-in going on with the likes of Joe Harper and Willie Donachie in natty light blue Scotland strips. The 1977 set also has Davie Cooper in his Clydebank days sporting a neat moustache which perhaps he was told to get rid of when he headed to Rangers later that year.

The final Scottish set was the 1979/80 one which is a pretty good looking set. However, you can only surmise that by this time Panini and their sticker sets had become the market leader and so no more Scots sets were produced. In England Topps Chewing Gum sets lumbered on for two more years but each individual card would be split into three player segments and as you can imagine they are quite small, although they did fit into a sticker album (surprise, surprise).

Of course, nowadays there are other card sets out there but to me it's just not the same. Maybe it's because I'm 40-odd years older and don't want to play dumb card games with them but maybe, just maybe, it's because the game and players were more colourful and full of character back then . . . or maybe it's just because Scotland never feature in any of the World Cup and European Championships sets!

USSR

The Union of Soviet Socialist Republics [USSR] was established in 1922 following the overthrow of the Tsardom of Russia, the Bolshevik revolution and then a civil war. It was dissolved in 1991, however in 1992 for sporting purposes such as the Olympic Games and European Football Championships a temporary arrangement was put in place whereby the former Soviet Union competed under the banner of the Commonwealth of Independent States [CIS] The demise of the USSR has resulted in the creation of over a dozen independent successor states of which Russia is the largest whilst Georgia is arguably the most troublesome (in a football sense) to Scotland.

The USSR were a major sporting power, however, winning the inaugural European Football Championships in 1960 and being runners-up in 1964, 1972 and 1988. They also won the Olympic Games football gold medal in 1956 and 1988.

Between 1967 and 1992 Scotland played the USSR/CIS on five occasions, winning one, drawing one and losing three.

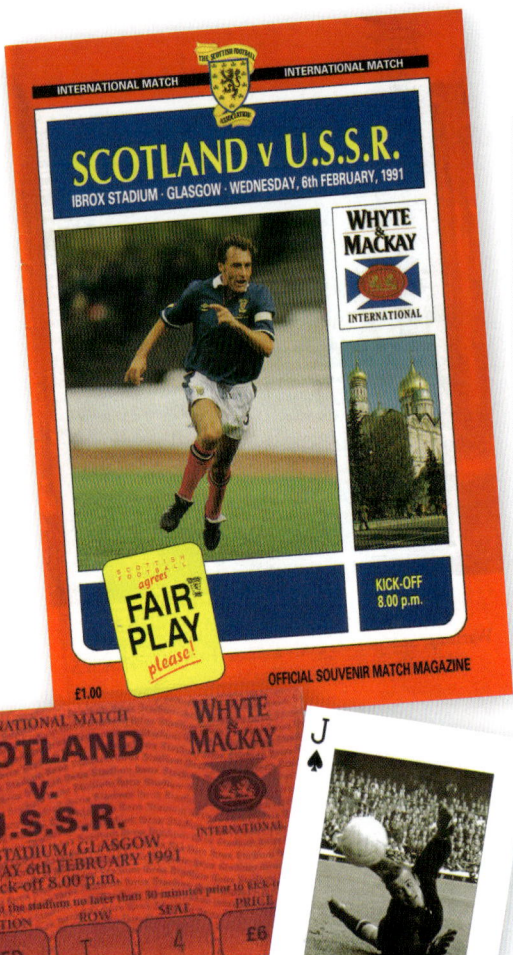

1967, Hampden Park, Glasgow,
Friendly, 0-2, 53,497

1971, Lenin Stadion, Moscow,
Friendly, 0-1, 20,000

1982, Estadio La Rosaleda,
Malaga World Cup finals group match,
2-2, 45,000

1991, Ibrox Stadium, Glasgow
Friendly, 0-1, 20,673

1992 Idrottsparken, Norkopping,
European Championship finals
group match, 3-0, 14,660

When the USSR first visited Glasgow in 1967 the Scotland team included seven Celtic players just 15 days before the Parkhead club won the European Cup Final. It was also Scotland's first game after the 3-2 defeat of England at Wembley so arguably our unofficial world champions crown then passed to the Soviets.

VINYLS: WORLD CUP VINYLS

First of all if you are a lover of vinyl records I will apologise for using the term vinyls in the title; it's just so wrong and yet so many people seem to use it now, in this so called age of vinyl revival. Heathens. Secondly I would like to apologise to lovers of music because as a rule, records made by football teams tend not to be on the musical side.

Personally I blame the English. Let's face it, if it wasn't for the success of the likes of the England World Cup Squad with 'Back Home' in 1970, followed by Chelsea's 'Blue is the Colour' then maybe some of Scotland's crimes against music might never have occurred.

Anyway, it's October 1973 and Scotland have just qualified for the 1974 World Cup and somewhere someone says 'let's do a record' and so is born 'Easy Easy' written by the songwriting team of Scotsman Bill Martin and Irishman Phil Coulter who had written hits around the time for the Bay City Rollers, Slik and many a Eurovision song. It was fairly bland but quite catchy all the same with its 'Yabba Dabba Do we support the boys in blue and it's easy, ea-zy' chorus. Shove in a few player mentions and you have a hit. Well, it did reach number 20 in the charts at the time.

A hit single did lead on to a hit album too. The *Scotland Scotland* album contained re-recordings of original songs by such Scottish luminaries as Gallagher & Lyle, Lulu and Middle of the Road [Chirpy Chirpy Shit Shit indeed] with squad members doing the backing vocals. And did the people buy it? Apparently, it reached numero 3 on the UK album chart.

Maybe it was the heady success of *Top of the Pops* appearances but for some unknown reason Scotland team-mates Sandy Jardine and Kenny Dalglish decided to release a single in 1975 called 'Each Saturday'. A decidedly cheesey 70s piece of pap it is, however it did get airplay on the John Peel show . . . once. Of course, this was years after it was released and at a time when Dalglish was the king of Liverpool and idolised

by Peel. I've seen it on eBay for £15, about £14.95p too much as far as I'm concerned.

1978, Ally's Tartan Army and all that World Cup fervour spawned a whole horde of musical tat. I suppose it was Ally MacLeod's exuberance that was so infectious that it set a nation down a path of joyful optimism and first out the box was comedian Andy Cameron with 'Ally's Tartan Army'. It was probably written on the back of a fag packet in five minutes, however despite its dodgy pedigree it did deliver the classic couplet 'We're representing Britain, and we're gauny do or die, England cannae dae it cos they didnae qualify.'

Andy got in there fairly early, releasing the record at the start of the year and by March it had reached number 4 in the UK charts. After this it became a bit of a free for all as everybody and their brother had to have a go at claiming the golden egg.

There was the Tartan Lads with 'Marching to Argentina'; Bill Barclay with Billy Rio and the Buenos Fairies singing 'Hoat Pies for me Argentina'; The Scottish Supporters with the imaginatively titled 'Ally MacLeod' among others; and of course there was the official song by Rod Stewart. From the mighty pen of the guy that wrote such classics as 'Maggie May', 'Tonight's the Night', and 'You Wear it Well' came the rather turgid 'Ole Ola (Mulher Brasileira)'. Rod did reach number four also but his timing wasn't that good, releasing it in late May and seeing it plummet salewise from about the moment Teofilo Cubillas scored his second for Peru past the despairing Alan Rough in Cordoba.

Andy Cameron did try to cash in further by releasing a second single and even an LP but somewhere, someone has a garage full of them. If only Scotland had won the World Cup, Andy could have been a millionaire.

Further crimes against music were to follow in the 80s with first 'We Have a Dream' released for the 1982 World Cup. At least it never took itself seriously with *Gregory Girl*'s John Gordon Sinclair screeching his way through B.A. Robertson's paean to our childhood football dreams.

Mexico '86 and does anyone remember 'Big Trip to Mexico'? No, that's because it was crap and never sold a copy it seems. I'm not sure if

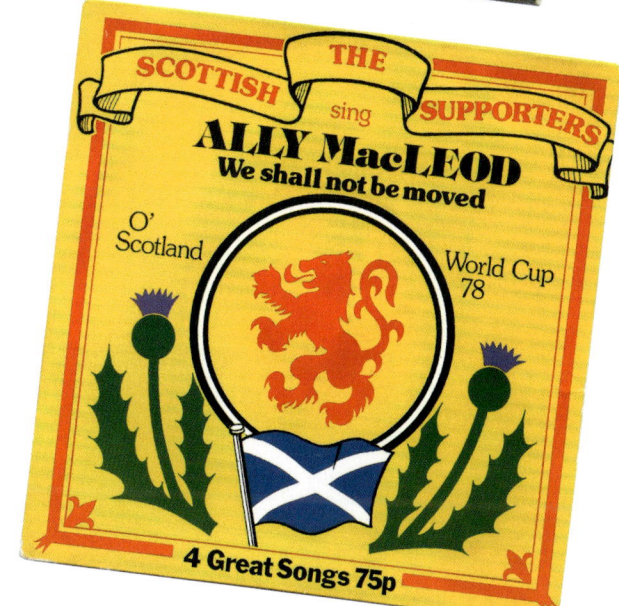

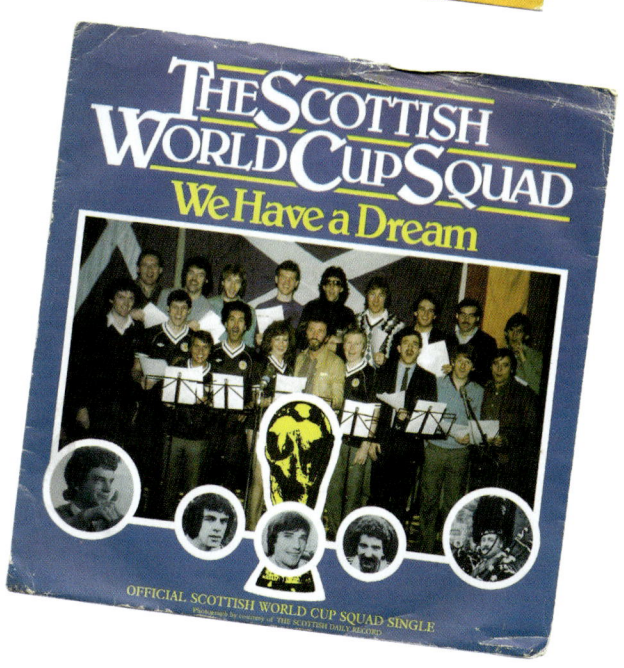

it was a sign of the times but England's World Cup song 'We've got the Whole World at our Feet' only reached number 66 but then again that was crap too having been written by the same trio of Hiller / James / James. Tony Hiller had been responsible for Brotherhood of Man's stomach wrenching Eurovision ditty 'Save Your Kisses for Me' previously as well. People have been jailed for less.

1990 and England step up their game with the New Order song 'World in Motion' whereas Scotland got a heartfelt [i.e. dreadful] song called 'Say it with Pride'. It would only get to number 43 perhaps due to the gaudy, God-awful shirts the players wore during recording which subsequently appeared on the cover of the single but more likely because striker Robert Fleck's rugged not-so-good looks scared people away from buying it. France '98 and Del Amitri release 'Don't Come Home Too Soon'. Nuff said.

VOGTS, BERTI
And so to the disaster that was the Berti Vogts era [March 2002 to October 2004]. First of all I do believe that an essential quality for a Scotland manager is that he is Scottish or at a stretch, British. In writing about Berti previously I have often talked about there being a curse attached to him and the players he gave debuts to but it is weird that so many have had injury problems and often had to quit the game prematurely. Among that list you can see players such as John Kennedy, Michael Stewart, Gareth Williams and Lee Wilkie and even those who have had good careers have had to suffer extensive injury plagued days including Darren Fletcher, James McFadden and Craig Gordon. Of course, fans of Nigeria and Azerbaijan will tell you the curse was that he was rotten. Oh and how he was at times.

Perhaps his biggest problem was in trying to change too much in too little a time, promoting players to full international duty when they had barely kicked a ball for their own first team, such as Kevin Kyle at Sunderland, Brian Kerr at Newcastle United, and Warren Cummings at Chelsea but then there was also all those goddam friendlies beginning with a 5-0 stuffing in Paris.

The Vogts era buckled under the sheer weight of these glorified training sessions — in just over two years we played 19 friendly matches, winning just four, drawing three and losing 12 although Robert Marshall reminds me that under the tutelage of Germany's successful Euro 96 coach, Scotland did manage to beat both Trinidad and Tobago in the one game.

People will tell you that at least Berti got Scotland to a play-off which nobody else has done since. Well, if you look at the qualifying group for Euro 2004 he would have had to have gone some to lose second place with Germany, Iceland, Lithuania and the Faroes making up the teams. And yet, he nearly did, for just 13 minutes into the first game in Toftir the Scots were two down to the mighty Faroe Islands. Scotland would come back to gain a desperate draw but the fallout would see Vogts lay the blame at the feet of Everton's David Weir who would then exile himself from international football over the next few years.

Vogts would win the next two games home and away against Iceland but defeat in Kaunas, Lithuania would see Scotland stutter towards second place. However a creditable draw with Germany was followed by a couple of golden moments and perhaps a glimpse of what could be achieved. In their final qualifying group match Scotland were struggling to overcome a staunch Lithuania rearguard action and so Berti brought on Manchester United's Darren Fletcher for only his second international in the 65th minute and by the 70th minute Fletcher had written himself into the Scotland history books with a well-placed volley from the edge of the box. Hampden went wild and a few weeks later it went even wilder as the two standout discoveries of Vogts' time, Fletcher and James McFadden, combined to give Scotland a 1-0 victory against the Netherlands in the play-off first leg.

The euphoria lasted a few days only however as we hit the earth with an almighty thump(ing). The 6-0 defeat was followed by a 4-0 loss to the Welsh in another friendly in which we were over-friendly and the clock was ticking on Vogts' time in charge. It would eventually come to an end following a poor start to the 2006 World Cup qualifying campaign and not a moment too soon.

However, to me Berti should never have got close to the job. After all, in his 'Focus on' feature from *Shoot!* magazine in the early 70s, his stated ambition was not to win the World Cup with Scotland but with Germany. Can you believe that? Some of his other choices are a bit strange though; not so much his choice of favourite singer — after all picking Tom Jones is not unusual for that era but to say your favourite country visited is Israel and then in the next question suggest roast pork as your favourite food is a bit off.

WALES

Scotland and Wales do not share a common land border that has been subject to dispute over the years. Equally important, it has never been common practice for Welsh sports commentators to demean the achievements of Scottish sportsmen and women. As such there has never been any major 'issues' between the two nations. Instead, it could be argued that we have a common 'irritant' which should bind us together.

The Football Association of Wales [FAW] was founded in 1876 making it the third-oldest behind England and Scotland. Not surprisingly then, Wales were Scotland's second, different, international opposition [our match no.6 which we won 4-0 in Glasgow].

Up until the First World War Wales played the vast majority of their home games against Scotland in Wrexham [birthplace of the FAW]. Cardiff, which only achieved city status in 1905 [and which was formally declared the capital of Wales in 1955], came to the fore in the 1920s.

Scotland have now played Wales on more than 100 occasions — most of them being British Championship matches — with Scotland well ahead in the series. The record book also shows that in the Victorian era Scotland gave Wales some serious seeings-to including 9-0, 8-0, 8-1, 6-1, 6-0 and 5-0 [twice]. However, as recently as 2004 they skelped us 4-0 in a friendly match at Cardiff's Millennium Stadium then 3-0 in 2009 in another friendly, this time at the Cardiff City Stadium.

Scotland have 'bested' Wales in four out of five World Cup qualifying campaigns. However, two of these [1978 and 1986] swung our way following a couple of dodgy penalty decisions which a number of our Welsh friends haven't forgotten or forgiven. [Mind you, I haven't forgiven them for inflicting upon us in the 1970s, the rugby-loving comedian Max Boyce].

The Millennium Stadium, Cardiff

Whilst Wales have not reached as many tournament finals as Scotland have, the harsh reality is that when they have got there they have progressed further than we have managed, eg, reaching the quarter-finals of the 1958 World Cup as well as getting to the semi-finals of the 2016 European Championships.

Some notable Welsh footballers who have given Scotland problems over the years include Ivor Allchurch, John Charles, Ron Davies, Mike England, John Toshack, Terry Yorath, Leighton James, Ian Rush, Mark Hughes, Robert Earnshaw and Gareth 'Bloody' Bale. Respect.

WAR AND VICTORY

During the Second World War there continued to be international matches between the Home Nations but these have never officially been recognised as full internationals. It is said however, some of the teams put out were as good as they could have been in peacetime, in fact for Scotland it was easier to get players released from the army than it was from some of the big English clubs right up until the early 70s.

England dominated throughout the war years with players of the calibre of Stanley Matthews, Tommy Lawton, Stan Cullis and Joe Mercer. There would be very few victories for Scotland in this era and perhaps it's just as well they are termed as 'unofficial'. After all, who wants to be reminded of scores such as England 8 Scotland 0 (Maine Road, Manchester, 1943), England 6 Scotland 2 (twice in 1944) among others... Still Scotland did win one 5-4 at Hampden in 1942 with Willie Waddell of Rangers and Billy Liddell of Liverpool making their first appearances in Scotland shirts.

Although not official there were some interesting tales from those days. The very first match between England and Scotland during the war took place at St James' Park, home of Newcastle United in September, 1939. England were to win 2-1 but prior to the kick-off two of their team failed to make it and so a pair of Newcastle United players in the crowd turned out for the England side, one of whom was Scottish. Tommy Pearson would play over 200 games for the Magpies and indeed would be capped twice for Scotland in 1947 including playing against England at Hampden.

For the first Hampden match on 11th May 1940 6,000 who had bought tickets never turned up, perhaps wary of German radio propagandist Lord Haw Haw's promise that the Luftwaffe would not let the match go beyond half-time. The game ended in an apparently drab 1-1 draw but thankfully with no sign of the German bombers. Crowds of over 100,000 would become the norm for these fixtures at Hampden with generally 75,000 attending games at Wembley.

In April, 1943 Scotland were defeated by England 4-0 at Hampden but the SFA had ran out of its clothing allowance coupons and so the team was fitted out with shirts belonging to Tommy Walker of Hearts from his previous appearances for the side.

Tommy Bogan of Hibernian was to make his one and only appearance for Scotland at Hampden in April, 1945 and it would last less than a minute as

he collided with England goalkeeper Frank Swift and ended up with a torn ligament. Sadly Frank was to lose his life in the Munich air disaster whilst travelling as a journalist with the Manchester United side of 1958.

Other players to make their debuts for Scotland in these years would include George Young, who would captain the Scotland team from 1946 to 1957 and Hibernian great Gordon Smith.

The Victory internationals were a group of games played in the immediate aftermath of the Second World War. A full league programme would not begin until the 1946/47 season so these matches that took place in 1945/46 are seen as unofficial which meant that Scotland's 1-0 victory over England at Hampden in 1946 which attracted a crowd of 139,468 would not be in the record books and indeed it would be 1962 before Scotland could record a home victory against the Auld Enemy for the first time since 1937.

To commemorate these matches Pepys International released the International Football Whist game in 1947. There were 44 cards in the set with eleven players each from the four Home Nations. In the Scotland side there would be a few players who had made their international bow in the war years including Willie Waddell, George Young and Gordon Smith as well as the likes of goalkeeper Bobby Brown, who would go on to manage Scotland, Willie Thornton, Willie Woodburn of Rangers and Partick Thistle legend Jackie Husband.

WEMBLEY '67

There have been thousands of words and photographs plus numerous videos relating to Scotland's historic 1967 victory over reigning world champions England at Wembley so for a change we will show each of the Scottish heroes in a contemporary football card in their club colours together with a small factoid or two.

1. Ronnie Simpson. Ronnie, along with Jim McCalliog, made his full international debut that day. [Incidentally there was a 16-year age gap between the two players]. Ronnie was also manager Bobby Brown's understudy at Queen's Park in the 1940s. Furthermore, Brown would cap goalies Bobby Clark (Aberdeen) and Jim Cruickshank (Hearts), both of whom were ex-Queen's Park players. Ronnie would win only four more caps, although a European Champion Clubs' Cup winners' medal with Celtic enhanced his cv somewhat.

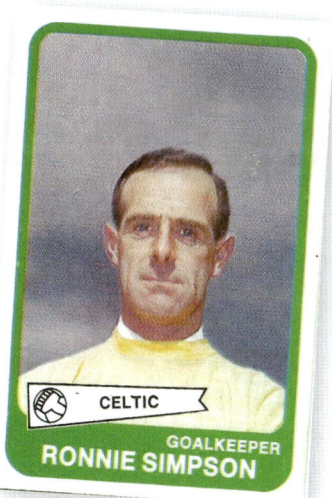

2. Tommy Gemmell. Tommy usually played at left back but to accommodate Eddie McCreadie he would play mostly on the right side for Scotland. Well known for his thunderbolt shot, Tommy would only score once for Scotland from the penalty spot but then again a few weeks after the

Wembley match he would score the first goal in Celtic's European Cup triumph. Tommy would also score in the 1970 European Cup Final against Feyenoord. Tommy would win 18 caps.

3. Eddie McCreadie. When Chelsea signed Eddie there was apparently, as part of the deal, a promise of two friendlies with his then club of East Stirlingshire. The Scottish club did try to get the second match played in 2014 but to no avail. Eddie went on to manage Chelsea but resigned after being refused a club car, a far cry from today's available money. Eddie played for Scotland 23 times.

4. John Greig. John's first 22 matches for Scotland were consecutive and had his club, Rangers, not refused to release him and his team-mates for Scotland's next international due to their upcoming European Cup-Winners' Cup Final he would have achieved a total of 37 consecutive matches – not quite a record though, as Kenny Dalglish holds that with 43. Greig captained the side at Wembley that day and won a total of 44 caps, scoring three times including a late winner in a World Cup qualifier against Italy in 1965.

5. Ronnie McKinnon. Ronnie would play in the Rangers side a few weeks after this match in which they lost the Cup-Winners' Cup to Bayern Munich with Sepp Maier, Gerd Muller and Franz Beckenbuer all in the German side. Franz Roth scored the only goal in extra time in the match in Nuremberg. Ronnie would miss out on Rangers' triumph in the final of 1972 due to being injured in an earlier round against Sporting Lisbon. Ronnie's twin brother, Donnie, played for Partick Thistle and went to Argentina with Scotland as a coach. Ronnie was capped 28 times, scoring once against Wales in 1967.

6. Jim Baxter. It is quite strange in some ways that when you google 'Baxter Wembley' you are always directed to 1967; it is amazing to think that he scored both goals in the 1963 victory over England and it almost seems forgotten. Maybe if he had played keepie uppie back then it might be different. Sadly Baxter would only play for Scotland two more times after this match and by the end of 1967 was finished as an international player at the age of 28, winning a total of 34 caps.

7. Willie Wallace. Willie was another player who within weeks of this match would go to become one of the famous Lisbon Lions. His first three caps would come as a Hearts player but it was Willie who called time on his Scotland career citing that he was frustrated at being a squad player often with no chance of playing due to substitutes not being allowed at that time. Willie won a total of seven caps. He emigrated to Australia in the late 70s and still resides there.

8. Billy Bremner. Billy is often remembered for that tantalising

SCOTLAND GLORY, TEARS AND SOUVENIRS

miss against Brazil in the 1974 World Cup finals but he did score three goals for Scotland. His first was against Austria in a World Cup qualifier in 1968 at Hampden that Scotland won 2-1, his second down at the Racecourse, Wrexham as Scotland won 5-3 v Wales in 1969 and his final one was against Spain in 1974 in the home defeat in the Euro Nations qualifiers. The victory at Wembley gave Scotland the upper hand in the Euro qualifiers for 1968 but this advantage was lost in a 1-0 defeat at Windsor Park in October 1967 to Northern Ireland. This game was known as the George Best match as he gave the Scots a torrid time. Bremner and indeed Baxter were both suspended by the FA for their clubs and country at the time. Who knows if Billy would have allowed Best to dominate the match so much?

9. Jim McCalliog. Jim was the real surprise pick for this match but he had scored the opening goal for the Scotland Under-23 side the month before this match in which Scotland beat England 3-1. Jim was sold by Chelsea to Sheffield Wednesday under Tommy Docherty in 1965 and would eventually be signed again by Docherty for Manchester United in 1974. Docherty would sell Jim on again less than a year later to Southampton. Jim would have the last laugh as he laid on the pass to Bobby Stokes to hit the winner against United in the 1976 FA Cup Final. Jim would only gain five caps for Scotland but would score what would prove to be the winner in this match.

10. Denis Law. Denis is, of course, Scotland's top goalscorer along with Kenny Dalglish on 30 goals including one in this match but he could have had one more had he not missed a penalty against Finland in Helsinki in May 1965. Fortunately Scotland won 2-1 that night. Denis once played against Scotland at Hampden although technically it was against the Scottish League as he turned out for the Italian League side in November 1961 during his time with Torino.

11. Bobby Lennox. Bobby was born and bred in the Ayrshire seaside town of Saltcoats and of the Lisbon Lions was born the furthest from Glasgow. Also hailing from the town was Stevie Clarke who was capped as a Chelsea player in the 1980s. Lennox played for Scotland on only ten occasions and scored three times including one in this match. In doing so he became the first Celtic player to score at Wembley; a feat that Kenny Dalglish would repeat in the 1977 victory.

WONDERFUL WINGERS

When Alf Ramsey led England to their World Cup win a long, long time ago [in a galaxy far, far away], it was a bit of a culture shock to us Scots in many ways but in particular, the fact he had done so without the use of any wingers – as opposed to wide midfield players. Such was the plethora of great Scottish wingers in that era that to play without one was almost heresy to the deities of football.

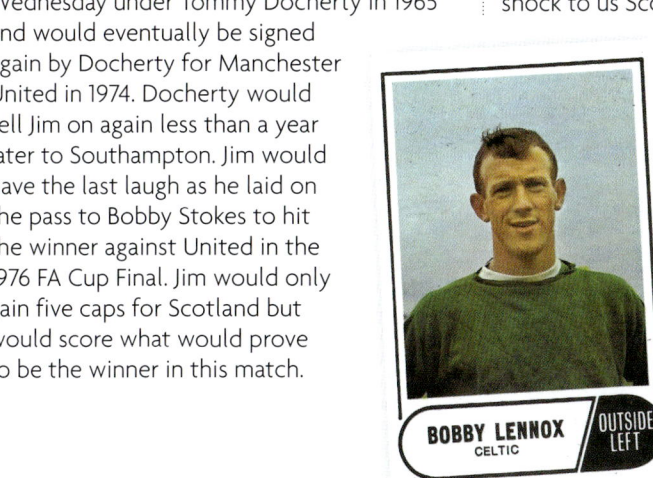

199

Long before the sixties Scotland always produced wingers with great speed, deft turns and a biting cross. Before the Second World War there was the Wee Blue Devil Alan Morton who was part of the Wembley Wizards team of 1928. The left winger won his first two caps as an amateur with Queen's Park in 1920 and would win a further 29 with Glasgow Rangers, scoring five goals playing for the national side up until 1932.

In the same year, Douglas 'Dally' Duncan would take up Morton's mantle playing 14 times for the national side as a Derby County player. 'Dally' would score seven times and would score both goals in the 1935, 2-0 victory over England at Hampden. On a number of occasions Duncan's right wing partner was Jimmy Delaney of Celtic. Delaney would be remarkable in being the only Scotland player who would receive caps either side of the 1939-1945 conflict. His first nine came as a Celt and after a nine-year gap he was capped as a Manchester United player. Jimmy would also net the only goal in the 1946 Victory International win against England at Hampden. His official goal tally would amount to six.

The war itself would see the debuts of another three wing maestros in unofficial matches; Willie Waddell of Rangers, Billy Liddell of Liverpool and Gordon Smith of Hibernian. Each were adored by their own fans and would have the status of legend enshrined at Ibrox, Anfield and Easter Road respectively. For Waddell and Smith there would be a continued dilemma for the selectors; which one to choose – Waddell was the more direct player with Smith the more elegant and so in the end caps were portioned out to both with Waddell gaining 17 and Smith winning 19. Billy Liddell could play on both wings and also through the middle so won out with 29 caps altogether. Liddell would score eight goals altogether with Waddell and Smith pitching in with six and four.

Despite their pedigree and talent none of this trio would ever grace the World Cup. For the 1954 World Cup in Switzerland Scotland relied on Johnny Mackenzie of Partick Thistle and another Hibernian legend and future Scotland manager Willie Ormond. Graham Leggat of Aberdeen and Stewart Imlach of Nottingham Forest were favoured for 1958 in Sweden.

1960 would see an oft forgotten winger of this period in Davie Wilson of Rangers making his debut. Denis Law in 1990 picked his all-time Scotland team and chose Davie not just for his wing play but as Denis put it, 'he also knew his way to goal'. Davie would score the opening goal for Scotland at Hampden in 1962 as Scotland recorded a 2-0 win and their first at home versus the Auld Enemy since 1938. Wilson would go on to score nine times for Scotland in only 22 Internationals.

If we think of the archetypal Scottish winger we do tend to imagine small diminutive figures and Willie Henderson of Rangers and Jimmy 'Jinky' Johnstone of Celtic typified that for many. Henderson would make the breakthrough to the Scotland side first at 18 and indeed is still one of the youngest players ever to be capped. Henderson scored in his first two Scotland matches and was part of the side that defeated England at Wembley in 1963 and at Hampden in 1964. Willie would finish his Scotland career in 1971 having amassed 29 caps and scoring five goals.

Enter Jinky in 1964. It's fair to say that Jimmy Johnstone is perhaps the most beloved of all Scottish wingers and not just for his skill and ability but for his bravery. Time and time again Jimmy would be hacked down and time and time again he would get back up for more. However, he would only ever gain 22 caps but not every Scotland manager fancied taking him on as he was a difficult player to manage and was often subject to fines and suspensions by his Celtic manager Jock Stein. Jock himself during his caretaker role of Scotland in 1965 always chose Henderson over Johnstone for the Scotland team.

Jinky would only ever play 23 times for Scotland, scoring on four occasions. The game for which he will always be remembered though is the 1974 Home International against England a few days after the famous rowing boat calamity. Willie Ormond, the Scotland manager at the time, received quite a bit of flak in the days that followed as did Jimmy and so told Jimmy, 'Just go out and prove them wrong.' Of course, Jimmy did and danced rings round the English defence as Scotland ran out 2-0 winners. In a final act of defiance Jinky would give the press box the 'V' sign... However, despite this performance it is still one of the great mysteries of Scottish football as to why Jinky was never allowed to grace the World Cup finals in 1974 by Ormond even taking into account some drinking sessions taking place on the pre-World Cup tour.

There were other sixties wingers I haven't covered yet such as Rangers and Everton winger Alex Scott who gained his first cap in 1957, winning 16 in total and notching up five goals. Then there's Bonnie Prince Charlie Cooke who was part of the great Chelsea side of the late 60s and early 70s and won 16 caps in total. Likewise an integral part of the Leeds United team from that era was Eddie Gray who won a mere 12 caps, scoring three goals.

There was also Willie 'Bud' Johnston who seemed to have two Scotland careers; one in the sixties with Rangers and the other in his West Brom days after a gap of seven years. Johnston was no doubt the quickest of the Scottish wingers and the fieriest too but to see him knock the ball way past the full back and sprint down the line was a sight to behold. Johnston's Scotland

Scotland

Willie Johnston

World Cup Appearances	2
World Cup Goals	0
International Appearances	21
International Goals	0
Height	5'7"

Germany. Around the same time others such as Tommy McLean of Kilmarnock, Tony Green of Blackpool and Jimmy Smith of Newcastle would play bit parts in the Scotland team.

Other wingers in later decades would grace Scotland sides including the likes of John Robertson of Nottingham Forest [28 caps including three at the 1982 World Cup finals, and nine goals] and Davie Cooper of Rangers [22 caps including two at the 1986 World Cup finals, plus six goals] and to a lesser degree the likes of Pat Nevin [28 caps, including two at the Euro 92 finals, and five goals] and Neil McCann [26 caps and three goals in the post-France 98 wilderness years] but never again would we see so many in such a short space of time as we did in that golden era of the 50s and 60s and so the next time someone complains why such and such a winger never won more caps just remind them of the choices the selectors had back then.

career would end in disgrace however following a failed drug test in the 1978 World Cup in Argentina. Johnston played 21 times for Scotland.

In one of Jock Stein's last games as caretaker he played three wingers with Henderson and Johnston of Rangers on the flanks and Charlie Cooke (then of Dundee) as an inside forward. Maybe he should have done it more as Scotland beat Wales 4-1 that night in November 1965.

The 60s was the great pinnacle for Scottish wingers and it also saw the careers of the likes of Willie Morgan and the tall and lanky Tommy Hutchison start to blossom, both of whom would actually play in the 1974 World Cup in West

WILLIE JOHNSTON (Rangers)

SCOTLAND GLORY, TEARS AND SOUVENIRS

X-RATED TACKLES

Them on us: Four examples from the hundreds, nay thousands, which we have suffered over the years:

1963 England v Scotland – This British Championship match at Wembley was only six minutes old when Scotland skipper Eric Caldow's left leg was broken in three places as a result of a tackle by Spurs' Bobby Smith. Descriptions of the tackle range from vicious to cumbersome and to make matters worse no substitutes were permitted back then. However, ten-man Scotland triumphed 2-1 to claim the British title. A long rehabilitation programme was required before Caldow could play for Rangers again but sadly he never added to his 40 Scotland caps.

1970 Scotland v England – In over 100 such fixtures this was only the second occasion in which the match finished goalless. That said, there should have been an opportunity for Scotland to have scored from the penalty spot when Everton's Brian Labone upended Colin Stein of Rangers in spectacular fashion. The Hampden crowd of 137,438 at this British Championship decider all knew it was a penalty but unbelievably the West German referee ignored his nation's injustice of four years previous and waved play on.

1986 Scotland v Uruguay – Scotland required a victory against the South Americans in order to progress at the Mexico 86 World Cup finals and our chances appeared to have improved after only one minute of play when Gordon Strachan 'took one for the team'. Jose Batista cynically clobbered the Manchester United midfielder from behind and duly received his marching orders from the French referee. Alas Scotland couldn't cash in on the numerical advantage and a 0-0 scoreline meant we returned home at our usual time.

2004 Scotland v Romania – Celtic centre-back John Kennedy was only 14 minutes into his international debut in a friendly match at Hampden Park when he suffered a horrific knee injury as a result of a 'late challenge' from Ioan Ganea of Wolverhampton Wanderers. To add insult to injury Romania

won 2-1 in front of 20,433. Despite several operations Kennedy never fully recovered and on medical advice was forced to retire from football in 2009 aged 26.

Despite international appearances by the likes of Doug Rougvie, Tom Forsyth and Kenny Burns, when it comes to *Us on them*, only one really bad example springs readily to mind:

1985 Iceland v Scotland – Scotland somehow managed to win this vital World Cup qualifier in Reykjavik 1-0, a match that is sometimes remembered for a tackle by that 'gentle giant' Graeme Souness which resulted in Sigi Jonsson being carried off on a stretcher and taken to hospital after 25 minutes. The Sampdoria-based Scotland skipper [whose thighs, in my mind, were second only to those of eighties songstress Laura Branigan] was booked which put him out of that fateful match with Wales in Cardiff four months later. Thankfully the Icelandic midfielder recovered fully and just to show there were no hard feelings he eventually signed for Dundee United.

YUGOSLAVIA

Yugoslavia [ie the Union of South Slavic Peoples] came into existence after the First World War in 1918 but started to disintegrate [violently] in the 1990s with the end result being seven independent successor states, most notably Croatia, Serbia and Slovenia. Yugoslavia were however a recognised football force having reached the semi-finals at the first-ever FIFA World Cup in 1930, finishing fourth in 1962 and being runners-up in the European Championships in 1960 and 1968. They were also Olympic Games football gold medallists in 1960 and silver medallists on three other occasions.

Scotland played Yugoslavia on a total of eight occasions between 1955 and 1989 winning twice, drawing five and losing just the once. [I'm perversely proud to be able to say that I was in Zagreb in 1989 to witness that sole defeat!]

1955, J.N.A. Stadion, Belgrade, Friendly, 2-2, 20,000

1956, Hampden Park, Glasgow, Friendly, 2-0, 55,521

1958, Arosvallen, Vasteras, Sweden World Cup Finals Group Match, 1-1, 9,591

1972, Estadio Mineiro, Belo Horizonte, Brazil Independence Cup, 2-2, 4,000

1974, Wald Stadion, Frankfurt, World Cup Finals-Group Match, 1-1, 54,000

1984, Hampden Park, Glasgow, Friendly, 6-1, 18,512

1988, Hampden Park, Glasgow, World Cup Qualifier, 1-1, 42,771

1989, Maksimir Stadion, Zagreb, World Cup Qualifier, 1-3, 42,500

When Scotland handed out that 6-1 thrashing in 1984, Yugoslavia actually had the temerity to take the lead after ten minutes, before six different Scotsmen got on the scoresheet. Unfortunately, there were less than 19,000 inside Hampden that evening to witness that all too rare event – Scotland stuffing some half-decent opposition – and to make matters worse proposed television coverage was disrupted by industrial action. Manager Jock Stein gave Steve Nicol his Scotland debut that evening and the Liverpool defender went on to win a total of 27 caps, three of which were against Yugoslavia.

SCOTLAND GLORY, TEARS AND SOUVENIRS

ZED NOT ZEE

How do you finish a Scottish international football A to Z when Zaire and Zico have already been covered elsewhere? Possible alternatives could include-

Zealous – 'Someone who spends a lot of time or energy in supporting something' – Your average Tartan Army footsoldier? See Tartan Army then.

Zero – The number of times Scotland have reached the second stage of a major tournament. Best not dwell on that statistic.

Zombie – 'Someone who seems completely unaware of what is happening around them, and who seems to act without thinking about what they are doing.' I'll let you nominate your own player, manager, referee, journalist, pundit, chief executive or fellow supporter.

Zurich – I had intended to indulge my schoolboy sense of humour here by mentioning the Wankdorf Stadium until I remembered it was located in Berne not Zurich. Furthermore, it transpires that Scotland have yet to play in Zurich, having faced Switzerland in Geneva, Basle, Berne and, er Birmingham.

Oh sod it, let's mention Zaire again, we know you want us to. Zaire [formerly the Belgian Congo and now the Democratic Republic of Congo] were the first team Scotland ever managed to defeat at a World Cup finals – 2-0 in the Westfalen Stadium, Dortmund, West Germany on 14 June 1974.

Zaire were also the first sub-Saharan African team to qualify for the FIFA World Cup and have twice won the African Cup of Nations – in 1968 and 1974. In West Germany however they lost all three group matches, conceded 14 goals and failed to score any at the other end. On returning home from the World Cup the Zaire team incurred the wrath of their all-seeing, all-powerful President Joseph-Desire Mobutu who took back his 'presents' given in reward for qualifying whilst promises of houses, cars and money never materialised.

Zaire's other main sporting claim to fame is its hosting, in October 1974, of the so-called 'Rumble in the Jungle' – a world heavyweight boxing title fight between the undefeated champion George Foreman and the challenger [and former champion] Muhammad Ali. 60,000 spectators at the 20th of May stadium in the nation's capital Kinshasa saw Ali win by a knockout.

Incidentally, on the 20th of May 1951 Scotland defeated Belgium 5-0 in a friendly match in Brussels with Aberdeen's George Hamilton netting a hat-trick in only his second appearance for his country. Is it possible that the good people of Zaire named a stadium in honour of the day that their former colonial masters were put to the sword by Willie Waddell, Lawrie Reilly and their mates?

PS: Thank goodness there are only 26 letters in our alphabet – the Cyrillic alphabet has 48. Russia 2018 would therefore be problematic for those of us who aren't cunning linguists….

James McFadden celebrates with teammate Darren Fletcher after scoring Scotland's winning goal against Holland in the 2004 UEFA European Championships first leg play-off. *[Unfortunately there was a bit of a hiccup in the second leg].*

BIBLIOGRAPHY

James, B.,
England v Scotland
(London, The Sportsmans Book Club, 1970)

Rippon, A.,
Gasmasks For Goalposts: Football in Britain during the Second World War
(Sutton Publishing, 2005)

Taylor, H.,
Great Masters of Scottish Football
(London, The Sportsmans Book Club, 1968)

Cosgrove, S,
Hampden Babylon
(Canongate, 2001)

Law, D.,
The King Denis Law an Autobiography
(Bantam Press, 2003)

Ross, D.,
The Roar of the Crowd Following Scottish Football Down the Years
(Argyll Publishing, 2005)

Gordon, R.,
Scotland 74 a World Cup Story
(Black & White Publishing, 2014)

Ward, A.,
Scotland The Team
(Derby: Breedon Books, 1987)

McDevitt, R.,
Scotland in the Sixties, The Definitive Account of the Scotland Football Team 1960-1969 (Pitch Publishing, 2016)

McColl, G.,
Scotland in the World Cup Finals
(London: Chameleon Books, 1998)

Keir, R.,
Scotland – The Complete International Football Record
(Derby: Breedon Books, 2001)

Hayes, D.P.,
Scotland! Scotland ! The Complete Who's Who of Scotland Players since 1946
(Edinburgh: Mercat Press, 2006)

Leatherdale, C.,
Scotland's Quest for the World Cup A Complete Record 1950-1986
(Edinburgh: John Donaldson Publishers Ltd., 1986)

Plus a website of fellow Scotland supporter Graeme McGinty which plugged half a dozen or so image gaps – www.scotlandprogrammes.co.uk. Cheers Graeme.

Football cards websites were also a great source of information, especially Nigel's Webspace cards, littleoak.com.au and the Football Cartophilic Info Exchange cartophilic-info-exch.blogspot.co.uk